SWEDISH DESIGN

EXPERTISE

**CULTURES AND
TECHNOLOGIES
OF KNOWLEDGE**

EDITED BY DOMINIC BOYER

A list of titles in this series is available at www.cornellpress.cornell.edu.

Swedish Design

An Ethnography

Keith M. Murphy

Cornell University Press

Ithaca and London

First published 2015 by Cornell University Press
First printing, Cornell Paperbacks, 2015
Printed in the United States of America

Library of Congress Cataloging-in-Publication Data

Murphy, Keith M., author.
  Swedish design : an ethnography / Keith M. Murphy.
    pages cm. — (Expertise : cultures and technologies of knowledge)
  Includes bibliographical references and index.
  ISBN 978-0-8014-5329-8 (cloth : alk. paper) —
  ISBN 978-0-8014-7966-3 (pbk. : alk. paper)
  1. Design—Anthropological aspects—Sweden. 2. Material culture—
Sweden—Philosophy. 3. Ethnology—Sweden. I. Title.
  NK1461.A1M87 2015
  306.4'709485—dc23   2014041686

Cornell University Press strives to use environmentally responsible
suppliers and materials to the fullest extent possible in the publishing of
its books. Such materials include vegetable-based, low-VOC inks and
acid-free papers that are recycled, totally chlorine-free, or partly composed
of nonwood fibers. For further information, visit our website at
www.cornellpress.cornell.edu.

Cloth printing   10 9 8 7 6 5 4 3 2 1
Paperback printing   10 9 8 7 6 5 4 3 2 1

CONTENTS

ACKNOWLEDGMENTS

Without the backing of a vast conspiracy of supporters, this book would not exist. I'd like to start by thanking Alessandro Duranti, Candy Goodwin, Chuck Goodwin, and Paul Kroskrity, who, when I came to them and said "hand gestures plus furniture plus Sweden plus anthropology," decided not to lose their faith in me. A number of other mentors at UCLA also helped shape the trajectory of this book, including Niko Besnier, Linda Garro, John Heritage, Doug Hollan, Elinor Ochs, Mel Pollner, and Manny Schegloff.

My colleagues, past and present, at the University of California, Irvine, have pushed my thinking and writing in directions I'd have never discovered on my own, and I'd especially like to thank Victoria Bernal, Tom Boellstorff, Angela Garcia, Julia Lupton, Bill Maurer, Sanjoy Mazumdar, Michael Montoya, Valerie Olson, Kris Peterson, and Kaushik Sunder Rajan. George Marcus has productively encouraged me to expand my views of both design and anthropology. All of my students at UCI—in particular Julka Almquist, Lilly Irani, Janny Li, and Stevie Rea—have in some way influenced this book. Iris Flores and Rachel Ulgado provided invaluable bibliographic assistance. And thanks to the Department of Anthropology staff, especially Norma Miranda, who takes care of all the things that need taking care of.

Over the years I have benefited immensely from conversations with a wide array of interlocutors whose voices echo throughout these pages. I was fortunate enough to be surrounded by a brilliant and generous group of graduate students at UCLA, including Steven Black, Anjali Browning, Mara Buchbinder, Cre Engelke, Inmaculada Garcia-Sánchez, Hanna Garth, Rachel George, Jeff Good, Anthony Graesch, Mi Kyung Kim, Heather Loyd, Angela Nonaka, Daisy Rooks, Merav Shohet, Jesse Summers, and Anja Vogel. I'd especially like to acknowledge the perseverance and dedication of Kevin Groark, Justin Richland, Kristen Schilt, and Jason Throop (the first person to hear of my plan to work in Sweden), all of whom have provided critical input at every stage of this project. For their own various bits of wisdom, insight, and assistance prior to and during the writing of the book, I'd like to thank Shoham Arad, Don Brenneis, Mary Bucholtz, Graham Jones, Susan Gal, Wendy Gunn, Cori Hayden, Jamer Hunt, Don Kulick, Lotta Björklund Larsen, Michael Lempert, Per Linell, Chris McCray, Lorenza Mondada, Howard Morphy, Smoki Musaraj, Constantine Nakassis, Todd Nicewonger, Mihir Pandya, Marina Peterson, Michael Silverstein, Ivan Small, Roger Säljö, and Marketa Velehradska. Thanks also to my friends Paul Connor, Jennifer Tsang, Kerry Tulson, Ann Walters, and Anna Krakus, who is not just a friend, but also the central pillar supporting everything in this book.

The list of people who have selflessly helped me in Sweden is long. I'd like to thank the office of the Swedish Fulbright Commission, Jeannette Lindström, Monica Dahlen, Nina Forsblad, and Antonietta Oppenheimer for easing my transition into the Stockholm way of living. Karin Junefelt, my "Swedish mom," demonstrated more kindness and generosity than I thought any normal human being was capable of. At Stockholm University, the Social Anthropology Department welcomed me with open arms, and I'd especially like to thank Ulf Hannerz, Christina Garsten, Shahram Khosravi, Johan Lindquist, Karin Norman, and Helena Wulff, as well as Laila Abdallah, Victor Alneng, Raoul Galli, and Johanna Gullberg. And for going above and beyond, Eva Lundgren and Renita Thedvall are true saints. I would also like to thank Mathias Broth,

Lucas Gottzén, Jonas Ivarsson, Oskar Lindwall, and Gustav Lymer, my staunchest intellectual supporters and interlocutors in Sweden. And without my friends Cameron Britt, Garrett Bucks, Jorg De Vries, Theresa Harmanen, Fredrik Johansson-Oviedo, Kjersti Knox, Cora Lacatus, Rebecca Lundberg, and Mia Marchner, fieldwork in Stockholm would surely have been a drag.

Many others in Sweden have contributed to the development of this project, but I'd like to thank in particular Jan Carl Adelswärd, Viveka Adelswärd, Karin Aronsson, Stella D'Ailly, Ronald Jones, Bronek Krakus, Urszula Krakus, Karl Lallerstedt, Lars Lallerstedt, Sara Lönnroth, Jonas Nobel, Dominic Power, Cilla Robach, Helena Scragg, Yngve Sundblad, Anna-Marie Svensson, Niklas Wolkert, Måns Wrange, and Christina Zetterlund.

I must profusely thank all of the folks who graciously allowed me a glimpse of their own small corners of the Swedish design world, especially the designers who opened their doors to me. Most will remain unnamed, but you know who you are. However there is an obvious exception in Peter, Matti, and Fredrik, whose work—in every sense of the term—has fundamentally made this book possible. Tack så jätte mycket.

Various pieces of this project were presented at a number of different conferences, colloquia, and workshops, and participants in those events have been instrumental in giving form to my otherwise inchoate ideas. These include members of the Department of Anthropology at the University of California, Santa Cruz; the Department of Communication and Rhetorical Studies at Syracuse University; the Departments of Anthropology and Sociology at the University of Chicago; the Social Anthropology Department at Stockholm University; Södertörn University College in Södertörn, Sweden; the Linnaeus Centre for Research on Learning, Interaction, and Mediated Communication in Contemporary Society (LinCS) at the University of Gothenburg; the American Anthropological Association; the International Conference on Conversation Analysis in Mannheim, Germany; and the Swedish Women's Education Association in San Francisco.

At Cornell University Press my deepest thanks go to series editor Dominic Boyer, for his unwavering advocacy; Peter Potter, for his careful guidance; Sara Ferguson, for her patience and efficiency; Marian Rogers, for her eagle eyes and cleverness; and Lisa DeBoer for compiling the index.

I'd also like to thank Svensk Form's Design Arkiv for granting permission to use images from the Stockholm and Helsingborg exhibitions, and the Swedish Post and Carl Zedig at Playsam for permission to include the Streamliner stamp. The Fulbright Program of the United States Department of State, the American-Scandinavian Foundation, and SWEA San Francisco all helped fund the research for this book.

And finally I'd like to thank my mother, Rosemary Murphy, my father, Richard Murphy, and my sister, Colleen Scott, for their love and support over the years. I've written this book in honor of my late uncle, Paul Kerrigan, who died suddenly and early while I was living in Sweden. Without his influence, this book would not exist.

Introduction

DISENTANGLING SWEDISH DESIGN

This is a book about design. More specifically this book is an ethnographic study of Swedish design, how design and designing work in Sweden, and how the ordinary things of the world there, the often-unnoticed accoutrements of everyday life, have come to acquire a certain political vitality. Over the course of the twentieth century, stemming from even earlier origins and continuing today, a powerful and pervasive discourse has emerged amid the parallel developments of both the Swedish model of welfare politics and a distinctive Scandinavian design aesthetic that endeavors to link social democratic ideologies to the forms and functions of mundane objects, like furniture and other household goods. Tables, lamps, and chairs are not just things, from this discursive point of view; they are *just* things, things that in their widespread presence politicize the everyday world through a subliminal semiosis that suggests, but does not necessarily impose, a significant, experience-near means for managing well-being in everyday life. Alongside an expectation that the Swedish political system is organized to "care" for its citizens, designed things in Sweden—especially those bearing simple and minimal forms—are expected to "care" for their users in ways that align with, if only unevenly, political and cultural values of social responsibility that hold long-standing purchase in Swedish society. What I present in this book, then, is an ethnography of this premise, of the culturally immanent claim that Swedish design is political in a particularly Swedish way, a claim that has essentially become a cultural theorem for explaining relations between people, things, and politics in Sweden. By following the actors, practices, and processes involved in producing Swedish design, I am deliberately sidestepping Langdon Winner's (1980) famous query, "Do artifacts have politics?"—though always keeping it in view—to address what could be considered a more fundamental question—*How are things designed to be political?* Or in even more basic terms, *How are things made to mean?* And in that making-meaningful, how do they help give shape to the social world?

Thus while this book is centered on the particulars of design in Sweden, it also offers an anthropological rumination on the very concept of "design" itself. Amid long-standing interests in art, aesthetics, production, consumption, and materiality, anthropologists have spent comparatively little effort closely exploring design as an analytic category and designing as a social practice. This is not to say, of course, that design has been entirely ignored—the recent development of "design anthropology" (Clarke 2010; Gunn and Donovan 2012; Gunn, Otto, and Smith 2013) refutes that—but perhaps when speaking of anthropology's view of design historically and in general, a better description might be "passed over." Anthropological treatments of topics like style, material culture, and architecture, among others, all at least implicitly attend to issues of design, while studies of artisans, craftspeople, and technicians at work often capture practices that constitute the small details of design work. What most of these accounts tend to pass over, however, is a serious engagement with the nature of design as a cultural phenomenon, as an assemblage of actors, practices, forms, and ideologies that all sit at the very core of what Nelson Goodman (1978) calls "ways of worldmaking." To be sure, design is a peculiar beast, encompassing "things" and "styles" and "practices" and "practitioners" all at once, but also "meanings" and "attitudes" and "behaviors," without any one of these receding too far into the shadows when others are brought into focus. Design shares many qualities with "art," and is often mistaken for "technology," but in most instances overlaps with both and neither of these things at the same time. Design is centrally concerned with making, preoccupied with form, and always accountable to particular social, economic, and ideological flows that lap against and surge beyond the designed objects themselves. In most instances design is a locally contingent and culturally elaborated process of production, a background scheme organizing the ways in which things are made. In other cases, such as in Sweden, design is granted a different kind of import, a degree of cultural significance that exceeds its simplest elements. Heeding Lucy Suchman's (2011:3) call for "a critical anthropology *of* design [that] requires, among other things, ethnographic projects that articulate the cultural imaginaries and micropolitics that delineate design's promises and practices," I submit in this book one path for exploring design as an anthropological object of inquiry.[1] What I present is not the only way to do so, of course—and it may not even be the best way—but my aim is to provide a working model, a prototype, for an anthropology of design that draws together the various nodes and links that all in their own ways help render design a critical aspect of the ongoing production and reproduction of social worlds.

I come to this project with training in linguistic anthropology, one by-product of which is an attunement to how certain kinds of language, certain registers, circle around and alight on the things of the world, and indeed, I was first drawn to exploring design in Sweden through the distinct ways in which it is talked about there. The most prominent, especially to outsiders, is a register of national identity attached to particular kinds of objects. *Svensk design*, "Swedish design," is unquestionably a conventional and popular branding device, with many companies—most notably, but by no means exclusively, the furniture retailer Ikea—explicitly promoting their products as examples of *god design*, "good design," with a relation of near identity holding between the two. But *svensk design* does not simply represent "good" design made in Sweden. It also projects a powerful, concrete rendering of a sort of essentialized "Swedishness" embedded in objects identifiable as emblems of nationalist pride. Thus in 2005 the Swedish Post issued stamps bearing the images of a number of highly recognizable pieces of Swedish design, including the Streamliner toy car made by Playsam (fig. 1), and the Speedglas welding helmet originally designed by Ergonomi Design, officially marking these commonplace objects as significant, state-approved tokens of Swedish culture alongside more tradi-

SVERIGE BREV

S.LUND   LEKSAKSBIL. ULF HANSES   INRIKES   L.SJÖÖBLOM sc 2005

Figure 1. In 2005, Posten (the Swedish postal service) issued a series of stamps celebrating six icons of Swedish design, including the Streamliner toy car, made by Playsam. Reproduced with permission of Posten AB and Playsam.

tional examples of cultural kitsch, like the *dalahäst*, a colorful, hand-carved wooden horse found somewhere in nearly every Swedish home.

But this linking of particular objects to national identity is not the only way design is talked about in Sweden. A second and in some ways more subtle register circulating around Swedish design and its objects, one advanced not only by scholars, critics, and other design-interested actors, but even by ordinary Swedes, is that which concerns the "social democratic" morality of everyday goods. Frankly, this kind of talk was more puzzling to me when I first visited Sweden. While symbolic connections between material culture and group identity are to be expected, I was hard pressed to see chairs and lamps as "moral" in any way. To me a chair was made for sitting—or maybe for reaching high shelves or piling my clothes on—and while I was able to identify the features that made different chairs look different from one another, I had no firsthand access to the seemingly taken-for-granted associations between design and politics that were so popular in Swedish design discourse. Of course my inability to see the chair like a Swede purportedly sees it could easily be attributed to something as vague as "cultural difference," and indeed a dynamic of alterity was at play. But rather than attribute the connections between politics and design to a factor

of socialization and move on, I chose instead to linger, to probe this relationship a little more deeply. Why these things? Why these forms? Why
these politics? What makes all of this hold together?

This book can perhaps best be described as an exploration, a "following" in Tim Ingold's (2012) terms, of the ways in which certain things are
given form in Sweden and why those forms matter, how those things are
rendered political objects, and how the tenuous synthesis between concrete shapes and abstract ideologies is reproduced and perpetuated as a
credible and culturally significant bond. To be clear, the claim that a chair
or any other object is political is at its core simply an assertion. It might
be an assertion based in some intuitive sense, but it is nonetheless an argument, and like all arguments it requires support and justification and
explanation in order to realize the potential of its persuasive effects. Thus
what I present in this book is a tracing of how a range of social actors
and institutions continuously, asymmetrically, and in most cases without
coordination, collectively contribute to the reproduction of a long-standing
cultural argument for the political nature of everyday things in Sweden.

I should clarify outright that this book is by no means a definitive history of Swedish design. Much is left out, and in many respects much more
is included than what is typically addressed by most design scholars. Anyone versed in the history of Swedish or Scandinavian design will probably
find the account I am presenting dissatisfying in many respects, partly because I am telling a story that, at least in its broadest silhouette, is already
well known, and partly because it does not dwell too long on the expected
icons—both people and things—of Swedish design. But another of those
sorts of accounts is not what I have set out to give, and indeed, they already
exist elsewhere in abundance.[2] In fact many such sources, because of the
ways in which they circulate as professional, institutionally backed assessments of Swedish design, act as data in my analysis, as some of the clear-
est visual and discursive representations of the cultural contours of design
in Sweden. Rather than replicating these sorts of accounts, I am trying
instead to get beneath them and around them, to explore how material
and ideological forms are made to correspond in credible ways, how this
relationship becomes cultural, and how it persists over time.

One of the chief characteristics of most scholarly treatments of design is
a tendency to focus on elite designers and their work—names and images
that for various reasons rise to the surface of public consciousness. While

elites certainly do exert a tremendous amount of influence on the practices, discourses, and emblems of Swedish design—or of any design tradition, for that matter—there is much more going on both "on the ground" and "in the air" that powerfully contributes to making things mean. Indeed, examining "design" as a sociocultural formation through a framework predominantly based on elites and the relatively restricted domains in which they operate does not capture the broad reality of designing in action.[3] While I certainly do deal with historical and contemporary elites of different sorts in this book, I spend more time with people whose names will probably never achieve the status of designers like Bruno Mathsson, Stig Lindberg, or Ingegerd Råman; companies too small to stand alongside Svenskt Tenn, Lammhults, or Kosta Boda; and objects far less iconic than a Hasselblad camera, a Tio Gruppen textile pattern, or Jonas Bohlin's famous *Concrete* chair. I stake the strong position that the kind of design expertise that contributes to the ongoing reproduction of Swedish design is fundamentally distributed across a wider range of people, practices, spaces, and institutions than an elite model is able to capture. Over the course of a year living in Stockholm, and shorter trips to Sweden spread out over another eight, I worked closely with dozens of designers, most of whom are young and trying to make a career out of their creative work—some quite successfully, and others less so. I attended design exhibitions of various kinds and interviewed their curators. I interacted with design students both in and out of the classroom, including at the annual *vårutställningar*, the exhibitions of graduating students' work that all of the design schools in Sweden put up each spring. I talked to designers, professors, curators, and political consultants who write about design in different venues and for different audiences, and I read the work they produced. I also spent a great deal of time with Swedish interlocutors who have no direct relationship to design other than as consumers of everyday goods, shopping with them, spending time in their homes, and moving through the city with them, all the while trying to document the *feelings and ideas* that design can evoke.

Let me here lay out the central thesis of the book: designers, at least those who work under that title, are only partially responsible for making *svensk design*—and as we will see, most of those I worked with do not even see themselves as doing so. To be sure, the social dynamics and practices of studio design work are absolutely critical for producing things, for producing "design"—and I will argue this vigorously—but these dynamics always run alongside other kinds of cultural flows. The most central contribution designers make is in the continual reproduction of form, of a standard kind of form that bears specific properties that afford the attribution of specific meanings. Those forms, instantiated in objects and released into the world, attract their ideological associations only through a constant circulation between different—and differently ordered—cultural domains. I follow design through a number of these domains, like museums, stores, and trade shows, in policies and media forms and other discursive imaginaries, to uncover the processes by which the forms given to objects in the studio acquire their ideological substances, the processes within which the political is applied to the material. While such processes tend to operate in relative isolation from one another, the reproduction and preservation of *svensk design*, the durable hybrid of minimalist aesthetics and social democratic ideology, is vitally dependent on all of them at once. What this means, then, is that design—or at least Swedish design—cannot be reduced to either the things themselves or to acts of designing, nor can we acknowledge both but favor only one. Things and practices, forms and matter, people and processes, and history and language, all of this and more is tightly entangled in the very existential fiber of design, and understanding design as a social force means following each of these as they move, tracing their relations, and accounting for their reciprocal effects.

Design in Stockholm

On a sunny afternoon in the late spring of 2006 I accompanied my friend Anders as he deposited his recycling at a facility a short drive away from his apartment in the Vasastan area of Stockholm. I had never been to this particular recycling center before—in fact, I never knew it existed, though I had passed it dozens of times in the ten months I had lived in the city. As we approached the familiar frame of the Wenner-Gren Center,[4] a shining skyscraper rising high above a neighborhood of midrise apartment blocks, Anders slowed the car and began to pull off the road. He angled his Volvo toward a concrete gate precisely carved into the craggy cliffs facing the Wenner-Gren Center tower, and without hesitating he drove directly inside. Simple fluorescent lights hung from the ceiling, and the rocky walls were moist. The air grew staler and stiller as we proceeded farther into the artificial cave, but, somewhat surprisingly, the light increased around us. Finally, the end of the tunnel expanded, and we entered a huge cavern lined with giant steel bins not unlike shipping containers. I was incredulous that this was the recycling center, but Anders only laughed as he stepped out of his car, handed me a paper bag full of random metal pieces, and pointed me to the ladder leaning against a nearby bin.

This was a recycling facility like no other I had ever seen. It was a former civil defense compound, I was told, abandoned at the end of the Cold War, but in subsequent years converted to meet the more urgent needs of an officially neutral and ecologically conscious nation. At that point I had been living in Sweden almost a year studying design and the people who make it, but only then, standing in that recycling center, a vast and obscure cavern hidden at the edge of the central city, did I come to realize what lies at the heart of the Swedish attitude toward design—and indeed, toward the politics of social life—a careful observation of the world as it is, and an unfaltering commitment to forming it and reforming it according to some collective definition of "better."

Throughout the city of Stockholm, and in other parts of Sweden, too, design is conspicuously present and unavoidably *sensed* in the rhythms of everyday life. In its most obvious guise it thrives as an explicit category of things set apart from other "mere" objects through their particular qualities, the ways they are described, and the places where they reside. Retail targeting different types of consumers—both those specifically interested in design and those who are not—crowds the urban landscape. Renowned specialty shops like Kosta Boda and Svenskt Tenn sell high-end glass and metalware to a predominantly wealthy clientele, while department stores like Åhléns and Nordiska Kompaniet (NK) pitch a wider range of designed goods to a wider range of middle-class consumers. DesignTorget, a chain of seventeen stores spread throughout the country (and one store in Oslo), sells a curated and continuously updated selection of designed everyday goods, mostly for the home, the garden, and other intimate sorts of spaces. Alongside this pervasive design-oriented retail presence, many of the city's museums and galleries feature exhibitions focused specifically on some aspect of design, or spotlight the work of particularly influential designers, like Stig Lindberg, Sigvard Bernadotte, and Bruno Mathsson

Figure 2. Poster for the *Design: Stockholm* exhibit at Stockholms Stadsmuseum, one of many permanent and temporary exhibitions dedicated to design in Sweden. Photograph by the author.

(see fig. 2). Even the Stockholm subway, billed as "the world's longest art exhibition," is designed not just as a public transportation system, but also as a *destination* for aesthetic experience, with 90 percent of its stations fitted with permanent or temporary art installations.

While these and other venues provide an accessible infrastructure through which the public is exposed to or can interact with design, in Stockholm design also operates in even more pervasive but less apparent ways. Moving through the city is eased and constrained by features of the urban environment structured to ensure that a positive "spatial acting-out of the place," as Michel de Certeau (1984:98) would say, is possible for all types of people. The grain of the tiled sidewalks is coarser at corners than in the block so that the blind, feeling the difference in texture through their canes, know where to stop and cross. There are no buttons for pedestrians to push to change the traffic signal, only small, low-hung boxes (reachable by children, the elderly, and people in wheelchairs) that, with only a gentle hand-press, respond with a loud beep as feedback. Elevators and escalators are architecturally endemic, and on small staircases in public and private spaces there are often ramps, usually two flat metal rails, installed for easily maneuvering baby carriages over otherwise unnavigable steps. And in the city center the facades of many buildings, especially residential ones, are famously painted in light colors, often pastels, that brighten the skyline's image during the gloomy days of winter. All of these small details, seamlessly integrated into the surface of the city and virtually unnoticed in daily life, indicate a certain deliberate *forethought* in urban design directed not simply at creating environments for some idealized city dweller, but at creating environments that anticipate the everyday needs of even the most overlooked sectors of society—design for all in a very real sense.

While the outward face of design in Sweden is largely, but by no means exclusively, geared to a public audience, a sensitivity to the force of design redounds just as powerfully in Swedish private lives and everyday practices. To a large extent this is no accident, a product of both explicit and implicit exposure to design and its effects over time. Most Swedes receive some basic instruction in Scandinavian design history during their early education, and many can at least recognize, if not recite in detail, the contributions of key artists and designers to modern Swedish culture.

The home is the primary site where design touches the surface of everyday experience at the smallest level of detail. Minimum room sizes and the dimensions and functions of certain kitchen equipment, like stoves and ovens, are regulated according to government standards, guided by a strong preference for maximizing the comfort and safety of users. Electric stovetops, for example, include a small light that, when illuminated, indicates that the surface is too hot to touch. Door handles on both public and private bathroom doors often include small red and green dials that indicate if a lock is bolted or unbolted from within, notifying the bathroom-needy whether or not it is safe to enter. And to the degree that it is possible, homes themselves are usually designed to maximize the available sunlight during the dark winter months, and light-colored walls and furniture help to keep open spaces bright.

Most workplaces, too, are constructed following similar principles. Bright, open spaces are thought to improve morale, and comfortable chairs and desks make long work hours more tolerable to workers and easier on weary bodies. Full kitchens are common in Swedish offices, and coffee, tea, and snacks are almost always on hand for an afternoon *fika*, the sacrosanct coffee break around which the workday is usually organized in a worker's experience. In one design firm I visited, four employees took advantage of the open floor plan of their office to play an impromptu game of soccer on a slow afternoon. While all workplaces are of course different, and each industry has its own architectural requirements, the overall attitude toward workplace design in Sweden is not one in which spaces *contain* workers, but one in which workers *inhabit* spaces.

Design, then, functions as a purposeful and thoughtful structuring of the lived world in Swedish society. In a word, design is *always there*, in the background of everyday life, and while its effects are usually hard to measure, they are often quite easily felt. Designed objects and spaces more or less permeate *all* societies, of course, yet because so many common objects and spaces in Sweden narrowly center on the enhancement of everyday life, Swedish design assumes a cultural significance beyond the necessity for *things*. Design becomes a tool for improving individual practices, common problems, and shared needs. It is not treated as a specialty service or an obstacle to profit, but rather the basic starting point for crafting a just society. In Sweden, so the cultural model goes, design is everywhere and belongs to everyone.

Methods, Narratives, and Forms of Life

The research for this book was conducted intermittently over ten years. This included a twelve-month period living in Stockholm between 2005 and 2006, supplemented by short trips, between two and six weeks each, almost every year between 2007 and 2013. The bulk of the work was centered in Stockholm, but I also spent time in Gothenburg and visited other smaller and larger towns. In order to grasp the extent and reach of the Swedish design world, I interviewed an eclectic set of people whose work and relations continuously reproduce it, including not only designers themselves, but also professors, design students, consumers, government officials, professional organization administrators, and others. In order to identify and extract the ideologies associated with Swedish design, and assess the domains in which they most prominently circulate, I applied discourse analytic methods to a range of design-related media sources (as well as my interviews). These included, among others, publications like national and local newspapers, popular and professional magazines (both contemporary and historical), design-themed books, museum and store catalogs, and a few televisual sources. And because museums, galleries, and exhibitions are significant spatial forums in which design objects and design discourse are mobilized, I spent time at as many of these as I could, mapping them, recording their contents, transcribing the copy from relevant museum labels, and talking with their curators, if possible. I also returned to these venues with native Swedes—sometimes design professionals, sometimes not—to try to evoke a "native" reading of these exhibits.

This project began, though, with a central focus on the practical work of designers. My interest in the production of Swedish design initially stemmed from a desire to understand designing from the designer's point of view—that is, through the mundane, linguistically mediated actions that comprise everyday design work. As a linguistic anthropologist I work from the assumption that language is not simply a means of representing ideas and things and feelings in socially sharable forms, but is also deeply constitutive of the various cultural activities that collectively give shape to lived reality. To be sure, language-in-interaction functions in many different ways to give meaning to the things that humans care about. But language also sits at the center of what Ludwig Wittgenstein (2009) calls "language games," the regulated, collaborative activities that serve as the machines with which meaning is socially produced, assigned, and distributed in everyday interaction. Everything we do with language—from simple actions like "referring" or "defining," to more complex ones, like "negotiating" or "convincing" or "glossing"—is, like a game, conditioned along particular sorts of regulating lines and performed through particular sorts of social roles. And almost every social action we perform in the world is thoroughly suffused with both spoken and embodied language. Thus understanding designing and the situated activities that comprise it requires paying close attention to the details of the "language games" that designers engage in as they work through producing their designs.

To that end I spent a lot of time inside design studios and design offices as part of this project, talking to designers and observing how they use their most typical tools, such as computers, paper, pens, and pencils, but also observing and inscribing how they talk to each other. To capture design work at this level of detail I relied primarily on a Canon GL1 video camera, which, when I was granted permission, I would set up in an inconspicuous spot and train on the center of activity in the studio. In some cases

I also audio-recorded interactions with a digital recorder. When I returned to the States these video- and audio-recordings were, with the help of a native speaker of Swedish, transcribed in detail using the methods of multimodal analysis (see, e.g., Murphy 2012; Streeck, Goodwin, and LeBaron 2011), including transcribing not only speech but also gestures and other embodied actions.

For Wittgenstein language games are not simply games—or really games at all—but what he calls "forms of life." That is to say, the language-centered activities that predominantly comprise the carrying out of everyday interaction are the force that gives shape and order to the lived social world. Life, as it were, is largely formed through the ways we use language. And yet the ways we use language are clearly not all there is to it. So while I began my research on Swedish design by focusing on the language games that designers perform in the studio, it became clear to me that these forms of life, in a quite literal sense, generate and are conditioned by other distinct forms of life that require their own kinds of scrutiny. Thus what I present in the rest of this book is a deep exploration of Swedish design as a series of interlocked and homologous forms of life—forms of work, forms of things, rhetorical forms, and political forms—all of which at least provisionally convene in social space and across time through what Wittgenstein (2009) calls "family resemblances," or similarities of various sorts that hold between different—but through their resemblances, related—phenomena. In following design across practices and discourses, spaces and things, rhetoric and politics, I treat different phenomena methodologically on their own terms. But at the same time I argue that these family resemblances are what tie together Swedish design as a resonant and forceful cultural category, at once both material and ideal, stable and dynamic, that continuously reinstantiates a certain political ideology in the everyday world.

A note on the role of history, and my use of it, in the text. In examining the role of historical figures and events in the development of Swedish design and politics, I generally fall in line with the interpretive approach to historiography forwarded by Paul Ricoeur (2004) and Hayden White (1973, 1978, 1987), both of whom grant narrative—as both form and method—a critical role in that endeavor. One of the many forms that the cultural object called "Swedish design" takes in Sweden is a narrative, at once both grand and demure—grand because it spans a long period of time and often seems just a little too neat; demure because its contours are deceptively simple. It is a narrative populated by a cast of well-known protagonists, like Ellen Key, Mats Theselius, Mårten Claesson, Eero Koivisto, and Ola Rune, but also by particular recognizably "Swedish" everyday objects. It is structured temporally, progressively from the nineteenth century until today, through a series of emplotments, crises, and resolutions. And of course so too is social democracy in Sweden, and its role in shaping contemporary Swedish society. I conditionally accept the narrative of Swedish design partly because it is the form in which ideas about both design and politics are organized in people's minds and on their lips, and partly because this narrative and its various elements, in their constant circulation, serve to establish core cultural conditions of possibility for the continued survival of both political and material forms. "The historical narrative," White (1987:21) asserts, "reveals to us a world that is putatively 'finished,' done with, over, and yet not dissolved, not falling apart." It is this apparent coherence and cohesion of the Swedish design narrative—its "not falling apart"-ness—that is one of my central objects of inquiry. Rather than simply assuming the narrative and taking its plotlines for granted, in my presentation I am pulling at its edges, plumbing depths that have not yet been explored—or that have been considered too inconsequential to consider much—and testing the strings that hold it together. In doing so I am of course partly overstating my point: in order to examine the narrative in its finest details requires accenting attributes that are certainly present, but also somewhat subdued in the flows of everyday life, and part of my task is to bring those attributes to the surface. In other words, what I am doing is offering an ethnographic autopsy of the narrative of Swedish design, examining its semiotic integrity as it is tossed onto the surface of the lived social world and taken up by the people who inhabit it.

Of course the story I am excavating is not without its detractors. As powerful as the narrative of Swedish design is in Sweden, counterdiscourses are also quite prominent, especially in recent years. Two books in particular, published in the early 2000s, initiated a turning point in the discourse of Swedish design—that is, its ostensibly positive political bent—and opened up new possibilities for critiquing the dominant model I am working with. Both books attacked what their authors characterized as the elitism of Swedish design and its moralizing commensuration of taste and form. In 2002, designer Zandra Ahl and journalist Emma Olsson

(Ahl and Olsson 2002) published *Svensk Smak: Myter om den Moderna Formen* (Swedish Taste: Myths of the Modern Form), in which they advanced a strong critique of the uniformity and significance of Swedish design. In the book they argued that the concept of "Swedish design" works more effectively as a global marketing device than as a description of real design conditions in Sweden. Rather than treating design as a benign manifestation of social democratic goodwill, they argued that modern design has been used in Sweden as a manifestation of power and dominance in everyday life.

Two years later, design historian Linda Rampell published a 750-page tome, based on her doctoral dissertation, entitled *Designatlas: En Resa Genom Designteori 1845–2002* (Design Atlas: A Journey through Design Theory, 1845–2002). While the title and topic seemed anodyne enough, the book was in fact quite controversial—so controversial that its first print run sold out almost immediately. In the book Rampell presented familiar material covering the development of design in Sweden—including people and events addressed in this book, such as Ellen Key (chapter 3) and the Stockholm Exhibition of 1930 (chapter 4)—but within her exposition she also detailed a scathing reinterpretation of modernism's viselike grip on design and politics in Sweden. In particular she targeted the decades-long obsession with linking rigid conceptions of "the good" with similarly rigid instantiations of "pure form" (see Akner-Kohler 2007), which, according to Rampell (2003), have led to a popular "enslavement" in Sweden—a characterization that many reviewers of the book (e.g., Jonsson 2003) were hard pressed to accept.

These two books and the debates they fostered not only cleared a space for discussing the dominant narrative of Swedish design in new, more critical terms, but also helped usher in a new chapter in contemporary Swedish design called *konceptdesign* (see chapter 4). Less focused on the use and practicality of objects, much of the work that fell under the *konceptdesign* rubric in the early to mid-2000s was directly oriented toward challenging deep-seated and taken-for-granted assumptions about the material world, including the particular kinds of people for whom design is designed. Many of these objects were deliberately crafted with humor or pique in order to excite reactions in users or viewers. While modernist forms conforming to traditional Swedish design were often used, they were also played with, through extension or elongation or asymmetry. And some objects were explicitly nonfunctional, or their uses were difficult to discern. As design historian and curator Cilla Robach (2005:7) phrased it in an introductory essay to a major exhibition of some of these works, "Konceptdesign is not an expression. It's an approach. A critical approach. A design that questions. That identifies and investigates problems. That asks questions. Complicated questions."

While problems of various sorts—social, political, economic—have been central in the production of Swedish design from the very beginning, much of what designers were producing in the early and mid-2000s was consciously reflexive in ways that were distinct from earlier critical design work. By embedding a critique of what design is and what it does in the forms and materials and functions of objects themselves, these designers attempted to use their products rather than just their voices to push Swedish design into new critical territory. And from a certain vantage point it worked. The debates and discussions that have developed since the mid-2000s have allowed new cohorts of design graduates—many of whom have been taught by the designers who matured in the *konceptdesign* space—to innovate more broadly in form and concept. And yet during that time and since then, in the pages of the major design journals and on the floors of the Stockholm Furniture Fair, in shops and galleries and in people's homes, the dominant forms of normative Swedish design have persisted, and have done so quite vibrantly. Indeed, even in the critique, the challenge to Swedish design interpellates and reinstantiates the dominant narrative.

Sweden as an Ethnographic Site

I ended up in Stockholm because that was where the designers were—or a lot of them, anyway—and that was also where the museums, shops, design schools, and politicians were. And when I got to Stockholm I spent quite a bit of time in a part of the city called Södermalm, because when it comes to contemporary design, that was, I was told, the place to be. Most of the studios I visited were located in this section of the city, and most of the designers I worked with lived there, or near there. While the institutional presence of design is dispersed throughout the city—in stores, museums, galleries, and schools—Södermalm is the epicenter for young Swedish creatives looking to make a name for themselves in design.

Södermalm is the southernmost and largest island of those that make up the central portion of the city of Stockholm. Historically dominated by working-class neighborhoods dotting the sheer cliffs at the shore and lining the hilly inland topography, Söder, as it is often referred to, is now Stockholm's intellectual and artistic center and one of the most important sites in the Stockholm design world. It also represents the cultural, if not geographic, counterpoint to Östermalm, the northeast section of Stockholm, which has traditionally been home to the city's moneyed and noble classes. While Östermalm's long, green, radiating boulevards were designed to give the city an air of Parisian opulence once thought befitting the bourgeoisie who lived there, Söder still retains much of its relatively recent working-class aesthetic.

Over the past several decades an affordable housing stock has drawn masses of young professionals and artists to Södermalm, transforming many of the island's formerly seedy and dangerous neighborhoods into chic, bohemian districts full of restaurants, cafes, boutiques, and nightclubs. This has, consequently, raised the standard of living there, and today Söder displays a level of luxury rivaling even Östermalm's, and does so along more than one symbolic axis. While Strandvägen in Östermalm has historically been and continues to be the richest street in Sweden, Södermalm's hip boutiques and design studios rival the many high-end and high-class galleries and design shops of Östermalm. And yet while these two sections of the city unofficially participate in a sort of civic status competition with one another, they continue to reflect the strict, essentially class-based divisions that have characterized them since at least Stockholm's expansion in the mid-nineteenth century (see Deland 2001). Politically Östermalm is one of the most conservative areas in all of Sweden, voting overwhelmingly in favor of the conservative alliance in the 2006 and 2010 national elections that installed Moderaterna, the center-right Moderates, as Sweden's ruling party for eight years. Södermalm's residents, on the other hand, despite voting more conservatively than in the past, have retained a healthy allegiance to political parties on the left end of the spectrum.

Thus Södermalm, as home to Stockholm's—and Sweden's—most vibrant art, design, and music scenes, is defined not only by what is produced there, in design studios and on nightclub stages, but also largely by what it does *not* offer. In broad strokes, where Östermalm represents an older social order dominated by establishment, conservative elites whose economic interests are today largely oriented toward the corporate sector, the image that Södermalm reflects is more progressive and independent: a place for young people who are still quite interested in making money, but who prefer to do it through innovation, creativity, and style. This is not to imply that Söder is unaffected by Sweden's push toward liberalization— for example, it is home to a rapidly emerging upper class, and housing prices there are now beyond the reach of most Swedes—yet in many ways the aura of Söder is a fitting example of social democracy's wider socio-political shift in contemporary Sweden: an embrace of overtly capitalist goals blended with traditional morals concerning how to go about achieving them. In other words, it is okay to make money, but it is best to do it in responsible ways.

Sweden has received comparatively little attention as an ethnographic location in recent years,[5] and most anthropological work has been directed to the details of specific practices and populations. Peter Stromberg (1983, 1986), for instance, has explored how congregants at a nonstate church in Stockholm build relationships of commitment to particular belief systems and religious practices, including some that share an underlying moral code with Swedish welfare politics. Gustav Peebles (2011) has critically analyzed the development of the Öresund Region, which bridges (literally) the city of Malmö, in southern Sweden, and Copenhagen, Denmark, alongside the attempted cultivation of the euro as a Pan-European currency. Don Kulick (2003, 2005) has examined complex cultural anxieties around sex, law, and politics in contemporary Sweden, and Cindy Isenhour (2010, 2011, 2013), working with groups and individuals who identify as ecologically minded, has analyzed the spread of sustainability as an emergent and powerful form of life in urban Sweden. And since at least the 1980s, immigration and immigrant communities have figured prominently in Swedish ethnography, including issues relating to ethnicity, race, and integration (Engelbrektsson 1986; Sawyer 2002), family planning (Sachs 1986), and language politics (Milani 2008; Milani and Jonsson 2012).

As Marianne Gullestad (1989b) has noted, much of the ethnographic and ethnological work on Scandinavian societies more generally has emphasized the home as a central cultural domain (Gullestad 1989a, 2001; Garvey 2003, 2005, 2008), and the minutiae of everyday life as the constituent material that underpins salient conceptions of national culture (O'Dell 1997; Frykman and Löfgren 1987). In Sweden such national identity often manifests in popular idioms of "Swedishness" (O'Dell 1998) or the "Swedish mentality" (Daun 1991, 1996, 1998; cf. Austin 1968), especially with regard to the preservation of tradition (Gaunt and Löfgren 1984), the construction of the Swedish middle class (Frykman and Löfgren 1987; Löfgren 1987), material culture and consumption (Löfgren 1993, 1997, 1999; O'Dell 1993), and Sweden's historical relationship with modernity itself (Frykman 1993; Löfgren 1991; Nilsson 1991). While the centrality of the home as a significant aspect of Swedish collective identity predates Sweden's emergence as a modern state, the home's position as a conceptual touchstone in contemporary society corresponds to the historical informalization of Swedish national culture in both public and private life throughout the twentieth century. Along with the development of the welfare state came the abolition of rigorous class and political structures (Löfgren 1988; Frykman 1995), and in the process social relations, both small scale and large scale, changed significantly. Government-directed informalization programs from the 1950s onward explicitly sought to alter people's behavior in order to promote equality and tolerance in everyday life, which led to, among other things, a severe reduction in the use of formal titles and pronouns, and an increase in the use of first names and informal pronouns—just as in the home—even in strict institutional settings (see Ahlgren 1978; Löfgren 2000).

The Political Textures of Swedish Cultural Life

Regardless of topic or perspective, though, it is virtually impossible to conduct ethnographic fieldwork in Sweden without somehow confronting the particular dynamics and values of the Swedish welfare state, first initiated by the Social Democratic Party (Sveriges Socialdemokratiska Arbetareparti, or SAP) in the early twentieth century. Social democratic politics—not necessarily the politics of the Social Democratic Party, but the welfare system it helped transform into a "cultural hegemony" (Tilton 1990:v)—either hums in the background or figures prominently in almost every previous ethnographic analysis of Sweden, and this book is obviously no exception to that trend. Indeed, the discourses and ideologies—the political ideas, as Sheri Berman (2006) calls them—are one of the central ethnographic concerns of the following chapters, and as such should be addressed in some detail.

The Swedish welfare state—first dubbed the "Swedish model" for an Anglophone audience by American journalist Marquis Childs in the 1930s (Childs 1936)—is typically considered one national manifestation of a more general "Nordic model" of welfare politics. The concept of the "Nordic model," which usually applies to the countries that constitute Norden, including Sweden, Norway, and Denmark in Scandinavia, as well as Finland and Iceland, came into prominence in the years following the end of World War II (Hilson 2008), when Norden itself emerged as a Cold War construct in a region searching for a voice within a cacophonous war-ravaged Europe (Waever 1992). The creation of a shared Nordic identity contributed to a kind of neighborly reconciliation. The centuries-long economic, cultural, and linguistic ties of the Nordic countries had been strained during the war, with Iceland occupied by the Allies, Denmark and Norway by the Germans, Sweden remaining officially neutral, and Finland staving off incursions from both the Germans and the Soviets (see Stenius, Österberg, and Östling 2008). Thus the concept of "Norden," with the Nordic model at its center, functioned as an affective bonding agent holding together a fragile regional postwar solidarity.

A number of other factors also contributed to the development of a shared Nordic identity and subsequently a general Nordic approach to welfare politics. At the time, all of these countries had relatively small populations, and historically, though not necessarily today, they were also, relatively speaking, ethnically and linguistically homogeneous. Moreover the geographical isolation of Scandinavia, which has been described as "the western part of Siberia" (Hagtvet and Rudeng 1984:227), necessitated some degree of cooperation both within national boundaries and across the region. But perhaps the strongest influence on the development of the Nordic model is the particular role played by the Social Democratic parties in the Nordic countries throughout the twentieth century (see chapter 2), parties that created through particular political operations and policy initiatives a welfare framework distinct from other "social market economies" (Pontusson 2011) developed in other regions of Europe and North America (Esping-Andersen 1990).[6]

Most characterizations of the Swedish welfare model tend to highlight four or five basic criteria—all of which are explicitly elaborated in Regeringsformen, or the Instrument of Government, one of the four fundamental laws that make up the Swedish Constitution—which provide the individual with a more or less high level of well-being in everyday life, and promote in their own ways values of care (*omsorg*), justice (*rättvisa*), and equality (*jämlikhet*), among others. According to this framework, the state should provide access to *employment* and job protections for all workers. This includes paid sick days and vacation, and agencies oriented to helping people find work and offering financial assistance to the unemployed. The state should also provide access to *education* for all citizens, the cost of which is subsidized by tax revenue. This includes primary and secondary education, but also higher education and professional schooling. A well-educated citizenry is a well-informed electorate, which is viewed by most Swedes as the backbone of a strong democracy. The provision of different kinds of insurance is the responsibility of Försäkringskassan, the Swedish Social Insurance Agency, including, among several others, *health insurance*. In recent years both the Social Democrats and the Moderates, who took control of government in 2006 but then lost control in 2014 (see below), have opened up the insurance and health-care markets to private business—with mixed results, according to many of my informants—but the core principle guiding even these reforms is that access to quality, affordable health care is a fundamental human right. The state also supplies *child-care assistance*, which takes the form of free or low-cost day care (*dagis*), after-school programs, money for some women who are unable to work during pregnancy (*graviditetspenning*), and generous parental leave options. Today in Sweden, after the birth of a child, mothers and fathers can share a total of thirteen months off between them while still receiving up to 80 percent of their normal pay, subsidized by the federal government. In addition, the state grants parents a small sum of money for each child every month to help meet basic material needs. Finally, the state should also offer and cultivate viable *pensions* for seniors, who have contributed to the growth of society and the economy over the course of their lives. Additionally in the Swedish case, in more recent years an emphasis on *environmentalism* and sustainable development has also become a prominent aspect of the welfare political economy (see Isenhour 2010).

The Swedish model—especially at its height in the 1960s and 1970s—has not been without its detractors in Sweden, of course. During the years of the SAP's dominance (almost the entirety of the period 1925–2006) the welfare state and its specific policies were unsurprisingly the target of deep and withering critique on the right (and left): banking regulations restricted economic growth, active labor market policies interfered with firms' global competitiveness, tax rates were insufficient for supporting social spending for an aging population (for two classics in the genre, see Langby 1984 and Rojas 1996). The ideal Swedish model that had been built between the 1930s and the 1970s (see chapter 3) had worked for a small, relatively homogeneous population, it was argued, but increasing immigration, expanding population size, growing participation in global markets, and steady European integration rendered the ideal version difficult or impossible to maintain. Yet from the 1970s onward, even as critique on the right decried the supposed antagonism toward liberalization of the welfare function in social democratic policy, Sweden's "strong state" had already begun its decline (Lindwall and Rothstein 2006), shifting away from an explicit emphasis on governance through research and expertise, a practice first established in the 1930s, toward a heavier reliance on market principles for handling social welfare and its provision. Faced with the difficulty of sustaining the strong state framework in a changing global economy—and mirroring trends in Scandinavia and other regions of Europe (Moschonas 2011)—the Social Democrats adopted increasingly liberalized models of governance beginning in the 1980s.

The most significant early outcome of this liberalization process was the Swedish banking crisis of the late 1980s and early 1990s.[7] Before the mid-1980s, banks, insurance companies, and other financial institutions in Sweden were subject to strict limits on how much money they could lend. They were also required by law to invest in government-issued and government-backed bonds. Deregulation in the mid-1980s did away with these restrictions, and in so doing created a new, freely competitive—but also higher-risk—credit market in Sweden, which in turn, by the late 1980s, rapidly produced a real-estate bubble not unlike that seen in the United States in the years leading up to 2007–8. But by 1990 the overheated economy began to run out of steam, and a number of securities firms, all losing money as increased interest rates began poking at the bubble, successively went under, threatening to take some of Sweden's major banks with them. In order to stave off the impending crisis, the Swedish government—by late 1991 controlled by a center-right coalition led by the Moderates, rather than the Social Democrats—stepped in to guarantee the deposits of every bank in the country and nationalize some of the worst affected.

Partly as a result of this banking crisis the SAP lost control of the parliament in the 1991 general election. This, consequently, ushered in a three-year period of steady rightward adjustment to the welfare system, including the privatization of aspects of the health-care system, tax code reform, and substantial cuts to public spending. Yet even though the center-right coalition's time in power was relatively brief, its liberalizing agenda managed to survive, and in some ways thrive, when the Social Democrats returned to power in 1994. Continuing with the deregulation regimes they had initiated before their electoral loss in 1991, the SAP endeavored to, among other decisions, push forward with schemes to financialize and partially privatize pensions (Belfrage 2008) and loosen housing regulations (Christophers 2013). Indeed, by the time they again lost power in 2006, the Social Democrats, once staunchly committed to a progressive economic policy, had become instrumental in producing a new "middle way" that, in contrast to the first decades of the welfare state's existence, leaned more to the capitalist right than to the socialist left.

In 2006 a center-right coalition led by the Moderates once again took control of government, and in 2010 this coalition, known as Alliansen (The Alliance) won reelection, marking the first time the Social Democrats lost two consecutive elections since the party first gained control of government. Several major (and quite different) events in the early 2000s have been linked to the SAP's initial failure in the 2006 election, including the government's poor response to the Indian Ocean tsunami disaster in late 2004, in which over five hundred Swedes were lost, and the SAP's failure to rally a national vote for inclusion in the Eurozone in 2003. A number of Swedes I talked to in the run-up to the election were suspicious of the discrepancy between Sweden's seemingly good economy and the high unemployment rate, which led to a widespread feeling of distrust in the party. Meanwhile, inside the political machine, the SAP was unable to secure a workable coalition with the Left Party and the Green Party to counter the growing center-right alliance (Aylott and Bolin 2007). But in 2014, having finally secured an informal "red-green" alliance with the major left-of-center parties, the SAP once again came back into power.[8]

While the modern Social Democratic Party has transformed rather drastically over the last several decades, and the center-right Moderates controlled government between 2006 and 2014, the welfare state that the SAP pushed to create nonetheless remains largely intact. Electoral politics and ideological commitments run parallel, but not in lockstep, and demand for social democratic policies in Sweden, as in other parts of Europe (Moschonas 2011), has remained strong. The Moderates did not engage in a widescale dismantling of the welfare state, and though it has taken on a much altered form from its original structure, it still persists in its broadest strokes. No longer simply a welfare state, contemporary Sweden can be more accurately described as a *welfare society*, "a social system in which welfare assumptions are an organic part of everyday life" (Robertson 1988:222; see also Lin 2004), where social, economic, educational, and health-care problems are primarily (though not exclusively) approached as requiring collective solutions, and where care of the self is not strictly the burden of the individual.

For a book about Swedish design I have not much addressed what exactly I mean about both the "Swedish" and the "design" components of the term. To that end, in chapter 1 I will present the analytic framework I am using for studying design as an anthropological object of inquiry and examine the parameters of Swedish design in particular—including what makes it "Swedish" in its forms and ideologies, or, more precisely, in the relations between them. I should stress again that when I talk about Swedish design in this book I am intentionally invoking a cultural model. It is a model with many real world tokens that match its idealized type, but the type is not itself monolithic. The objects designed in Sweden by Swedish designers do not, of course, all look the same or fit this cultural construct, and much of what has been created there, both in the past and today, challenges normative Swedish design in form and conceptualization. Even some of the most celebrated contemporary designs—for example, the ornate glassware of Per B. Sundberg, the austere interiors of the design collective Uglycute, or the one-off art pieces by the group Front (see chapter 4)—are difficult to square with the dominant abstractions that typify Swedish design. And of course, as I have noted, there is wider debate in the Swedish design world about the status and role of Swedish design, in terms of both designers working in critical dialogue with the history of Swedish design, and those who think and write about it. But rather then dissecting the continuously unfolding debate about Swedish design itself that persists in Sweden, in the following pages I am more concerned with attempting to understand and recover the tones and textures of the debate's central

object of concern. Within the frameworks of design history and design education in Sweden, arguments tend to revolve around whether or not it is
possible to claim *that* design has a politics. But the question I am asking is
in some ways more primitive than that: How do we get to a point where
this debate is even possible? Indeed what I am getting at in this book is directed toward exploring the complex ways through which design is constructed, abstracted, distributed, operationalized, and given meaning in
Sweden, and thus I am intentionally sidestepping the question of whether
or not the claims of Swedish design are true. That is not for me to decide.
However, I definitely think they are real, inasmuch as the model of Swedish design, even for those who are explicitly working in a critical mode, is
an ever-present metric against which almost all design work produced in
Sweden is gauged.

The remainder of the book is then dedicated to exploring four separate
cultural domains in which Swedish design is produced and thrives. The
first domain I will analyze is the beautiful home. In the late nineteenth
century, around the time that social democratic politics first began to fo-
ment, the home entered into a long and complex process of politicization
in Sweden, both as a discursive formation and as a real place of social interaction. Alongside this move, activists, artists, and early designers began
to promote beauty—a beauty based in simplicity and functionality—as a
mechanism for increasing social equality, and household goods as the most
effective vectors for shepherding beauty into the everyday world. This resulted in the parallel development of a conceptual infrastructure for leading social democratic ideology into the home through objects that embody
political values, which in turn helped construct a physical infrastructure
for marking and enacting those ideologies in everyday life. A comprehensive system of governance like the Swedish welfare state, which relies on
often obscure and invisible entitlements, subsidies, and tax codes as the
central mechanisms for effecting social policy, faces the challenge that
those who gain the most from these policies often have no sense of the full
benefits those policies afford them. Suzanne Mettler (2011) calls this the
"submerged state," a kind of indistinct governance that operates opaquely
in the shadows of policy, which, if left immersed in the realm of the unex-
pressed, can lead to increased social inequality and dangerous misunder-
standings of the political process. Health-care provisions, tax credits, and
workplace protections that cover large segments of the population can be

drafted, passed, and enacted without much or any straightforward attempt to inform the public of what they will provide. While such policies may in fact bring about the on-the-ground results their authors intend, lacking any articulation and demonstration of the benefits of these policies, the public is largely incapable of drawing links between specific political actions and their consequential outcomes. Thus one solution to the problems of the submerged state is to employ different techniques for increasing the visibility of governance in action, generally through explicit indications, visualizations, and materializations that render clearly the connections between policies and their benefits. As we will see in chapter 2, through various discursive and material social engineering processes, several key figures in the nineteenth and early twentieth centuries—among them artists, activists, politicians, and intellectuals—all targeting the home from different angles, brought forth the first renderings that would dominate Swedish design for decades to follow.

The second domain of Swedish design is the design world itself (see chapter 3). Communities organized around certain aesthetic regimes—at least ostensibly—like art worlds (Becker 1982) are generally replete with particular discursive formations that capture, project, and elaborate particular social values. Given the salience of Swedish design discourse, it might be expected to be commonly heard among the Swedish design world's most central players. Yet a politicized way of describing things and enlivening forms is not only rarely used explicitly by designers themselves, but doing so tends to be actively resisted. Instead, the main focus of most young designers is, understandably, building careers, negotiating alliances, and finding ways to acquire status within the confines of what is, ultimately, a small and competitive domain. However despite designers' reluctance to engage directly with promoting the politics of Swedish design, they do play a critical role in its advancement. In seeking to grow their businesses and gain professional success, designers subject their designs to particular processes that can generate economic and prestige value but that also simultaneously render their work amenable to politicized redescriptions. The moments in which designers "let go" of their objects, releasing them into contexts controlled (directly and indirectly) by others, are critical pivot points mediating the relation between design as a practice and design as a cultural category.

To inspect the third domain we must travel deeper into the practices that constitute designerly action, into the studio where the forms of Swedish design—straight lines, soft curves, and so on—are most radically considered and worked, in a very literal sense. The design studio is a particular site of cultural production (see chapter 4). In some respects it resembles a number of other technical domains that have been studied ethnographically, including scientific laboratories (Dumit 2003; Latour and Woolgar 1986; Montoya 2011; Sunder Rajan 2006), engineering firms (Vinck 2003), advertising firms (Mazzarella 2003), and architectural studios (Murphy 2005; Yaneva 2009). But the everyday work of designers—especially the furniture and product designers I spent most of my time with—is also akin to the sorts of craft work carried out by creators as varied as chocolatiers (Terrio 1996), mat weavers (Venkatesan 2009), potters, woodworkers, and leatherworkers (Herzfeld 2004), producers of "traditional" handicrafts (Esperanza 2008, 2010), and even factory workers (Kondo 1990). Some studies have focused in particular on the embodied expertise required for certain forms of situated craft production (Gowlland 2009; Makovicky 2010; Marchand 2010). With few exceptions (Cohn 1987; Jones 2011) such studies tend to emphasize individuated embodied skill and action while passing over—or treating as "context"—the dynamic interactional and indeed conversational frameworks in which much creative work is embedded. But I take very seriously the contention that the details of making things, in the moments of making them, matter; that "in the act of production, the artisan couples his own movements and gestures—indeed, his very life—with the becoming of his materials, joining with and following the forces and flows that bring his work to fruition" (Ingold 2012:435). When exploring form giving in action, my approach treats the messiness of interactions between designers in the studio, the suggestions and assessments they make, the sketches they draw not only for themselves but for one another, their ways of talking and habits of movement through space, as not simply context for some greater embodied expertise, but in fact what constitutes the very conditions within which a designer's skill is performed, calibrated, evaluated, and controlled. In other words, I locate creativity *between* designers rather than *in* them. One effect of this is a destabilization of the image of the singular designer imbued with unique technical skills, a resonant character inhabiting both popular and scholarly imaginaries. In making this move the intent is not to question the skills of individual craftspeople, or to challenge the notion of skill itself—although moving beyond, or perhaps below, lionizing depictions of design and designers is a critical aspect of this project. Instead the goal is to resituate the analysis of creative action within the multiple coincident spheres of contingency in which craftspeople operate, including not only economic, historical, and political spheres, but also, as we will see, conversational and interactional spheres, which directly, in moments of creation, influence the way things are made, and how they acquire meanings in other domains.

The final domain I examine is comprised of what can be called displays of force, the exhibitionary sites and indexicalizing practices that present a politicized Swedish design to a consuming public (see chapter 5). There are different kinds of sites here—stores, museums, trade shows, and civic expositions—and they exist chained together through family resemblance across space and through time. But despite the diffuseness of these various sites they together act as a more or less coherent machine stitching together ideology and form and compelling the Swedish public not only to see Swedish design as a specific class of things, but also to experience it holistically, including the attendant welfare politics that are proposed to subsist around everyday objects. Greg Castillo (2010) has repurposed Joseph Nye's (2004) concept of "soft power" to describe the potency of staged domestic displays used as semiotic weapons by both the United States and the Soviet Union during the Cold War—perhaps best exemplified by the infamous Kitchen Debate between Vice President Richard Nixon and Soviet premier Nikita Khrushchev in 1959, which unfolded primarily inside a transected, prefabricated faux suburban home on view at the American National Exhibition in Moscow. Both the Americans and the Soviets invested heavily in constructing public exhibitions of mundane domestic environments as precise, to-scale models of the material benefits offered by their political-economic systems, socialism and capitalism, respectively. Indeed at multiple exhibitions both before and after the American National Exhibition, the Cold War's two central combatants engaged in a steady semiotic arms race centered squarely in the imagery and materiality of home life—focusing in particular on kitchen appliances and other modern conveniences—pitching battles that "cultivated national prestige" (Castillo 2010:xi), all in the hopes of persuading both internal and foreign audiences to view one side, and not the other, as providing the best pos-sible standard of living.[9] This same process, through which soft power is enforced in the curated experience of everyday forms in controlled envi-ronments with controlled messages, has long been operating in Sweden, and is crucial even today for the ongoing maintenance of Swedish design in the public consciousness.

1

THE DIAGRAM OF SWEDISH DESIGN

Exploring design from an anthropological perspective requires establishing some parameters around what sorts of objects, practices, ideologies, and other phenomena fall under the rubric of design. And exploring Swedish design in particular requires laying out not only what makes Swedish design "Swedish," but also what separates it from other kinds of design. In the first section of this chapter I will describe what I mean by "design" in general and how studying it anthropologically relates to important work in material culture studies and science studies. I will then detail the specific qualities and characteristics of both the ideological/political and the formal/material aspects of Swedish design. Finally, I will situate both Swedish politics and Swedish modernist design in relation to other similar political systems and modernist traditions, to identify the specific relationship between politics and design in Sweden.

Defining Design

"Design" is a curious term. It can describe very different sorts of things depending on who utters it, and for what purposes. In some instances "design" is conflated with the adjective "designer," which describes a type of commodity typically reserved for the wealthy and elite, or those who aspire to such a station. In other cases "design" is a code word for "added value," as when companies like Apple in the United States, or Volvo and H&M in Sweden, explicitly prioritize an attention to detail—of aesthetics, functionality, materials, and the like—as what distinguishes their goods from what their competitors produce.

Other characterizations of design focus on practicalities. In both professional and academic conceptualizations, design tends to fall squarely in the realm of the technical. There is often a marked emphasis on design as a systematic and rigorous *method* for creating things from specific kinds of inputs. The diverse practices of engineering, architecture, city planning, and software development, along with graphic design, industrial design, landscape architecture, and a host of other design disciplines, are all based in sets of precise principles—some of which are shared across these fields, many of which are not—that when purposefully applied to raw materials allow designers to create new objects—buildings, landscapes, posters, chairs, services, user experiences, town plans, and so on. In other words, design in this sense is a kind of controlled and cultivated creativity, with a stress on the particular practices involved in planning and creation.

An even more general sense of design, one that flows from its technical connotations, is as a basic *way of making*, situated somewhere between raw labor and artistic production. Design is not simply work, not simply labor, because the effort involved is carefully considered and usually subject to reflexive evaluation. Design is also not quite art—though it often bumps up against it, as we will see in chapter 4, because the objects of design, even those that foreground aesthetic qualities, are usually made to be used, to serve some practical function. From this broad perspective, design is not restricted to those with technical training or institutionally recognized skill, but applies widely to any kind of creative action that involves planning and forethought. What follows from this view is that the differences between various kinds of making are based less in what they make, or even how they make it, but more in the relative degrees of professionalization, institutionalization, and cultural prominence each is accorded.

Where, then, does that leave us in approaching design as a sociocultural practice? Design concerns process, an active, almost teleological ordering of raw materials into some resultant thing, sometimes conceived as a physical object, but oftentimes as things with less obvious contours, like "activities," "services," and "experiences." I say "almost teleological" because while the general kind of thing strived for in designing is usually anticipated by its makers, other contingent specifics, like forms, functions, materials, and costs, are more subject to manipulations and unexpected outcomes in the process. Autonomous expressiveness is not necessarily design's central concern, though neither is it indifferent to it. Instead design is primarily an intentional structuring of some portion of the lived world in such a way as to transform how it is used, perceived, or understood. Design both delimits and affords relational configurations between people, spaces, and things, and does so in considered and unconsidered ways. Design can also capture specific meanings, and constrain or facilitate interpretation. The meanings that adhere to the objects of design are always situated and contingent, and linked both to the form of the designed product and to the contexts in which it is embedded. In other words, design is a kind of directed creativity with meaningful social consequences, a gradual and granular enstructuring of the everyday world.

While makers—designers, in typical parlance, though any given case may involve "designers" who are not trained as such—are absolutely central to design as a sociocultural practice, design and designing do not begin and end with the human actors responsible for driving design processes. The people who cultivate design and designing are always subject to the particular cultural flows of history, ideology, and politics on which "moments of designing"—when "ideas" are transfigured into "forms"—travel. Moments of designing matter, of course, but only insofar as they are considered alongside and in complementarity with other processes that shape and form designed things. Understanding how design makes things—and makes things mean—requires understanding how objects are shaped to tolerate meanings (Murphy 2013), the processes through which they are given those meanings, and how those meanings are negotiated and argued through different suasive processes.

Material Culture and the Force of Things

The assertion that design nudges the social world in certain ways as it enstructures that world—giving it shape and meaning, even if only ambiently—assumes that designed things retain a certain social power, and the anthropology of design I am advocating draws on a number of arguments that previous social scientific studies of materiality and technology have critically addressed in this regard. These arguments include the capacity of things—in particular artificial things—to impart some effect on the world; the agency of the people who make those things and who use those things, including reference to ideas about both intentionality and unintended consequences; the particular properties of the things designed and how they relate to other phenomena; and the nature of relations between people and things (and things and other things, and things and ideas), phenomena that may not always exist as distinct from one another in the world, yet which for analytical purposes often require at least some demarcation, in order to straighten out our concepts.

There are two particular lines of influence that have significantly informed the analysis that follows, both of which are built around a critique of the deep dualism, both ontological and analytic, separating human subjects from the nonhuman objects that always already surround them. I share this antidualistic stance, along with a more general concern these approaches share for closely attending to the mediated interactions that hold between people and things. But furthering these fundamental debates is not my specific goal. Instead I use these works as both delimiters and points of departure for the discussion of design and the power of things that follows.

In a series of monographs (1987, 2010, 2012) and edited volumes (1998a, 2005), Daniel Miller has carefully developed an influential theory of materiality primarily focused on consumption. Through deep ethnographic engagements with particular consumption practices, like shopping (Miller 1998b, 2001b) and the crafting of domestic interiors (Miller 2001c, 2008), or with particular artifacts like cars (Miller 2001a), cell phones (Horst and Miller 2006), and clothing (Banarjee and Miller 2003; Miller and Woodward 2012), Miller and his colleagues have been principally responsible for drawing material culture out from the shadows of bare context and bringing it to the fore in contemporary anthropological analysis. The central tenet of this perspective is that buying, using, and interacting with objects transform not only the objects themselves and their meanings, but also the people who consume them within culturally inflected courses of action. Humans exist in complicated constellations of interaction, wherein things, people, space, time, and ideas all converge to form the social world. We give order to that world through the bonds and associations that we form with things, through which we make divisions, categories, and groupings, discern patterns, and draw connections. But what emerges from these relations is no static system. Because our interactions with objects are ongoing and shifting, these divisions are constantly subject to recasting, the categories are subject to reordering, the groupings to dissolution, and the connections to redrawing. Indeed our identities cannot be understood without reference—or even deference—to the role played by material artifacts in our identities' processual unfolding and modification. From this perspective humans and things are always mutually constitutive, and agency—whether it seems attributable to either humans or artifacts—is fundamentally embedded in their relations (cf. Winner 1980; Johnson 1988).

The second line of influence—though the influence is somewhat less direct—is the study of sociotechnical systems, or actor network theory, most commonly associated with the work of Bruno Latour (1993, 2007), Michel Callon (1986, 1987), and John Law (1987, 1992). Perhaps even more forcefully than Miller, the sociotechnical perspective, which derives from science studies but has in recent years been applied to a wider range of social domains, advocates the complete disavowal of analytic frameworks that grant primacy to human agency in processes responsible for manifesting the social world. Where Miller sees agency as constituted in the relationship between people and objects, actor network theory treats agency as more widely distributed both synchronically and diachronically across objects, inscriptions, people, practices, events, and spaces, all of which are assumed to be equally agentive. Viewed through this lens, an empirical field of action is leveled across its various constituents, as all parties—human, artificial, and natural—become mutually invested stakeholders in the collective production of knowledge and knowledge systems. By deprioritizing the role that humans play in complex social action and elevating the role of nonhuman objects, actor network theory posits a deep structure of agency within objects and networks of objects that is largely invisible to the people who interact with them, but that is nonetheless contributory to their effective possibilities.

These areas of research represent some of the most intricate and detailed frameworks not only for thinking about how humans and objects interact, but also for thinking about how objects contribute to the broader production and reproduction of particular material and nonmaterial conditions in society. In drawing together these lines of influence to circumscribe an ambit for the anthropological study of design I have absorbed their shared critique of dualism, almost to the point of unrecognized orthodoxy, although my more humanist reflexes will admit that the sort of flattening of agency that actor network theory insists on is less preferred than Miller's retention of distinctly human modes of agency.

For Miller and the material culture school, objects are not simply instrumental for people in carrying on courses of action, but are deeply meaningful to them in many ways in their everyday lives, and thus help give form and content not only to the physical world, but also to the concomitant cultural worlds humans inhabit. The meanings that occupy the relations between people and things can be partly idiosyncratic, but also partly shaped by social forces, practices, and channels of circulation that continuously recast objects as they move between and across different sociocultural domains. What follows is that people and things, when examined through lenses of every resolution, are not empirically distinct from one another—though discussing them as distinct may be required by language and for clarity—but are instead always mutually constitutive: people make things, but things also make people.

One of the core advantages of actor network theory is its ability to handle practically any phenomenon it is applied to, including not just humans and artifacts, but also inscriptions, images, discourses, practices, and more. Relying on the principle of "generalized symmetry" (Callon 1986), according to which every element of the network must be accounted for with the same methodology, thereby not privileging any one node over another, actor network theory can easily incorporate any object of inquiry into an analysis without generating much methodological anguish—though matters like power, intentionality, consciousness, and concerns that never surface (Winner 1993) are more difficult to account for. While the methodological rigidity attached to generalized symmetry is not, I think, a tenable approach—from my point of view, regarding different kinds of phenomena on their own terms respects their particular integrities and makes for better analysis—the basic ecumenical stance of actor network theory, in which a diversity of factors at multiple scales are viewed as contributing to the social reproduction of larger distributed systems, even when the contribution is not immediately visible or direct, is critical.

Latour (2008), noting the "weakness" of the concept of "design," which can encompass practices, styles, collections of things, attitudes, discourses, and more, has attempted to identify some of its most basic components within an actor network theory framework, and highlights five features in particular. First, because design is, in a sense, doing something less than "building" or "constructing" and is instead focused on incremental changes to the world, Latour claims that design is a particularly modest creative endeavor. Second, design is also a domain dominated by skillful pedants preoccupied by "a mad attention to the details" of what they make (Latour 2008:3). Third, design is a process of sign making, concerned with manipulating not only materials but also meaning and interpretation. Fourth, design does not seek to reinvent the world from scratch but to transform what already exists. Finally, design is inseparable from ethics, from evaluations of good design and bad design not just in terms of taste, but also in terms of its material effects. All of these criteria, loose and unaligned as they may be, are indeed central to delineating design.

Finally, I will add that Alfred Gell's (1998) emphasis on indexicality for facilitating the force of artifacts to affect the world is essential for evaluating how design connects to and interacts with practices, discourses, ideologies, and objects of various kinds, and in the process helps identify family resemblances between them. Indexical relationships are key for establishing and sustaining family resemblances across different phenomena. But rather than treating indexes as "natural signs," as Gell does, linking objects to creators, I treat them more as "naturalized signs," that is, signs that undergo cultural, social, and political procedures whereby the abductive field is reduced by degree, and indexical objects with some degree of "fit" are specified. Moreover, indexical signs are not the only kind of signs involved. Attending to multiple design practices, operating at multiple scales, that give cultural form to objects, not just as blunt artifacts but also their specific qualia and the semiotic "bundling" (Keane 2003) that those qualia entail, reveals how designing generates and distributes "dynamic interconnections among different modes of signification at play within a particular historical and social formation" (Keane 2003:410). In other words, design is, in part, a process of naturalizing signs and sign relations.

Diagramming Swedish Design

Bearing in mind this framework for studying design in general, I will be arguing in the remainder of this book that in Sweden *svensk design* in particular operates as a *diagram*, in Gilles Deleuze's (1988) sense, a set of relations linking the everyday world—composed of objects, spaces, people, and more—to the cultural ideologies that motivate the persistence of a social democratically infused "way of life." For Deleuze a diagram is a sort of map of social relations—and forces between social relations—that is agnostic as to the ontological state of its components, marking "no distinction between content and expression, a discursive formation and a non-discursive formation" (Deleuze 1988:34). Animate human subjects and inanimate artifacts, institutions and the discourses that help shape them, temporal events and atemporal flows are all gathered and delineated and rendered real within the diagram. As Jakub Zdebik (2012:1–2) describes it, the diagram "values the unformed, the state of flux, the dynamic, the movement towards actualization. It also deals with organization, forces at work in social and cultural constructs; it is a way to travel from one system to another. The diagram allows a glimpse of the state that comes before the formation of an object, and of what goes into its formation." In other words, while the phenomena captured by the diagram may themselves subsist and circulate precariously, the diagram supplies them with a provisional stability without fundamentally transforming them in any way.

As a diagram that maps Sweden's sociopolitical landscape, Swedish design is composed of lines drawing together people (designers, consumers, curators, citizens, politicians), things (everyday objects, their particular forms and arrangements), and ideologies (of care, responsibility, equality, justice, beauty) such that the modern sociopolitical formation of Sweden, with all of its attendant norms and cultural values, is constantly marked and remade at the level of everyday life. In this sense a diagram is also *machinic*, "a precise state of intermingling of bodies in a society, including all the attractions and repulsions, sympathies and antipathies, alterations, amalgamations, penetrations, and expansions that affect bodies of all kinds in their relations to one another" (Deleuze and Guattari 1987:90), which through the forces that hold between these elements "constructs a real that is yet to come, a new type of reality" (142). The diagram of Swedish design does not simply *represent* relations between these different bodies, between people, things, and discourses; it actively and continuously *reproduces* and transforms—or in some cases, preserves—these relations. In its machinic composition the diagram of Swedish design is composed of innumerable separate but interlinking machines—the domains I analyze in the following chapters are, in a sense, four of those machines—all producing and reproducing and stitching together various qualities of Swedish design.

But how? For Deleuze diagrams are delineated according to two broad classes of lines—lines of enunciation, that is, "whatever can be articulated" (Deleuze 1988:32), and lines of visibility. To understand how the diagram of Swedish design is formally composed, and how its machines collaboratively reproduce Swedish design as such, requires some attention to how these two kinds of lines are made manifest.

Lines of Enunciation: The Final Vocabulary

As I climbed out of a taxi in the town of Visby in the summer of 2012, my eye caught the cover of a magazine peeking out from a bundle of reading material stuffed in the driver's seatback pocket. Its title was *Form & Design*. Having lived in Stockholm several years prior, I was not surprised that a glossy design publication would be considered light reading for a short cab ride. But Visby is not Stockholm. The biggest town on the island of Gotland in the Baltic Sea, Visby is far removed from the country's capital and other major cities in Sweden, in both its geography and its disposition. It is not a backwater town, by any means, but neither is it especially central to the contemporary Swedish design world. Yet even here, beyond the reach of the hustle and bustle of Stockholm, the lines that give shape to the diagram of Swedish design are tacitly articulated in the most mundane of spaces.

Lines of enunciation in the diagram of Swedish design trace out the boundaries and contours of what is pronounceable about objects and forms. They conjure the very category of *svensk design* itself, undergirding a fiat ontology that interpellates a cultural class simply by giving it a name and a face and a place to thrive, like magazines tucked away in the seatbacks of local taxicabs. In doing so these lines render dispersed objects examples of the same kind of thing, while simultaneously constituting the discursive arena within which claims about the category and its tokens can be staked. They also help cement relations between particular material forms and the social bodies—individuals, institutions, media forms—that make and perpetuate those claims. Lines of enunciation are most typically manifest in what Deleuze (1988), following Foucault, calls "statements," ideologically loaded propositions and descriptions about the world that in their appearance quicken some portion of social reality. Statements are not always entirely linguistic (e.g., organized grammatically) or bounded fast in space or time. They are "never hidden, yet are not directly readable or even sayable" (Deleuze 1988:53). Individual statements constantly emerge in practice, sometimes in talk, sometimes in writing, sometimes in images, and often in how we interact with material objects or physical space. They are sometimes direct and sometimes oblique, and while no single instance necessarily defines any particular power position or ideology, each appearance, each line of enunciation, contributes to the reproduction—and sometimes the transfiguration—of the given order of things, even if by small degrees, without generating much recognition or critique. Together the lines of enunciation delineated by statements set the parameters within which rational thought and action can take place and constitute the terrain of the socially acceptable. These lines are intimately connected to history while at the same time remarkably liberated from precise temporal anchoring, providing social actors with the raw ontologies they need for making sense of social life.

Statements regarding the politics of Swedish design assume a number of guises. Formulations explicitly predicating ideological qualities of Swedish design have circulated since at least the late nineteenth century (see chapter 2), echoing across a century of political and social change in Sweden. In 1939, design historian and activist Gregor Paulsson, one of the most influential early proponents of modernist design in Sweden, published a book detailing in images—mostly photographs and architectural plans—the successful architectural reforms Sweden had undergone over the previous decade. In his preface he described this work as having two interrelated goals—developing a new aesthetic style for buildings and home furnishings, while at the same time attempting to reduce inadequate living conditions across the class spectrum:

> These two motives were in their turn based on the development of democratic ideals. The new shapes in architecture denoted a style of liberty, their

social function was to express equality; the idea being to remove class contrasts and differences also where the community's outward appearance was
concerned, and to raise the standard of the surroundings in which the ne-
glected strata of the population lived. (Paulsson 1939:7)

Almost twenty years later Paulsson offered a more pointed distillation
of that same sentiment with regard to everyday objects, what he called
formade kulturföremål (designed cultural objects), identifying "use" as a
central concern for design. He specified three different kinds of use that
matter: "Practical use concerns how to handle the thing; social use concerns
how to be with the thing; the aesthetic use concerns how to see the thing"
(Paulsson and Paulsson 1957:13). Sidestepping trends that downplay the
person as a component of design, this simple array of uses simultaneously
emphasizes beneficial functionality, an attention to aesthetics, and a recognition that the object plays a social role in the life of a user.

In more recent years similar kinds of predicating statements have
served as the basic building blocks of Swedish design discourse, including
an even more elaborate set of criteria. Describing the guiding program of
his organization, the director of the Swedish Society of Arts and Crafts (see
chapter 4) wrote in 1982:

We are trying to enrich the concept of "good design" and to expand the
traditional idea of quality to include issues that go well beyond function
and form. This comprehensive view means that products are well made in
a human and pleasant working environment, produced without wasting
valuable and irreplaceable natural and human resources, and sold at reasonable prices to satisfy real needs. (Lindkvist 1982:260)

Books focused on Swedish design or Scandinavian design, found in almost every bookshop in Sweden, are also suffused with these sorts of statements. A large volume celebrating Swedish design at the beginning of the
twenty-first century described designing as

[a] creative act by someone who wanted to express a feeling, a function or
simply a powerful form. Whose goal was to satisfy his or her—and the
universal—ambition to experience surroundings as aesthetically meaningful, both at home and in public settings. . . . Design that, when good, appeals

to the eye and heightens our pleasure and well-being—that is to say, our quality of life. (Helgeson and Nyberg 2002:12)

And as one of Sweden's best-known design critics phrased it,

Contemporary modern design is a symbol for a good future, freed from conventions and filled with ambitions for a better and brighter life. . . . With modern design one can show that democracy can be strengthened in practice by a better and more beautiful everyday. (Hedqvist 2002:102)

These are just a few of the countless explicit statements that delineate and articulate the ideological aspects of the diagram of Swedish design. They are composed around a particular descriptive paradigm—*democratic, social, equality, good, satisfaction, pleasure, quality, better, beautiful*, from the examples above—that, following Richard Rorty (1989), I am calling "the final vocabulary" of Swedish design. A final vocabulary generally consists of sets of words for describing things or states of affairs that are so close to other vague, yet powerful terms, like "true," "right," and "good," that when applied prevent alternative linguistic formulations from ever taking root—they are *final* in that those who sincerely employ them cannot conceive of any other legitimate means of expression. Final vocabularies are nimble and lean, not overburdened with complicated abstractions, and widely recognizable and repeatable (if not always believed) by those who hold some stake in the things they describe. This is not to say that final vocabularies are actually "true" in any absolute sense. Indeed, multiple final vocabularies can be used by competing factions to describe the same entity. Rather, the use of a final vocabulary signals that such descriptions are largely taken by their users at face value and assumes that they reflect an observable reality not open to critique or competing descriptions. In other words, final vocabularies represent the lexical concentration of ideology, an essential and essentializing rhetoric meant to highlight specific qualities while simultaneously preventing the acknowledgment of others.

Where statements exploiting the final vocabulary attempt to bring together political ideology and the objects of Swedish design, most lines of enunciation are less straightforward in their operations. Instead they manifest more prominently as *preoccupations*, concerns that circulate around design, designers, and designing practices without tangibly settling on particular materialities. During the height of the Swedish welfare state in the 1960s and 1970s, this was particularly evident in the pressing social questions tackled by popular design periodicals like *Form*, the official publication of the Swedish Society of Arts and Crafts. Throughout most of the 1970s each issue would be devoted to a particular theme, introduced on the cover by a provocative question and addressed through in-depth articles and images within. For instance, one issue in 1970 dealing with design for the elderly asked, "Can we live how we want when we grow old?" Another from 1974 asked, alongside a montage of nine "typical" Swedish faces, "Is the family changing?" (the short answer, according to the articles inside: maybe). And an issue from the following year explored cases in both Sweden and *u-landet*, the developing world, to answer the question, "Is society child-friendly?" Very little of the text contained in these publications, and similar others of the period, utilized the final vocabulary to describe the work and objects of Swedish designers. Nonetheless by intently confronting the very sorts of problems that progenitors of the final vocabulary like Paulsson had earlier argued should be the central concern of design, the old lines of enunciation retained the same fundamental profile, even if the paths they followed and the pitch of their curves had shifted just a bit.

Today the statements that articulate these lines of enunciation, suffused with tones of equality, social justice, and care precisely dispatched though functionality, beauty, and simplicity, have become utterly taken-for-granted qualities of *svensk design*, in terms of both how it is done by designers and how it is normatively understood—so much so that most designers, as I will discuss in chapter 3, do not align with these statements as explicit aspects of what they do. These statements also appear quite frequently in various mediated contexts, a "murmur without beginning or end" (Deleuze 1988:7) that consistently and regularly reproduces a publicly shared and recognizable discursive field. In Stockholm and other cities, design has all but saturated the urban landscape. Magazines delineating lines of enunciation, like *Form*—but also a number of others, like *Forum, Hemma*, and *Arkitekten*—aimed at both popular and professional audiences, are regularly sold at newsstands and convenience stores. Images of various household goods, high-tech objects, interiors, or even designers themselves adorn their covers, while descriptive articles inside dissect the intricate meanings of design, including the Swedish and Scandinavian types. Indeed, there is a certain reflexive, almost self-obsessed tenor permeating much of the media attention that surrounds design in Sweden. Books both large and small showcasing the best of historical and contemporary Scandinavian design or instructing readers how to decorate their homes modernly and efficiently are prominently displayed in major bookshops, and many department stores construct—and proudly exhibit—entire sections of floors devoted specifically to "Swedish design." But as indispensable as these lines of enunciation are to the integrity of the diagram of Swedish design, they trace out only part of the picture.

Lines of Visibility: The Cultural Geometry

Of course what is articulable about design must be articulable about something in particular. Lines of enunciation, statements about Swedish design, are only, in their barest forms, claims about the sociopolitical status of objects. There is nothing inherently "correct" in the claims themselves, no infallible logic that makes them indisputably credible. Like any claim, lines of enunciation require evidence and argumentation in order to bend toward persuasion. They need something to cling to, to adhere to, something that somehow scaffolds their propositional content in ways that, at least provisionally, grant the premise outlined by the final vocabulary an anchor in material reality. They need other lines, lines of a different sort, with which to intersect.

For Deleuze (1988) lines of enunciation are counterbalanced by what he calls lines of visibility, or what can be seen. These lines sketch out the domain of the sensible, the surfaces, planes, and curves that compose the silhouette of the materially experienceable, and give weight, size, and shape to matter and substance. They are diffuse and immanent in the everyday world, yet while "visibilities are never hidden, they are none the less not immediately seen or visible" (Deleuze 1988:57), lingering unnoticed and unremarked in the basic structure of spaces and things. They are also not strictly a visual phenomenon, but rather "are complexes of actions and passions, actions and reactions, multisensorial complexes, which emerge into the light of day" (59) through mediated interactions that call them into being.

Elsewhere I have called these lines of visibility the "cultural geometry" of Swedish design (Murphy 2013), the basic set of form preferences that constitute the core qualities of what emerged over the twentieth century as Swedish style. These preferences—dominated by straight lines, clear angles, and simple curves—are often associated with modernist aesthetics in design, art, and architecture more generally, the origins of which can be pinned to a number of non-Swedish sources, including the World's Fair of 1851, the Arts and Crafts movement, the Deutscher Werkbund, and most notably the Bauhaus school in Germany (Crouch 1999; see below).[1] It is an aesthetic regime that is "Calvinist in its rigor" (Goldhagen 2005:144), firmly committed to the unambiguous disavowal of constructions overburdened by complexity as a means for advancing a particular political agenda: constructing a new social world made up of "objective" forms freed from the constraining class markers associated with older styles. According to the logic of modernist design, minimalist forms provoke minimal social distinctions, and thus fit comfortably within broader political programs aimed at dismantling class hierarchies and other social configurations of inequality.

While modernist forms came to characterize design and architecture globally in the twentieth century, in Sweden they assumed the status of what Jan Mukarovsky (1977:53) calls a "technical norm," or "certain habits, petrified residues of the long evolution of art." From the 1920s onward, through periods of contestation and revolt and reassessment and embrace, straight lines, squares, rectangles, and cubes—shapes composed of right angles, or near right angles—have ossified as the kinds of forms normatively captured by the "Swedish" part of Swedish design. Since the 1960s, with the advent of ergonomic design, though stemming from even earlier origins, simple curves—not intricate or convoluted, but organic, following the bends of the human body—have also fallen under this label. Symmetry and proportionality are critical as well. The angles and surfaces that arise from the arrangement of basic forms in designed objects should reflect the same kind of simplicity as the component elements. These forms and surfaces can give shape to practically anything, from apartment buildings, chairs, and tables to lamps, cutlery, and the typography marking book covers and public space. Collectively this cultural geometry has become for Swedish design what Roman Jakobson (1971) calls "the dominant" of an aesthetic work, the abstractable—if not extractable—quality of the thing that specifies its typological character, granting it a sense and identity of its own. Not everything designed and produced in Sweden is based in the cultural geometry, of course. But inasmuch as the cultural geometry manifests as the dominant, if not exclusive quality of the everyday built environment, in both public and private spaces, it substantiates most directly the lines of visibility that, together with lines of enunciation, constitute the diagram of Swedish design.

From one point of view, the straight lines, right angles, and simple curves that dominate Swedish design amount to what Robin Evans (1995) calls a "dead geometry," forms so worked over, so thoroughly understood that they no longer incite interest or experimentation. They are predictable and expected, a known quantity, and routine. But from another perspective their very predictability is precisely their strength. Through decades of use in innumerable designed cultural objects, the integrity of these forms is thoroughly means tested, a ubiquitous "inoculation against uncertainty" (Evans 1995:xxvii) in the everyday world and a material analogue of the careful, positive rationality that underpins social democratic ideology. In Sweden the fundamental building blocks of design—point, line, and plane—have been transfigured and reassembled into critical vectors of cultural value. A once-dead metric geometry of mere distances and structures flourishes vibrantly as a projective geometry thick with shadows and images textured and given conceptual mass by lines of enunciation.

For these different sorts of lines to hold together as a diagram of design, as a materialized depiction of the Swedish social imaginary, there must be some semiotic tolerance (Murphy 2013) between the dead geometrical forms and the ideological claims that revitalize them. This is not to say that there is always a clear and direct match—indeed, as we will see, the matching of lines is an ongoing cultural achievement—but rather that there must be qualities of both that at least credibly correspond in experience. There is a basic consonance between "simple" forms and democratic idealism. They are raw and unelaborated, the rudiments of form, really, and are thus less prone to class-restricted appropriations. However, the dominant manifestation of this correspondence is the cultural geometry's capacity to reflect and perform two core values of social democratic ideology, *trygghet* (security) and *omsorg* (care), and to do so along at least three dimensions, the first of which is security and care through *economics*. Minimalist forms like straight lines and right angles are easier to mass-produce than more complicated shapes. They are easier to machine-cut, and easier to transport—both from factory to store and from store to home—all of which tends to reduce costs for consumers.

The second dimension is security and care through *functionality*. Functional design does not strictly mean that an object *does* something (a stopwatch as opposed to a lapel pin), but more that an object works to address a perceived problem, and does so in an obvious and rational way. For instance, one designer I talked to named Petra S.[2] noticed that water would pool on her garden table after a rainstorm, and the table would have to be drained and cleaned to be used again. As a solution to this problem she devised a small circular table with a short ridge along the tabletop's edge to capture the rainwater like a shallow bowl; she also included a small notch in the ridge to channel the water off the tabletop. But rather than allowing the water to pour down onto the ground, she designed a small bowl, attached to the table's base directly under the notch, which collected the rainwater and repurposed it as a water source for local birds, an ecologically conscious solution solved through a new implementation of the cultural geometry. Moreover, ergonomic design relies on curves to provide for users quite directly through objects that are, for example, crafted to conform to the contours of human hands or the curves of human backs, thus making interactions with everyday things more comfortable and less stressful on the body.

A third dimension of the correspondence between form and care—a kind of *psychological* care—is achieved through a particular culturally elaborated conception of beauty. Since the late nineteenth century, beauty has been discursively linked to simplicity of form in Sweden, along with the parallel promotion of interaction with beautiful things as a means for engendering happiness in everyday life (see chapter 2). To craft beautiful objects, to create environments that resonate with positive aesthetic details, is to attend to the affective well-being of people who use those objects and inhabit those spaces. As a designer named Jenny L. explained it, expressing an alternative to overt political descriptions of design, "It could be as interesting to say, 'Ah, this furniture is all about the world, and the people and the emotions in the world. . . . It's beautiful, it's a happy life! I want you to be a little bit more happy,' or whatever." Playing the part of "an active engineer of atmosphere," to borrow Jean Baudrillard's (1996:25) phrase, a designer working with the cultural geometry helps construct a secure and caring everyday world precisely by giving beautiful forms, simple forms, to her objects.

Drawing the Lines Together

But as I have been saying from the start, this is all a kind of cultural achievement. The lamination of ideological claims to specific forms, the twisting together of lines of enunciation and visibility to form a materialized diagram of social relations—in other words, to produce something meaningful called *design*, and in this case called *svensk design*—requires a tremendous amount of work from a range of social actors, from designers to activists to curators, policymakers, artists, professors, consumers, and others. It requires an ongoing commitment to *form giving* of all different sorts, with all sorts of material across all sorts of domains. As Tim Ingold (2010a, 2010b, 2012) has argued, a focus on creativity that narrowly emphasizes an archaic Aristotelian "hylomorphic" model, which treats matter (*hyle*) and form (*morphe*) as distinct phenomena, unproductively reduces "making" to the actions of goal-oriented producers pressing pregiven forms onto pregiven materials. It is a position that grants too much agency to both creators and the completed artifacts they produce, without accounting in any serious way for the "fields of force and currents of material wherein forms are generated" (2010b:92). Too heavy an emphasis on inert, artificial "objects" over the matter that constitutes "things"— which he describes as a "gathering together of the threads of life" (Ingold 2010a:4)—leads us to overlook the constituent elemental qualities that accord those objects their social vitality. Building from Deleuze and Guattari (1987), Ingold (2012:433) argues alternatively that "the generation of things should be understood as a process of ontogenesis in which form is ever emergent rather than given in advance." From this point of view, then, the role of the expert creator—the designer, the curator, the journalist—is not to impose form onto matter, but instead to guide the *becoming* of things by channeling "fields of force and currents of material" in considered ways that shape and fashion a novel configuration of existence.

Unlike the kinds of artistic production that Ingold is primarily concerned with, design is typically a much more dispersed and elongated creative process. Beyond prototyping and small handmade production runs, designers typically spend more time in their studios giving forms in pixels, ink, and hand gestures than in the matter that composes their objects. And besides, designers are not the only ones giving forms to objects, since the work of other players in the Swedish design world is absolutely critical to shaping the overall contours of design. Ingold forcefully maintains that in critiquing hylomorphism his goal is not simply to identify the model's weakest points, but "to overthrow the model itself, and to replace it with an ontology that assigns primacy to processes of formation as against their final products, and to flows and transformations of materials as against states of matter" (Ingold 2010a:2–3). To be sure, this is a virtuous proposition, one that has helped pattern the trajectory of my analysis. But what is left unclear in this move is the status of matter and especially of form as empirical entities, for both anthropologists and our interlocutors. Creation may not entail the imposition of pregiven forms onto pregiven matter, but design as a kind of creation makes clear that forms, at least, do subsist in and circulate through domains beyond those in which formation processes are distinctly marked, like the studio. Challenging the ways in which we conceive of the relations between form and matter is critical for advancing a more refined understanding of the meaning of things in their cultural contexts, but it should be done with a sensitivity to the ways in which forms often live their own cultural lives independent of the things they in turn help enliven.

Form giving is emergent from the many vagaries of production, from the tiny little motions of putting hands, tools, and machinery to material; from talk about the thing itself and the other things it is somehow "like," or "not like," according to the various stakeholders who intervene in its making; from the interlocked cultural, social, functional, and political statements that help shape things as they are "born" and into which they are thrown, even if against their will; and from the ways in which things are rhetorically displayed, the ways in which lines of enunciation are trued with lines of visibility. While individual things are truly made in instances of production, they are also, especially though not exclusively in the context of mass production, *remade* as specimens of a type that displays a particular form and a particular function, and can "reflect" the same kinds of meanings and associations as every other specimen. Making things that conform to a type with particular indexical associations is what Asif Agha (2003) calls "enregisterment," or

> social processes—processes of value production, maintenance and transformation—through which the scheme of cultural values has a social life, as it were, a processual and dynamic existence that depends on the activities of social persons, linked to each other through discursive interactions and institutions. . . . Cultural value is not a static property of things or people but a precipitate of sociohistorically locatable practices, including discursive practices, which imbue cultural forms with recognizable sign-values and bring these values into circulation along identifiable trajectories in social space. (Agha 2003:231–232)

In other words, treating design as a kind of enregisterment, as a dynamic set of interrelated processes of value production, reveals that making things mean in a cultural way is the result of activities carried out by asymmetrically distributed actors tasked with reproducing, preserving, and augmenting indexical connections between forms and other meaningful entities—objects, people, places, ideas, relations, and so on. It is here, in the practical activities and procedures that relentlessly suture sign to object, and do so in a range of contexts, that cultural value resides, rather than in the things themselves or the wider contexts that they inhabit. To be sure, stitching together lines of visibility and lines of enunciation is by no means a neat affair. Because these lines are ontologically quite distinct— "anisomporphic," as Deleuze describes them—their integrity as a complete whole is rather imprecise, "the result of a certain 'jiggery-pokery'" (Deleuze 1988:62) rather than consistent compatibility. Deleuze (65) notes further: "Between the two there is a perpetual irrational break. And yet they are not any old voices on top of any old images. Of course, there is no link that could move from the visible to the statement, or from the statement to the visible. But there is a continual relinking that takes place over the irrational break or the crack."

This relinking over the crack between the visible and the articulable, between forms and ideologies of design in Sweden, is what the rest of this book will explore. In what follows I present four different "enregistering machines" of Swedish design—and these are only four among innumerable others. In processing relations between bodies, enregistering machines do not simply *give* lines and forms; they also give *to each other* lines and forms that are otherwise anisomorphic, such that something new emerges in their comingling. Each of these enregistering machines is composed of its own constituent parts and operates according to its own logic. Each also processes and produces its own material for its own ends. Yet because of their particular relational configurations in Swedish society, they all work together, unorchestrated but still in concert, to continuously redraw the diagram of Swedish design.

Untangling the Swedishness of Swedish Design

To understand the ways in which the diagram of Swedish design has emerged and persists requires some attention to the particularities of how each of these sets of lines has developed in relation to wider sociopolitical contexts outside Swedish borders. The lines of enunciation and visibility of Swedish design do bear similarities to both political forms and design forms apparent in other national contexts, and I am not claiming that Swedish design is a singular phenomenon in the world. Indeed, I am arguing that it is a manifestation—and a relatively clear one at that—of a more general set of complex relations between objects, ideologies, practices, and people that hold in many sociopolitical contexts, each with its own particular local contingencies. To unpack how design has been "made Swedish" in Sweden, then, means turning to the specifics of both social democracy and modernist design in Sweden and beyond.

Social Democracy in Sweden and Elsewhere

As a political form, social democracy is of course not unique to Sweden. It has origins in strains of Marxist thought that spread throughout Europe in the nineteenth century, and it began taking shape differently in many countries over the course of the twentieth century, especially in the fractured aftermath of World War II (Padgett and Paterson 1991). And while a preoccupation with "welfare" is generally considered a hallmark of social democratic political systems, it is not solely the purview of Social Democratic parties, as the influence of those parties has seeped into a variety of political contexts. As Gøsta Esping-Andersen (1990) has argued, "liberal" welfare states, like Canada, Australia, and the United States (Hacker 2002: cf. Fennell 2011, 2012) have tended to promote a minimalist welfare program through market-driven mechanisms designed to address "basic rights," while "corporatist" welfare states, like Germany, France, and Austria, are more likely to use the power of the state—often in complicated collusions with the church—to protect the rights of citizens without universalizing them or engineering away status differences. However, in contrast to these models, only "the social democrats pursued a welfare state that would promote an equality of the highest standards, not an equality of minimal needs" (Esping-Andersen 1990:27), and the Nordic countries—Sweden, Norway, Denmark, and Finland—are where social democrats have held the most sway.

In the various national contexts in which social democrats have thrived, the ideas and values underpinning social democracy share a number of core features (Esping-Andersen 1985), most of which differ in their degree of emphasis within a given political system and the mechanisms through which welfare is provided. The most common of these include the provision of particular public services, like health care and public education, poverty reduction programs, labor protections, and a recognition of the right of collective bargaining. And in states historically controlled by Social Democratic parties there is typically a more explicit emphasis on promoting social equality, class solidarity (as opposed to class struggle, as advocated by Communist parties), and social reformism through parliamentary democracy. In all of these respects Swedish social democracy fits a normative model of the social democratic political form.

At the same time, though, social democracy has developed in some very particular ways in Sweden, even in relation to the other Nordic countries, marking Sweden more as the exception than the ideal. The Swedish Social Democratic Party (SAP) was the first social democratic party in the world to take control of government through an electoral process, and despite having lost control of government in 2006, it remains the most successful social democratic party in history, having continuously served as the largest party in the Riksdag (the Swedish parliament) since 1917. In its early days, while social democratic parties elsewhere in Europe grappled with how exactly to align with some core issues of orthodox Marxism, including class struggle and historical materialism, the SAP instead adopted class cooperation, a flattening of social hierarchies, and cross-class inclusion as core party values. Indeed, in contrast to social democratic parties in Germany and France, the SAP was decidedly undogmatic about its Marxism. Whereas these other social democratic parties, working in a more Marxist vein, viewed democracy as a bourgeois approach to reform (Berman 2006:155), in Sweden the SAP saw democracy as a pragmatic and primary mechanism for enacting social change.

Another significant factor influencing the development of social democracy in Sweden was the state's political posture during both world wars. In the aftermath of World War I, but especially in the context of the global depression of the 1930s, Sweden was in a more or less equal position to other countries in Europe. Sweden had been neutral during the war, but was also much less industrialized and developed than European countries to the south, so despite not having suffered much direct damage during the conflict, the country was nonetheless in similar need of rebuilding. The interwar years, as Sheri Berman (2006) has forcefully argued, served as a political incubator in Europe where emerging parties espousing utterly distinct ideologies all sought to solve the social and economic problems that the war and depression had wrought, through a number of shared basic goals. Both left-wing parties (the Social Democrats) and right-wing parties (the National Socialist Party in Germany, the Fascists in Italy) were fundamentally concerned with reshaping society from the ground up, primarily through the political process; they all also emphasized collective solidarity and the role of "the people" in each party's development; and they were all explicitly in favor of constructing a middle way between socialism and capitalism. Of course the left-wing and right-wing parties diverged drastically beyond these fundamentals, and for much of the 1930s into 1945 it was not clear whether a left-leaning democratic or a right-leaning authoritarian orientation to social reform would prevail in Europe. The Nazis outlawed social democratic parties in all of the countries they occupied, including Denmark and Norway, but social democracy was able to survive and thrive in Sweden because of the state's official neutral status. Thus while the development of social democracy in Sweden greatly benefited from a Pan-European wave of reformist political sentiment in the 1920s and 1930s, the system was able to ride out Axis imperialism in the early 1940s, which in turn led to the entrenchment of social democratic policies

occurring earlier there than in other Nordic countries whose social democratic frameworks, unlike Sweden's, required considerable reconstruction
following the war.

Finally, from the start the SAP exhibited a strong dedication to forwarding social reform through technocratic empiricism, a faith in the
power of research that other social democratic parties of the early twentieth
century lacked (Berman 2006). Rather than assuming the role of vanguard
party and treating the desires and beliefs of party leadership as dogma, the
SAP initiated a program of targeted, rational social improvement in which
problems were identified and studied, and reforms were implemented
based on the results of those studies. By approaching reform in this incre-
mentalist manner the Social Democrats broke strongly from their original
Marxist influence. Whereas in Russia, for instance, revolution had been
kickstarted into existence, its unfolding accelerated by a political movement
too impatient to wait, the SAP preferred to slow the revolution down, to
forge it piecemeal, bit by bit, allowing enough time to consider each problem on its own, each process used to address the problem, and all of the
potential consequences of reshaping society as that reshaping unfolded.

And in this project design was critical. As modernist design spread
from Germany to other parts of Europe, both its forms and ideologies of
social transformation tended to remain, to some degree, as it was adopted.
But in Sweden, modernism found a home, literally and discursively, that
was largely unrivaled in other countries.

Modernist Design in Sweden and Beyond

The origins of modernist design in the first few decades of the twentieth
century are most often associated with a small number of personalities and
institutions, including architects Le Corbusier in France and Walter Gropius and his Bauhaus school in Germany. Known eventually as the International Style, or Neue Sachlichkeit (The New Objectivity) in German,
European modernist design would become the twentieth century's "most
concentrated systematization of surface" (Ward 2001:9), a style dominated
by simple forms that spread from Germany to other parts of Europe, including Sweden, and to the United States, where it mixed with both indigenous American modernist styles and consumer capitalism, and then
eventually to the rest of the world. While its origins can be traced back to

at least the late nineteenth century, modernist design began to flourish in Europe most strongly in the immediate aftermath of World War I. The war itself had represented a distinct point of transition between old traditional warfare technologies like horses and rifles, and more modern machines like tanks, airplanes, and flame throwers, whose destructive power left most of Europe, and especially Germany, in ruins. In the face of the widespread devastation of both population and infrastructure, modernist design, partly influenced by the technological advances that drove much of the fighting during the war, emerged as a means by which the reconstruction of German society could take place.

The Bauhaus school, founded in Weimar, Germany, in 1919 under the leadership of Walter Gropius, became the foremost institutional progenitor of modernist architecture and design, in Germany and beyond, during its short existence. Originally focused on projects as varied as architecture, textiles, painting, and typography crafted without any particular specificity of style, over the course of the 1920s Bauhaus instructors increasingly developed an emergent functionalism—a simplicity of form, an acceptance of mass production, an eschewal of unnecessary ornament—as their dominant design framework. This turn was in part motivated by the usefulness of mass-production technologies that functioned most efficiently with simple forms, but also by a strong desire to sever connections with the staid, elaborate forms associated with Germany's long imperial past. Modernist architecture and design, it was hoped, so visually distinct from what came before, would give new form to a brand new world.

But this was not to be, at least not in Germany. Having thrived during the brief democratic period of the Weimar Republic, the Bauhaus shuttered its activities in 1933, under pressure from the new Nazi government, forcing many of its prominent members, including architect Ludwig Mies van der Rohe, to flee to the United States. Then in 1937, in the same political move that simultaneously identified and censored so-called degenerate art, the Nazi regime banned functionalism and the International Style in architecture and design. In direct opposition to modernism's break from Germany's past, Hitler and his principal architect, Alfred Speer, imposed dominating neoclassical architectural forms in an attempt to signal the strength and power of the German nation by visually referencing ancient Roman styles. In that same vein Hitler and his minister of propaganda

Joseph Goebbels banned the use of most modern typefaces in graphic design, relying instead on the heavy use of Fraktur, an old Germanic variant of a Gothic font whose form had been linked to German-language printing for centuries. Yet despite Hitler's explicit antimodernist orientation and the imposition of *völkisch* aesthetics, a minimal pluralism of design styles did manage to persist in Nazi Germany (Aynsley 2000; Betts 2002; Miller Lane 1968). Even Goebbels himself saw the utility of functionalism's emphasis on simplicity and reduction of form for effectively reaching large numbers of people (Welch 1983). Nonetheless, the period from 1933 to 1945 represented a severe suppression, if not outright withdrawal, of modernist design in Germany.

Following the end of the war, functionalism was given an initial brief reprieve in the East. In another attempt to use design style as a visible line of differentiation separating the current regime from its predecessor, the Soviets, intent on expelling the *völkisch* styles promoted by the Nazis, invited formerly evicted Bauhaus-trained architects and designers to settle and work in the East (Rubin 2006). This renewed enthusiasm for modernism was short-lived, however, and by 1950 the ruling Socialist Unity Party rejected functionalism as overly imperialist and internationalist, and as such not sufficiently connected to the German nation they hoped to revive (Ulrich 2004). This proclamation led to a ban on modernist design for the first half of the 1950s, but this ban, like the previous bout of enthusiasm, was also short-lived. Recognizing that the need for managing a large population through modern mass-production methods outweighed the ideological restrictions on modernist design, the East German government lifted the ban in 1956, and by the 1960s the popularity of functionalist goods exploded in the East (Rubin 2006).

In the West the trajectory was a little different. As in the East, modernism was reintroduced to distance the current regime from associations with the Nazis, and soon enough "industrial design emerged as a primary site for fronting a new West German cultural order" (Betts 2004:2). Yet unlike what unfolded in Sweden starting in the 1930s, and what at least lightly concerned members of the original Bauhaus, functionalism in West Germany was less oriented toward advancing class solidarity through everyday design and more conspicuously linked to liberal ideologies of consumer capitalism primarily imported from the United States. As

Czech-born, American art historian Lorenz Eitner described the state of industrial design in West Germany in the late 1950s,

> For all the publicity which "modern design" has received in Germany, industrial products designed with originality and a sense of beauty continue to be rare and expensive. In industrial design, as in other forms of art, modernity remains the prerogative of the unusually discerning or the unusually rich. (Eitner 1957:3).

In other words, whereas in Scandinavia and East Germany modern design was initially entangled (though in different ways) with an inclusive concept of "the people" or "the masses," in postwar West Germany it assumed a more explicit association with cultures of consumption and industrialism, in particular in the case of internationally recognized brands like Braun and Volkswagen.

After reunification in 1989, while both East and West had embraced and developed their own versions of modernist design during the years of separation, realigning these modernisms as part of *die Wende* turned out to be a rather difficult process. One symptom of this difficulty was manifest in a variant of *nostalgie* (Boyer 2006), a widespread cultural nostalgia felt by former East Germans for life in the East, which in some cases would settle on particular objects, often those from the post-1960s modernist period, and the affective associations they evoked (Berdahl 1999; Betts 2000; cf. Fehérváry 2009, 2013). Thus despite both East and West forwarding versions of modernist design during the Cold War, the years following *die Wende* revealed just how different those modernisms had been.

Italy, too, eventually embraced modernist design, though its course there both parallels and diverges from the German case.[3] As in Germany, the period immediately following World War I saw the rise of a dictatorial political party—the Fascists, led by Benito Mussolini—whose leaders viewed design and architecture as both significant visual representations of political power and critical mechanisms of governance. But unlike in Germany there had been no indigenous school of art and design equivalent to the Bauhaus, or at least none as prominent and productive—and thus threatening to the ascendant Fascist regime.

Mussolini himself, like Hitler, was partial to neoclassical architecture, and the claim to a long lineage extending back to ancient Rome was a central component of the Fascists' overwhelming nationalist and imperialist project. But unlike Hitler, Mussolini was not explicitly anti-modernist. As an associate of Filippo Marinetti, the founder of Italian futurism, Mussolini was deeply influenced by avant-garde movements in art, literature, and fashion, and subscribed to a number of futurist ideologies, including a faith in technology and industrialism, and a reliance on violence for achieving desired political goals (Doordan 1995). He also embraced mass-production methods developed by Henry Ford in the United States, treating them as essential for the success of Fascism's new corporatist economic system designed to overcome the weaknesses of both Marxism and capitalism. Meanwhile, in contrast to the liberal period before the 1920s, the Fascist regime was initially decidedly isolationist, promoting trade primarily within imperial boundaries rather than in international markets. One result of this was that while the ideas and objects of modernist design spread from Germany to other countries in Europe in the 1920s and 1930s, they had little early purchase in Italy. Indeed, not until after the war, in the 1950s, did modernist aesthetics begin appearing in Italian design, but rather than entering through Germany, these new styles mostly surfaced through the influence of American consumer capitalism—and, as in West Germany, it was largely stripped of socially oriented ideological readings that had survived and thrived in Scandinavia.

Modernist forms of one kind or another have appeared, circulated, transformed, and disappeared in various national cultural contexts throughout the twentieth century and into the twenty-first, but they of course have not lived the same sorts of lives in all of those environments. Even in Germany, the most significant site for modernist design's early cultivation, there has not been a consistent relationship between the style's core forms, their political meanings, and the kinds of work these forms are mobilized to do—including under one (at least nominally) consistent political regime. What the German and Italian cases reveal is that even in countries internationally recognized today for their successful modernist design projects, the integration of design, politics, and the everyday world is always variable and contingent. Moreover, a historiographical orientation to the sociopolitical qualities of design that simply lumps together forms (e.g., modernism) and ideologies (e.g., welfare politics) because of surface similarities visible at one point in time does not do justice to the consequential cultural and historical particularities that contribute to design's role in shaping a given society.

2

Building the Beautiful Home

There is a common Swedish aphorism that neatly captures the special relationship between politics, particular historical figures, and the significance of design in Sweden: "Per Albin Hansson byggde folkhemmet, Ingvar Kamprad möblerade det" (Per Albin Hansson built the *folkhem*, Ingvar Kamprad furnished it). Hansson, an early prime minister from the Social Democratic Party, is credited with establishing the political basis for the Swedish welfare state, which during its early years was termed the *folkhem* (people's home). Kamprad, the founder of Ikea, the Swedish furniture retailer, helped introduce inexpensive mass-produced chairs, tables, and beds into practically every Swedish home by the 1960s. While the emergence of the early welfare state and the growing social significance of design in Sweden were ultimately motivated and propelled by different forces, their parallel development, both in time and texture, was no coincidence. Politicians, artists, and social activists, all influenced by the same conceptual currents of social reform circulating in Sweden over the course of the twentieth century, instantiated their own unique but thematically similar movements for progress in satisfying the common material needs of all Swedish citizens. And during one significant period in the 1930s there was direct, interpersonal influence between several key figures in the construction of the welfare state and the introduction of functionalist design in Sweden. Understanding the historical formulation of the lines of enunciation of Swedish design, how the final vocabulary was first assembled and rendered applicable within a particular "social democratic" framework, requires close attention to the early, often intertwined roots of both design and welfare politics. In many ways neither story can be fully understood without reference to the other, because in important instances, especially early on, their characters and plotlines have largely overlapped.

The theme of this chapter is the home, considered both as a *real place*, a real building composed of lines of visibility and occupied by a real family, and as a *concept*, a resonant political metaphor used as an organizing principle by a political party intent on transforming society. In Sweden the home has been both the motivation for and the object of large-scale social engineering projects shaped by a utopian vision to improve the conditions of society as a whole by addressing the everyday problems of each of its members (Berner 1998; Hirdman 1989, 1992, 1994; Carlson 1990). A long-standing central theme in Scandinavian cultural life (Gullestad 1989a, 1989b, 2001; Löfgren 1987, 1999; Hansen 1976), the home today stands as the best representation of how the moral order is ideally configured in Sweden. It is where the family resides, the most basic unit of social organization, bound together by warmth and care, and the primary locus where essential needs can be satisfied. An individual can find comfort in the home and can seek refuge there in times of trouble, either in solitude or in the company of others. It is both an intimate place and the point from which interactions with the wider world are launched. But the home is also quite politically significant on a much grander scale. In establishing the welfare state the Social Democrats explicitly exploited the affective associations that Swedes had invested in their homes and home lives, and they recast the home as a primary site for political reform. The home, then, both materially and ideationally, and largely through the efforts of specific politicians, intellectuals, and designers, is the foundational source of the enduring poetic entanglements between Swedish politics and Swedish design.

Kollektivhuset

On a chilly evening in late spring, with the sun still looming in the sky but sleepily eyeing the horizon, my friend Leif and I walked along the water on the island of Kungsholmen in Stockholm. The grass around us was covered with dozens and dozens of rabbits, a fact I have to this day never been able to get over, and I found it hard to concentrate on our conversation. "There's an apartment building up there," he said casually, pointing to the right as we passed a street intersecting our path at the perpendicular. "It's an old modernist building from the 1930s. It has dumbwaiters." Momentarily swayed from the rabbits, I asked him a few questions about the building, but he didn't know much more than what he'd already said. I made a mental note to come back to the neighborhood soon, to see if I could find my way into the building. But I never was able to get inside.

"And I am building a house," wrote Alva Myrdal, a sociologist and Social Democratic operative, in a letter to American friends, in 1932. "Together with another architect which is not in Gunnar's group, a more realistic than articulate person. We have an idea about building a 'kollektivhus,' an ideal family hotel with cooperative organization to take care of all your material needs and unload your responsibility also for your offspring" (quoted in Hirdman 2008:154). It would be a building to house many families, designed to take care of their most basic needs *together*, a perfect model for a new form of living (see fig. 3).

And indeed Alva did build that house, and many others besides, though her involvement in the others was much less central. For Alva, a critical figure in the construction of the welfare system in Sweden, housing—both its standards and its affective manifestation as *home*—was the most important aspect of an effective plan for social and economic reform, a plan that she and her friends in the Social Democratic Party, including her husband, Gunnar, were desperately intent on carrying out. Arguably, without Alva's attention to the home and home life in their reformist project, the development of the Swedish welfare state—itself taking on the qualities of a home for the people—would not have unfolded as it did. Her insistence on the home became both a rational focal point linking ideology to practice, and a forceful ratchet point that by degrees shifted political debate on social reform in a direction favored by the Social Democrats. But getting there, to where the new home was given form, took some time, and some effort.

Figure 3. The *kollektivhus* designed by Sven Markelius, with Alva Myrdal; Stockholm, 1936.

Laying the Foundations for Welfare: Nineteenth-Century Politics and Social Agitation

The history of the Swedish welfare state is, in its earliest years, coextensive with the history of the Social Democratic Party, which was founded in 1889 and came to dominate Swedish politics for most of the twentieth century. Like social democratic parties then springing up elsewhere in Europe, the early SAP was heavily influenced by Marxist thought, although the nascent party's embrace of socialist ideology was not wholehearted or without debate (Berman 1998, 2006). As a result of some particularities of Sweden's political roots and the strong influence of particular party members, the SAP took on a very distinct character over the course of its maturation.

Since 1809, Sweden has officially operated as a constitutional monarchy. Representational governance has a long history in Scandinavia. Beginning in the sixteenth century the Swedish parliament, or Riksdag, was organized as four separate houses, each representing one of the four traditional estates—nobles, clergy, the bourgeoisie, and landowning farmers. In 1865, bowing to pressure placed on them by rapidly industrializing economies at home and in the rest of Europe, the estates voted to abolish the old system of representation and replace it with a new parliamentary system, this time composed of two houses whose members were elected by a wider swath of the population. The First Chamber, composed of the old aristocracy and bourgeoisie, maintained a higher degree of power than the Second Chamber, representing the peasantry and the emerging working class, and this arrangement more or less resulted in continued governance through plutocracy through the late 1800s.

For several decades the two houses struggled over the interrelated complexities of economic development and political enfranchisement, the consequences of which severely threatened the grip on power then held by the upper classes. One of the biggest problems confronting Sweden was poverty in the face of strong population growth. By most measures the country was extremely poor, and while industrialization was taking root, the promised economic benefits that came along with it were not immediately apparent, and certainly not appearing as quickly or forcefully as in other parts of Europe. Despite an upward swing in urbanization, by 1900 almost 80 percent of the population was still rural and poor, and from the 1860s to the 1890s almost one million Swedes emigrated to the United States to escape the economic crisis. Meanwhile, the population in Sweden continued to expand rapidly, including a growing number of immigrants from Finland and the lower Baltic states, and Sweden's infrastructure soon weakened under the strain. Amid these pressing concerns, the Second Chamber of the Riksdag, the lower chamber, pushed for an expansion of suffrage among the lower classes so as to increase its parliamentary power, a move the First Chamber flatly opposed. By the turn of the century, however, it was clear that political liberalization was inevitable, and through a series of reforms over several decades, different classes received the vote, culminating in true universal suffrage in 1921. It was in this sociopolitical climate that the ideologies underpinning the Swedish "third way" between capitalism and socialism began to develop.

The people themselves, and not just elected politicians, were instrumental in developing this project. During the last few decades of the nineteenth century, folk movements began springing up throughout Sweden, taking the form of cultural associations, social societies, and work federations. Some of these groups were overtly political, and others were not, but most were more or less democratically structured. The guild system had been dissolved in 1846, and it was not until the 1870s, stemming directly from these folk movements, that true trade unions began to appear. Workers gathered together according to particular professions and skills, and over time various smaller unions consolidated into larger, overarching labor organizations like Landsorganisationen (LO), which is still today Sweden's largest trade union. But collective organization was not just the purview of the working class, as more industrialists entered the growing economic field, and employers' federations began mobilizing to advocate for their own collective agenda. Amid this arrangement were planted the seeds of what would become the core social democratic tradition of cooperation—admittedly not always pleasant—between workers, employers, and the government.

Influenced by the momentum of increasingly active international social movements, official modern-style political parties also began to take shape in Sweden in the late nineteenth century, most notably the Liberal Party and the SAP. While the ideological substrata on which these parties were founded were, respectively, economic liberalism and socialism—and were thus ostensibly incompatible—the leadership of both parties at the time saw substantial overlap in their missions for freedom and social justice. However, this alliance was, at first, slow going. Because the bulk of their membership was in large part a holdover from earlier political periods, the Liberals, drawing their ranks from the First Chamber, were able to gain a substantial foothold in the Riksdag, while the fledgling Social Democrats managed to seat only one member, Hjalmar Branting, over a six-year stretch starting in 1896. Early in his life Branting tended to subscribe to an orthodox Marxist interpretation of socialism, a political outlook that did not have wide support in Sweden. But partly through cooperation with the Liberals during his first years in parliament, Branting came to view peaceful political reform as a viable alternative to socialist revolution (see Berman 2006), and his political work left a lasting imprint on subsequent generations of Social Democratic politicians.

Social Reform through Aesthetic Reform: Art, Design, and Mass Production

During this same early period much of the very ideological material that inspired the SAP's developing political platform also circulated in the intellectual milieu dominated by artists, social activists, and other players on Sweden's cultural stage. The most influential force in the late nineteenth and early twentieth centuries was the national romantic movement in art, literature, and architecture, which had swept across Europe in the 1800s, though assuming a different tone and timbre in Sweden than it had elsewhere. With origins in the earlier romantic movement in art and architecture, national romanticism "sought to transcend established boundaries, including the social constructs of class, the geographical constructs of regionalism, and the temporal constructs of history" (Facos 1998:3) by emphasizing national unity through affectively resonant imagery. While most national romantic artists in Europe, at least those influenced by the German tradition, drew extensively on idyllic, pastoral imagery to create and celebrate an imagined national past (see Eade 1983)—often in direct refutation of the advances of industrialism and modernity—Swedish national romantics were more interested in cautiously embracing modernity than in rejecting it outright (Facos 1998). To be sure, Swedish artists, as in other national traditions, did work with imagery of a mythologized national past and did attempt to move viewers emotionally by focusing on the idealized beauty of the Swedish landscape and connecting it to the concept of "homeland." But unlike in other nations Swedish national romanticism did not necessarily appeal directly to some *genetic* Swedishness grounded in a shared and purportedly pure ethnic identity, but instead appealed to a *geopolitical* Swedishness based on location and a set of common core values—a love of nature, social equality, and individual liberties. Partly "because the movement functioned as a cultural and spiritual complement to social democracy" (Facos 1998:3), national romanticism would have a deep and pervasive impact on twentieth-century Swedish culture and politics, despite no formally arranged contact, at least at that early point, between artists and politicians.[1]

Romancing the Home

One of the unique characteristics of Nordic national romanticism was its particular emphasis on the home and home life in its aesthetic reimagining of the national. While the nation as "home" or "homeland" was a theme in most national romantic traditions (Eade 1983), artists and architects working in Norway, Denmark, Finland, and especially Sweden treated the relationship between home and nation quite literally. The most important figure in the Swedish national romantic movement was Carl Larsson, a painter and author who, along with his wife Karin, revolutionized—this is not an overstatement—the way Swedes conceive of home life and home decoration. Since the 1880s the Larssons have attained iconic status in Sweden, with Carl's instantly recognizable paintings of Karin's interior designs not only visible today in coffee-table books and on mass-reproduced prints and posters, but also adorning almost every conceivable kind of home knickknack, from plates and mugs to postcards, coffee canisters, and laptop computer sleeves. Many older Swedes (and even some younger ones) display Larsson imagery in their homes, though in differing degrees of prominence, and on several occasions in Sweden, on learning of my interest in Swedish design, friends or their family members gave Larsson memorabilia to me as a gift. One older friend even insisted that "this is where Swedish design began."

While Carl Larsson, like other influential artists of his generation, was skilled in painting grand landscapes in the national romantic tradition, he differentiated himself and his work—and touched so many viewers—by reducing his vision in scale and situating it squarely in depictions of intimate activities and private spaces. As one contemporary art critic from the United States described it, Larsson "found his inspiration amid the endearing association of family life and became the foremost Swedish intimist" (Brinton 1916:406–407). In his influential book *Ett Hem* (A Home), Larsson depicted his family in vibrant colors and nearly realistic lines, all of them typically going about their everyday business. The most common setting for these portrayals was the Larsson home, called Lilla Hyttnäs, which "immediately became the most beloved house in all of Sweden" (von Zweigbergk 1968:12)—and which has since been transformed into a popular tourist destination. In his illustrations Carl paid considerable attention to presenting the details of Karin's decorations as realistically as he could. Tables, chairs, and benches, sofas and framed wall art, potted plants and flowers, are often granted equal or even greater prominence in Larsson's paintings than the people inhabiting the same spaces. In a sense, Lilla Hyttnäs itself took on the status of a member of the Larsson family in Carl's portraits. Because the intimacy of these images is so striking, and a profound feeling of care shines powerfully through their art and affects so many Swedes, the work created by the Larssons has come to represent a touchstone for Swedish interior design, enduring as an accessible model for decorating the home and constructing a comfortable domestic life.

Ellen Key and the Reformation of Beauty

Closely related to the national romantic movement, another international source of influence on late nineteenth-century Swedish aesthetic culture was the Arts and Crafts tradition, which thrived fervently in Great Britain and the United States from the 1860s into the first decades of the twentieth century. This movement, which in many ways was an early manifestation of a kind of person-centered design, focused on promoting the skill, uniqueness, and creativity of the craftsperson. The foremost inspiration for the Arts and Crafts movement, though not himself a member, was John Ruskin (1890, 1907; Daniels and Brandwood 2003; Henderson 2000), a British poet, artist, and social critic who famously upheld a strict interrelationship between architecture and morality and, like Carl Larsson, encouraged a positive, idyllic image of home life and the pleasures of nature.

Ruskin's writings on social justice influenced the development of the La-
bour Party in Britain and inspired William Morris (1882, 1902; Štanský
1985), an artist and writer, to fight for accessibility and affordability in art
and design and to explore the power of architecture for reshaping social
conditions.

The ideas of Ruskin and Morris were primarily introduced to Sweden through the work of Ellen Key (Nyström-Hamilton 1913; Lengborn
2002; Linden 2006), a prominent feminist and social critic active at the
turn of the century. Today Key is best known internationally for her pio-
neering polemics on pedagogy and family life, but she was also a major
voice advocating widespread social reform as industrialization began to
take hold in Swedish society. Influenced by the Arts and Crafts movement, though not as skeptical of industrialization, Key over the course of
her lifetime developed a political stance that was in large part committed
to liberalism but mixed with a socialist penchant for egalitarianism and
social justice. Key made a name for herself in Stockholm as an advocate
for working-class women and by penning a number of widely read com-
mentaries on education, parenting, and suffrage, which helped establish
her reputation as one of Sweden's most important intellectuals. Through
her activities she also developed close ties with the founding members of
the SAP, despite her bourgeois background. Though her influence on the
development of Swedish design is wide ranging, it is most evident in three
particular features—the refashioning of the concept of "beauty" to include
simplicity and functionality; the recasting of beauty as a necessary quality
of everyday goods; and the promotion of the home as a critical site for
actively instantiating social reform—all of which had a lasting impact on
Swedish design.

Key was intrigued by the metaphysics of everyday life, and in particular
the power of *beauty*, a mundane kind of beauty, to help shape an emergent
Swedish sociopolitical cosmology. In 1899 she published a short collection
of essays whose title—*Skönhet för Alla* (Beauty for Everyone)—quickly became a foundational statement for Swedish design, a call to arms for artists,
designers, and industrialists to reconceptualize the place of the beautiful in
mass-produced goods. It was in one of the essays in the collection, "Skönhet i Hemmen" (Beauty in the Home) (Key 2006, 2008), that Key offered
her most in-depth, and ultimately persuasive, explanation of how to make
"the beautiful" accessible to everyone through everyday goods.

The essay "Beauty in the Home" took the form of a primer for modern home decoration. Over thirty-four pages Key offered plenty of sensible advice, making no attempt to conceal her disdain for homes "lacking in style," and scornfully describing their "ugly rooms" in minute detail. (Words like "gaudy" [*prålig*], "imitation" [*oäkta*], "flimsy" [*sladdrig*], and "uncomfortable" [*obekväm*] make numerous repeat appearances in the text.) Indeed, Key argued forcefully that from her point of view, "the beautiful" shares unquestionable identity with "the good." But in the midst of laying out this practical guide, Key simultaneously leveled a devastating critique of the social organization of taste in Sweden—a critique with deep implications for the expansion of social justice at a time when inequality, according to almost any metric, was devastatingly high.

The thrust of Key's argument originated in an acute sensitivity to the symbolic violence caused by uneven *access* to beautiful goods: "Först när inget fult finns att köpa, när det vackra är lika billigt som den fula nu är, kan skönhet för alla bli full verklighet." (Key 2006:29; Not until there is nothing ugly to buy, when the beautiful is as inexpensive as the ugly is now, can beauty for all become a full reality.)[2] Unlike many of her contemporaries, Key recognized that "good taste" is linked to class; that it is not innate, but learned; and that it develops over time and emerges through practice and experience. Theories of the beautiful that were then current tended to skew heavily toward Kantian formulations of "pure beauty" and almost exclusively to situate beauty—or at least the artificial kind—in traditional forms of fine art. While such theories sought to explain how individuals confront, sense, and understand the aesthetic world, Key was more interested in finding ways to *actively use* aesthetics to maximize the experience of improved material conditions for as many people as possible. And what this required was a redefining of the very criteria by which beauty should be judged.

Key's first order of business was to expand the contours of beauty beyond *art* into the domain of *everyday things*. In her theory of aesthetics, distinctions between art and nonart were rendered irrelevant. She dismissed the idea that a beautiful object, such as a painting or sculpture, by its nature "has no function" and instead fully embraced functionality as part of an object's beauty. Unlike most artworks, the objects of everyday life crave manipulation. Key stressed that benefits derived from an object's *use*—how it actually performs its intended purpose—contribute to its inherent beauty:

På en stol skall man kunna sitta bra, vid ett bord skall man kunna äta eller ar-
beta, i en säng skall man kunna vila väl. Den obekväma stolen, det vingliga
bordet, den smala sängen är därmed redan därför fula. Men det är ändå inte
säkert att den bekväma stolen, det stadiga bordet, den breda sängen är vackra.
Saken måste, liksom varje vackert föremål i naturen gör det, fylla sitt än-
damål med enkelhet och lätthet, förfining och uttrycksfullhet, annars har den
inte uppnått skönheten, även om den motsvarar nyttans krav. (Key 2006:28)

One should be able to sit well in a chair, one should be able to eat or work
at a table, [and] one should be able to rest well in a bed. The uncomfortable
chair, the wobbly table, and the narrow bed are accordingly already ugly.
But it is not yet certain that the comfortable chair, the steady table, and the
wide bed are beautiful. Just as it is with every beautiful object in nature, the
thing must fulfill its purpose with ease, simplicity, refinement and expressiveness, otherwise it has not attained beauty, even if it satisfies the requirements for use.[3]

The implication of this formulation is that by *interacting* with objects,
and not merely by sensing their visually pleasing appearances, people will
come to *holistically experience* beauty in the everyday rather than simply to
intuit it.

Key also explicitly linked beauty with simplicity, treating formal extravagance as the exact antithesis of beauty in domestic objects. Such
details, according to Key's calculus, are dangerous, and she repeatedly
stressed the importance of formal austerity: "För dem, som inte själva har
säker smak är det bästa rådet att undvika vridna och tillkrånglade former
eller pråliga, mångbrokiga och skrikande färger, och välja enkla former
och entoniga färger." (Key 2006:43; For those who don't themselves possess infallible taste, the best advice is to avoid distorted and complicated
forms and loud, ostentatious, multi-hued colors, and [instead] to choose
simple forms and monochromatic tones.) By working with only the most
basic of colors and simplest of shapes and avoiding wrong choices like
"loud colors" or "distorted forms," the threat of ugliness is mitigated.
Moreover, Key explicitly correlated the beauty of simplicity with an object's functionality:

Det är helt klart att var och en som har skönhetssinne kan åstadkomma
en viss harmoni mellan det nyttiga och det vackra, om man inte förväxlar

det senare med överdåd, som ofta är ett hinder för det verkligt vackra. Det senare kan ordnas med enkla medel och för ett billigt pris. (32)

It is obvious that each and every person who has a sense of beauty can achieve a certain harmony between the useful and the beautiful, so long as she doesn't confuse it with extravagance, which is often an obstacle to the truly beautiful, which [itself] can be realized through simple means and at a cheap price.

What emerges in Key's aesthetic theory, then, is a portrait of beauty generated in the simple forms of everyday things put to use. Moreover, she consistently underscored the socioeconomic implications of simplicity throughout the text—since formally and functionally simple objects tend to be cheap to produce, they are thus cheap for most people to buy. This is beauty for all in the most immediate of senses.

For Key, merging beauty with simplicity was a way to "universalize" recognition and appreciation of the beautiful. To reduce an object to the simplest of forms and to ascribe beauty to this reduction minimizes noise in the social systems in which judgments of taste are embedded. In one sense this represents a "smallest common denominator" theory of beauty, a pruning of taste that trims away what makes the beautiful "beautiful." But such pejorative interpretations misrecognize the flexibility of "defining down" beauty. Key's aesthetic did not directly *preclude* embellishment and complexity from "the beautiful," but simply reconfigured the core foundation of beauty to be widely inclusive rather than exclusive.

There is a brutish quality to Key's argument, an insistence that simplicity is unquestionably beautiful on her say-so. But Key was no authoritarian; she was not interested in pursuing class revolution or pushing a regime of social hygiene. Instead, Key viewed the large-scale and egalitarian redistribution of *symbolic capital* as central to any project advocating social progress, starting with the normalization of aesthetic currencies used to carry out the transactions of everyday life.

But reconfiguring beauty was only part of Key's goal. Advocating "beauty for all" in the everyday world required *locating* a redefined beauty so as to affect as many people as possible, and Key understood the political implications of declaring "the home" an irreducible primitive of large-scale social reform. Because of its near-universal ubiquity, the home became—and remains—the most logical site for instantiating aesthetic

reform at the level of experience. And over the next several decades it became evident that Key was not the only one who felt this way.

Raising the People's Home

In an address published in the 1927 Christmas edition of *Morgonbris*, a pe-
riodical printed by the SAP's women members, party leader Per Albin
Hansson offered his estimation of the work that women do, alongside his
particular vision for the future:

> Vi ha hunnit så långt att vi kunna börja reda det stora folkhemmet. Det är
> fråga om att där skapa trevnad och trivsel, göra det gott och varmt, ljust och
> glatt och fritt. För en kvinna borde det icke finnas en mer lockande upp-
> gift. Kanske behövdes det blott att hon får ögonen på den, att hon får väck-
> else, för att hon skall komma med hela sin iver och hänförelse. (Quoted in
> Hirdman 1989:90)

> We have come so far that we are now able to begin to prepare the big home
> for the people. The task is to create in it comfort and cheer, to make it cozy
> and warm, bright and gleaming, and free. There is probably no more entic-
> ing task for a woman. Perhaps she need only set her eyes upon it to be in-
> spired to throw herself into it with all her zeal and devotion. (Quoted in
> translation in Hirdman 1992:25)

Having steadily gained a larger number of seats in the Riksdag over the
first decades of the twentieth century, becoming the largest party after
1921 (and the inception of universal suffrage), by the late 1920s, despite
losing its grip on parliamentary control for several years in the middle
of the decade, the SAP was poised to begin implementing its agenda for
workers' rights, economic equality, and individual liberty.[4] Drawing partly
from Key's influential campaign for domestic reform, though less concerned with her critique of beauty, the SAP seized on the home primarily as a rhetorical tool in conceptualizing and expressing its political task.
But as significant as the home seemed to be to the Social Democrats' plans,
its position as an actual political target remained ambiguous. Key had argued that everyday material existence should be the object of political reform, with women and children, both subjugated classes, as particularly

in need of their benefits. While the home—what it was, who composed it, and what it represented—remained uncomfortably present in social democratic ideology, showing up often without having much to do, for all its prominence there was very little sense as to the precise nature of its reality for the party's future programmatic plans. What was it about the home that mattered so much?

Because the domestic sphere was first and foremost a female domain, party leadership was ambivalent about how exactly to reconcile the home as an actual lived space with the specific policy positions represented in the party platform (Hirdman 1989, 1994). On the one hand, male members of the SAP did tend to find solidarity with women, acknowledging their work in the home as a necessary and important form of labor, and advocating—though not entirely selflessly—for more lax attitudes toward sexual liberation. On the other hand, there was a worry that overpoliticizing the home would result in an imprudent release of women from the constraints of the domestic sphere, which would in turn both add more competition to the labor market and leave serious blemishes on women's moral stature. So at this point, rather than investing any serious political capital in leading politics directly into the home, the SAP decided instead to bring the home, in the form of what would become a very powerful metaphor, directly into politics.

In 1928, only several months after his address to the women of the SAP was published, Per Albin Hansson explained in a monumental speech a new social democratic framework for a better organized society:

> The home's foundation is community and a feeling of togetherness. The good home does not recognize any privileged or neglected [members], any favorites or stepchildren. [In the home,] no one looks down on another or tries to gain advantage at another's expense, nor do the strong push down or plunder the weak. In the good home, consideration, cooperation, and helpfulness prevail. Applied to the great home of the people and the citizens, this would mean breaking down all social and economic barriers that now divide citizens into privileged and neglected, into rulers and dependents, into rich and poor, into landed and impoverished, into plunderers and plundered. (Quoted in Berkling 1982:227; my translation)

This speech introduced the concept of *folkhemmet*, "the people's home," which became over the following decades the dominant analogy used to describe the emergent welfare system. Just as Key had turned to the home as a site in which to begin the eradication of class barriers, so too was the leadership of the SAP inspired by the home in remaking a centrally governed society. Moreover, as the party's political center of gravity gradually shifted away from its original focus on workers' rights to a more inclusive agenda of broader social reforms, the home shed its ambiguous status and gained more prominence as a specific physical site within Social Democratic planning. But while the idea of the home was an appealing one for Hansson to draw on to make his point, it was still just an idea without much substance. In order to move from plan to structure, the *folkhem* needed an architect, or maybe two. And, as it turned out, some interior designers as well.

Gunnar and Alva Myrdal: Engineering the Structure of a New Society

Those architects were named Gunnar and Alva Myrdal.[5] There were other collaborators, of course, but the level of influence the Myrdals were able to exert on both the SAP's leadership and the Swedish people themselves, starting in the 1930s and extending until their deaths, was unparalleled in the twentieth century.

Gunnar Myrdal (1898–1987) was raised in modest conditions, first in the rural part of Sweden where he was born, then in the capital city after the age of six. His father was a railroad worker from an agrarian family with conservative political roots, which undoubtedly influenced Gunnar's early political leanings, though never stridently so. In 1918 he enrolled in law school at Stockholm University, and a year later he met Alva Reimer (1902–1986), whom he would eventually marry in 1924. After earning his law degree Gunnar decided to abandon the legal profession, preferring instead to study economics at Stockholm under Gustav Cassel, then one of the world's foremost economists. Over the next several years, primarily under the sway of Alva, Gunnar's politics grew increasingly in line with those of the SAP, and in 1932, the same year the party took what would become near-permanent control of the Riksdag, Myrdal officially signed on as a member.

And then, after assessing the condition of the *folkhem*, he got to work. In 1933, along with his friend Uno Åhrén, an architect and chief planner of Sweden's second largest city, Gothenburg, Myrdal petitioned members of the SAP's new cabinet to sanction a study of housing conditions there, with the intention of issuing a report on future plans and possibilities for a national housing policy. Myrdal and Åhrén published their findings that same year as "The Housing Question as a Problem of Urban Planning," (Myrdal and Åhrén 1933), which led directly to the establishment of Bostadssociala Utredningnen, a more substantial and powerful state-sponsored commission tasked with researching and steering questions of national housing policy. Both Myrdal and Åhrén were appointed members.

During this same period, the new minister of finance, Ernst Wigforss, a linguist by training with a predilection for planned economies, tapped Myrdal to serve on the Committee on Unemployment, a group charged with tackling the severe labor problems that had befallen Sweden during the ongoing global depression. After several months of research on this topic, the solution that Myrdal offered is what today is generally labeled Keynesian expansionist monetary policy (though Myrdal seems to have developed the ideas first; see Barber 2008): increased government investment in widely beneficial public works projects, like transportation infrastructure, housing, and public utilities. This intentionally generates government debt—though, importantly, debt that can be monitored and controlled—but also in the process helps produce goods and services the country needs while simultaneously employing large numbers of workers. The economy would recover, Myrdal argued, from the injection of new wages into the market, and the accumulated debt would be paid down through new tax revenues collected off those wages. The SAP leadership ultimately followed Myrdal's recommendations, and, much to their relief, they worked. After only four years the government recorded overall budget surpluses and lower unemployment rates, scoring, under Myrdal's guidance, the first large-scale political victory for the young Social Democratic Party.

But this was only Myrdal's first maneuver. While he was researching, writing, and helping to implement his monetary policy recommendations, Gunnar was also hard at work with Alva on a book that would shake Swedish society to its core when it was published in 1934. The book was entitled *Kris i Befolkningsfrågan* (Crisis in the Population Question) (Myrdal and Myrdal 1934), an erudite, controversial, and unexpectedly popular exploration of declining birthrates, population control, and sexual morality in a transforming Swedish society. While the population had increased overall throughout the previous few decades, the growth was primarily due to the effects of improved living conditions on adults, which in the long run kept older people living longer. At the other end of the spectrum the birthrate was steadily declining, in part because of the population's urban migration during the same time frame: children were more of a hindrance to families living in dirtier, smaller homes in the city than they had been on the farm, where they could contribute to the home more directly through their labor. For several years Gunnar had argued that the declining birthrate and the attendant danger of a shrinking population, what he called "the liquidation of a people" (quoted in Barber 2008:56), was the biggest threat to Sweden's continued prosperity, even its very existence. He felt that attempts to *increase* the population, which some politicians had proposed, were less important than stopping its potential free fall. Thus what the Myrdals tried to offer with their book was not so much a full-scale reversal of the declining birthrate trend, but a more modest friction that might slow it down—specific policy recommendations designed first and foremost to prevent economic catastrophe.

The central thrust of *Kris i Befolkningsfrågan* was a forceful critique of unreflexive, demographically driven population control strategies, especially those concocted within the Malthusian tradition. Of particular concern was the status of poverty in a given population and its deleterious effects on the whole of society. Rather than treating poverty as a personal characteristic refracted across poor individuals and inextricably woven into the fabric of any given population, as had been the prevailing view, the Myrdals argued that poverty is instead a social condition exacerbated by state policy, but also quite solvable though technological, political, and cultural intervention (see Gille 1948). Using massive amounts of data to paint a vivid portrait of 1930s Swedish society, the Myrdals mounted a two-pronged attack against population decline and social inequality, targeting wages and employment, on the one hand, and families, home life, and housing, on the other, each reflecting the interests and expertise of one of the book's two authors. One of the central aspects of this strategy was a concentration on population as a metric for social improvement, which avoids threats of class warfare by instead implicitly promoting class solidarity. Policies targeting the relatively abstract concept of "the population," which necessarily includes all citizens regardless of class, have the effect of rendering everyone something close to *the same* from the point of view of the state. A concentration on "family" reform in essence has similar effects, cutting across class lines by ensuring that any couple intending to have children and build a home, irrespective of their means, is afforded by the state the same basic level of economic security to do so. To be sure, this was in a sense a state-sanctioned *policing* of the family, in Jacques Donzelot's (1979:6–7) phrasing, aimed foremost at "developing the quality of the population and the strength of the nation" with only secondary consideration for the citizens involved. Nonetheless, the Myrdals viewed their project more expansively: Why can't we fix both at once?

In a political world controlled by men and dominated by the power of economic determinism, Alva's contributions to this critique were especially significant to both the book's initial success and the eventual enactment of its specific policy recommendations. On the basis of her academic and professional background in social psychology and education, Alva saw the family, and everything surrounding the family—parenting practices, schooling, the home and its accoutrements—as eligible for political reform. Like Gunnar she believed in a technocratic vision for change. She encouraged supplying parents with scientifically derived knowledge about child rearing and home hygiene, arguing that children would thrive most vibrantly in good social, material, and affective environments. She also supported new forms of collective living, including domestic architecture that fostered and facilitated shared responsibility for common everyday needs, like child care and food preparation. Many of the most fundamental aspects of the modern Swedish welfare state, like parental insurance and the Swedish daycare system, were originally Alva's ideas. Working from a firm belief that maintaining the status quo would lead Sweden to its inevitable demise, Alva made the case that state intervention into family life and everyday economic activities, if carried out properly, could nudge a new kind of social order into being at the most basic level of material existence.

In 1936, two years after the publication of *Kris i Befolkningsfrågan*, Gunnar was elected to the Riksdag, which allowed him to help guide the implementation of the proposals he and Alva had carefully crafted. Soon enough the SAP's *folkhem* began to develop from a thin, largely theoretical frame into an increasingly substantial political edifice, as a number of significant policies were enacted, including improved nutritional standards for foodstuffs, benefits for higher education, universal health-care coverage, loans to couples for starting a new home, and policies for improving the nation's housing stock. The home, which had first been used as a symbolic organizing principle for an emergent political system, was now, thanks in large part to the work of the Myrdals, the very domain in which that political system was rendered present in, and directly relevant to, people's own lives.[6] By the late 1930s even the Myrdals' home—"a white, functionalist-style residence in the Stockholm suburb of Bromma, the stronghold of Swedish Social Democracy" (Hirdman 2008:134)—was well known throughout Sweden.

The Myrdals were unrepentant idealists, believing fully in the transformational power of social engineering to create a better society. Their vision for how best to effect progress on as wide a scale as possible involved enlisting experts and specialists trained in specific fields to observe, analyze, and rationally interpret the data that to them constitute everyday social reality—a targeted improvement of social conditions through what Karl Popper (1971) calls "piecemeal" social engineering. Though the Myrdals certainly expressed a utopian vision in their work, they were not true utopians, according to Popper's framework. In Popper's sense, "utopian" engineering describes not so much an actual outcome, but the motivation and techniques of implementation that precede it. In an attempt to construct an ideal society according to predetermined parameters and rationalize its structures and functions down to the smallest detail, utopian engineers, Popper claims, engage in planning practices intended to effect very specific, anticipated outcomes that are generally preferred by the engineers themselves. The target of their work is *society as a whole*, with specific projects designed to manipulate its constituent elements so as to reshape what currently exists according to a predrafted blueprint or plan. While remaking society in a "utopian" image may in some cases sound laudable, according to Popper, it too readily lends itself to totalitarian modes of state organization favored in dictator-controlled regimes, for only in such power arrangements is an uncontested concept of "the good" able to be carefully cultivated across diverse social and economic domains.

The alternative to this kind of social engineering, the Myrdals' preferred method, is Popper's "piecemeal engineering," whose targets are *specific social problems* instead of society as a whole, and whose outcomes are not resolved in advance. As Popper (1971:158) explains, "The piecemeal engineer will, accordingly, adopt the method of searching for, and fighting against, the greatest evils of society, rather than searching for, and fighting for, its greatest ultimate good." To be sure, the difference between these two types is subtle, but it is also important. Popper's version of utopian engineering grants social planners too much power in determining how society *should* be organized, as well as over which of its aspects must be reassembled in order to achieve that new organization. It promotes un-compromising adherence to an original blueprint, regardless of history or context. And its idealistic vision admits no room for disagreement, no space for debate, and as a consequence tacitly condones the use of violence as a potential means for attaining its goals. Piecemeal engineering, in contrast, because its projects are relatively small-bore, with no aspirations to trans-form the entirety of an existing social structure, is inherently less disruptive to society and its members. It also involves a "search" for social problems, signaling that the engineers do not begin their task having already decided what needs to be fixed. And because its goals are prefigured rather than predetermined, in its design and implementation, piecemeal engineering incorporates both anticipated and unanticipated results into a plan whose natural state is one of flux and instability. In other words, whereas utopian social engineering is closed, rigid, and opaque, piecemeal engineering is open, flexible, and transparent.

To the Myrdals a given policy aimed at changing some aspect of society was only a crude tool, itself only as good as the materials from which it was made. In order for a policy to work most effectively on the problems for which it is created, its details should derive from empirically observable conditions, and it should be enacted with an acute sensitivity to those very same conditions. Thus the power of politics was for the Myrdals based in science, knowledge, and reason—put to use in bounded and controlled contexts—rather than on the whims and predilections of party leaders or party members. By turning to technical practitioners, they argued, and re-lying on their specific areas of expertise to craft and implement relevant policies in a piecemeal fashion, politicians would gain a level of control over their efforts, and an ability to test, tweak, and improve their imple-mentations, that had never been possible before. And the Myrdals knew just which kinds of practitioners were needed.

Accept the New Reality

In an essay predating the publication of *Kris i Befolkningsfrågan* by two years (Myrdal 1932; excerpted as Myrdal 2005) and written while collaborating with Uno Åhrén on Sweden's housing problem, Gunnar Myrdal carefully laid out his preference for a new system of governance. In particular, he invoked three specific types of rational technocrat—an economist "to study the employment problem," a sociologist to address "the family problem," and an architect "to ponder over the cities' housing problems"— each of whom would be responsible for improving a different corner of lived reality, though all according to a shared general set of guidelines. Gunnar the economist and Alva the sociologist had already assumed their roles. What they needed was an architect—but this time, an architect in the most literal of senses. Instead they had five, and an art historian, too.

"And I am building a house," wrote Alva.

Though she described the house to her friends in mostly aspirational tones, it was certainly real. Or at least the plans for it were real. In part using recommendations that she and Gunnar had put forth in *Kris i Befolkningsfrågan*, she and a friend, an architect named Sven Markelius, had set out to design, fund, and build an actual real-world example of the kind of collective living—including shared nurseries, rationalized floor plans, and dumbwaiters to transport food from a central kitchen—that Alva had envisioned as part of her reimagined social order. The building, which was given the name Kollektivhuset (The Collective House), was completed in 1935 and still stands today as a national landmark—though it has lost much of its original functionality—a block or so off the strand on Kungsholmen near the patch of grass where rabbits like to gather.

Before undertaking his joint project with Alva, Markelius had gained some notoriety through his efforts in the Stockholm Exhibition of 1930, where he and his colleagues helped introduce functionalist design to the Swedish public (see chapter 5). As significant as that event was—and it was very significant—it was the official publication that the organizers produced after the exhibition, called (and styled) *acceptera* (Accept) (Åhrén et al. 1931, 2008), that helped propel Markelius, along with his five coauthors, directly into the center of political debates around housing, public health, and the future of Swedish society. The book landed with a raucous splash, less so among the general public than among the governing elite. The ideas first presented as only possibilities in *acceptera* in 1931 would go on to form the basis for the concrete policy proposals outlined in the Myrdals' more popular work, *Kris i Befolkningsfrågan*, three years later.

The essay, first published by *Tiden*, the SAP's official journal for theoretical and political debates, takes the form of a massive manifesto. It is long, full of both text and images often laid out using avant-garde techniques—typographical play, collage, unexpected juxtapositions—and its tone is strident and suasive. But *acceptera* is also in many ways a precise technocratic instrument, full of charts, figures, and plans derived from recent research and industrial developments. And its authors were no agitators, but respected architects and academics. Markelius cowrote the book with architects Per Eskil Sundahl, Wolter Gahn, and Erik Gunnar Asplund, the latter one of Sweden's most notable architects and a late-in-life convert to functionalism (see Wrede 1980; Jones 2006). Uno Åhrén, Gunnar Myrdal's friend and research partner—and also a former disciple of Asplund—was also a major contributor. The sixth author was Gregor Paulsson, an art historian and director of Svenska Slöjdföreningen, the Swedish Society of Arts and Crafts (now known as Svensk Form; see chapter 3), who had penned his own influential *propagandapublikation*, called *Vackrare Vardagsvara* (More Beautiful Everyday Things), in 1919 (Paulsson 1919, 2008). Together these men crafted what would become a deeply influential urtext not only for social democratic housing policies, but also for the development of Swedish design, presenting "a distinct and unusual emphasis on a new form of social engineering that not only attempts to adapt modernism to a Swedish context, but also to portray the theory itself as a specifically Swedish phenomenon" (Mattsson and Wallenstein 2009:33).

The central preoccupation of *acceptera* is a critique of the status quo in Swedish society, along with the presentation of a detailed and motivated program for improving the housing problem in Sweden, and doing so in a way that is sensitive to the social and material worlds in which Swedes of the time were embedded. The authors' argument, demonstrated with photographs, drawings, and charts, spans every design scale, from city blocks to entire buildings—mostly residential, but also schools, workplaces, and public architecture—to apartments, rooms, and the furniture, cutlery, and art pieces that fill them. As the authors move from topic to topic, almost no aspect of everyday life is overlooked. Embedded in their argument is a strong case for embracing mass production, as the supposed stark separation between industrial and handicraft modes of production, they maintain, is largely overwrought. Although the rhetorical thrust of *acceptera* is strongly hortative—the title of the book is the imperative form of the verb—the authors are not unsympathetic to their audience's worries. Fearing that the public will cling too tightly to the forms—both concrete and abstract—of the past, the authors leave room for the old in their new scheme, although only as affective objects. To those skeptics reluctant to embrace this new way of life they say, echoing Ellen Key, "Keep these familiar old friends and enjoy them. They have sentimental value that we do not despise. But do not be surprised that *we want to create objects that we can both feel an attachment to and that will work well and beautifully*" (Åhrén et al. 2008:259; original emphasis). Indeed, the emotional mode of relating to things was critical to their project. They hoped that people would *care* about how they interact with the material world, which would in turn help shift their orientation to their placement within it. The quiet revolution the *acceptera* authors attempted to set in motion with their book was not intended to destroy and replace the familiar textures of the everyday world, though some critics initially read it that way. Instead their intention was to fundamentally redefine how people relate to their material conditions and instill in them a belief that changing those conditions for the better was possible. The cover of the book stated their position quite plainly: "Accept the reality that exists—only in that way have we any prospect of mastering it, taking it in hand, and altering it to create culture that offers an adaptable tool for life."

The lines of enunciation tracing out Swedish design today stem from many different sources and display various inflections, but the most significant point of origin, in terms of their enduring content and organization, is without a doubt *acceptera*. Many of the final vocabulary's most common words and phrases are featured prominently throughout, especially "beauty," "functionality," "quality," and "modesty," along with recognizable descriptors like "comfortable," "pleasant," and "affordable." Several discussions of the need for homes and objects to "satisfy needs" are woven through the text, and even more concerning the benefits of light and sunshine in enclosed spaces. The link between these terms and other values is also quite clear. At one and the same time the book's argument contends with aesthetic value, social value, and economic value, either flowing seamlessly between concrete examples of each or exploiting ambiguous language that works equally across these different domains. Again, the book's opening salvo, "Accept the reality that exists—only in that way have we any prospect of mastering it, taking it in hand, and altering it to create culture that offers an adaptable tool for life," can be read as an entreaty to politicians, designers, and ordinary citizens alike, each endowed with the same capacity to improve the social world. Even the structure of the arguments the architects make displays a formal symmetry with arguments made by SAP politicians in their official rhetoric, highlighting prominent dualistic oppositions—for politicians, rich versus poor, urban versus rural, men versus women; and for architects, technology versus art, beauty versus functionality; and for both, the individual versus the masses—in order to break them down systematically in favor of advocating a space for social and conceptual inclusivity.

One of their most cogent arguments, following the path first forged by Ellen Key, is for a redescribed and more broadly applied notion of beauty. From their point of view the traditional separation between "art" and "technology" is largely artificial, the unfortunate result of a long-term historical habit of narrowly constraining beauty to art and utility to technology. In addition to misrecognizing that each quality also subsists in both kinds of things, this division disregards entire classes of objects, objects we see and interact with and rely on each and every day, that do not fit easily into either category. And while everyday objects tend to lean closer to the technological because they do often serve some particular purpose, they are not granted the same status as more vaunted examples of technological achievement, like automobiles, bridges, and airplanes, and thus miss full inclusion in most evaluative formulas. To rectify this oversight the *acceptera* authors propose a new category, "utilitarian art," which includes practical everyday objects, and which, like fine art, traffics in beauty, but a different kind of beauty, in which a thing's "form must express its purpose and provide a clear visual embodiment of its functions" (Åhrén et al. 2008:277). This kind of beauty does not merely inhere in the physical composition of utilitarian art. Form, color, and lines matter, but the object is not itself beautiful, they insist, until an actual user is brought into the contemplation. Thus the beauty of utilitarian art, of the material things of the everyday world, is fully experienced, fully laid bare, only in meaningful, purposeful interactions with forms that appropriately suit the actions to which they are put to use.

Having made their definitional move, the authors caution that incorporating utilitarian beauty into everyday goods should not entail a clumsy layering of aesthetic features onto otherwise drab, practical objects, stating flatly that "in recognizing the functionally beautiful, we repudiate the opinion that art is something that is added to the technological" (Åhrén et al. 2008:278). Nor, they maintain, are they repackaging what was by then an old argument that practicality is itself identical with beauty. Without mentioning her by name, but with clear allusions to her influential work, the authors suggest that Ellen Key's agitations had helped advance the idea that beauty could be *attached* to an object as an amendment to its practicality, which from their point of view had in some ways degraded industrially manufactured household goods. "Down with beauty" they say, or at least down with a notion of beauty still mired in "impractical aestheticism" (281), adding that " 'Too much beauty' could be adopted as the motto for the cultural life of the last decades" (281). They protest that despite Key's good intentions, her particular reformulation of beauty, though valuable, was not a radical enough departure from the old, elitist version she was attempting to overturn. While many manufacturers in the first few decades of the twentieth century did heed her call for "more beautiful everyday things," the criteria for judging their aesthetic worth matched those long preferred by the upper classes, leaving beauty still a clear marker of distinction only granted to the lower classes through a misguided sense of noblesse oblige. For the *acceptera* authors Key's critique ultimately missed the mark. The beauty of utilitarian art, they insisted, now defined as "spring[ing] from the desire to give logical clarity to the workings of [an object's] form" (278), should not be something that conspicuously stands out in an object, that makes itself known in direct opposition to the noticeably *not beautiful* qualities of other objects. Instead, beauty should be so immanent in the built environment, so deeply integrated into every single facet of the everyday world, that finding a *not beautiful* thing would be a nearly impossible task.

Expanding the *Folkhem*

By 1939 the effects of *acceptera* and the work of the Myrdals were plain
to see. That year Gregor Paulsson, one of the *acceptera* authors, published
in Sweden a book with bilingual Swedish-English text called *Ny Svensk
Arkitektur/New Swedish Architecture*. The volume, a follow-up to an earlier treatment of Swedish architecture he had published in 1916 (Paulsson 1916), was replete with photographs and drawings of the seemingly
innumerable examples of newly built structures of the sort he and his collaborators had advocated, all "arranged in the order of their actual importance, starting with the housing of the lower and middle classes" (Paulsson
1939:5) and continuing on depicting schools, social welfare buildings, industrial, retail, and bureaucratic architecture, and ending with buildings
dedicated to recreation and sports. The book was a testament, a collection
of evidence, that the social engineers' goal to "build for the people in such a
way that their humanity may, as far as possible, be justified by their external environment" (9) was a resounding success.

During the Second World War and the decades immediately following
it, the Swedish welfare state expanded rapidly and extended its reach into
an ever-widening spectrum of social and political domains. Every person
in society became familiar with the *folkhem* on a very intimate level. The
concept of the *folkhem* directly exploited Swedish nationalist sentiment,
but rather than casting it as an exclusive form of nationalism, SAP leaders draped it in a rigid inclusivity, stressing "the party's desire to help not
merely workers, but the 'weak,' the 'oppressed,' and 'people' more generally" (Berman 2006:167). Within this new political system *class struggle* was
finally replaced by *welfare*, a mechanism designed to effect social progress
by providing "unfettered opportunity for the individual" (Scott 1988:526),
regardless of his or her position in society. Crucial to the project was ensuring the kind of safety and security that people experienced in their homes,
but applying it to Swedish society as a whole. This also meant building
many more actual homes to house the growing population and ensuring they were of better quality than what had existed before the 1930s.
Because the original housing plan enacted in the shadow of the Myrdals'
work was so successful, the strategy was later formally reprised during
the Miljonprogram, or Million Homes Program. One of the largest and

most important social planning initiatives in Sweden's history, the Million Homes Program set out to construct a million new housing units across the country between 1965 and 1975, which helped established the rings of satellite suburbs that surround Sweden's major urban centers today (see Hall and Viden 2005; Rörby 1996).

The Social Democrats continued to renovate and upgrade the *folkhem* through almost forty-five years of uninterrupted control of the Swedish government, well into the 1970s. In the late 1960s and early 1970s the notion of *jämlikhet*, "social equality," arose as an explicitly articulated goal for workers and politicians interested in finally abolishing the class system, along with *jämställdhet*, a similar term more specifically aimed at gender parity in employment. During this period there was a strong push for laws, policies, and regulations to recognize the same basic equality of all individuals regardless of class, gender, age, or any other demographic traits. In 1974 the Instrument of Government was added to the national constitution, and it included the following proclamation (Chapter 1, Article 2):

Public power shall be exercised with respect for the equal worth of all and the liberty and dignity of the individual. The personal, economic and cultural welfare of the individual shall be fundamental aims of public activity. In particular, the public institutions shall secure the right to employment, housing and education, and shall promote social care and social security, as well as favourable conditions for good health.

The public institutions shall promote sustainable development leading to a good environment for present and future generations.

The public institutions shall promote the ideals of democracy as guidelines in all sectors of society and protect the private and family lives of the individual.

The public institutions shall promote the opportunity for all to attain participation and equality in society and for the rights of the child to be safeguarded.

The public institutions shall combat discrimination of persons on grounds of gender, colour, national or ethnic origin, linguistic or religious affiliation, functional disability, sexual orientation, age or other circumstance affecting the individual.

The opportunities of the Sami people and ethnic, linguistic and religious minorities to preserve and develop a cultural and social life of their own shall be promoted.[7]

With the basic ideological outlines of the social democratic welfare system enshrined in the Swedish Constitution, the state was officially christened as the primary guarantor and protector of individual rights, independent of which political party controlled parliament. For the SAP this was a good thing, because starting in 1976, after forty years in power and amid raucous national debates about economic and environmental issues, it lost control of the Riksdag, and for the first time in a long time found itself working as an opposition party. After years of ongoing construction, this marked the beginning of the end for the strong *folkhem* model, both as a metaphor and as a system, having reached its zenith in the 1960s. The SAP did regain power in the 1980s, but since then has traded parliamentary control with a center-right coalition led by Moderaterna. Yet while over the past several decades increased attention to the economic motors of state-sponsored sociality has led to a steadfast adherence to certain economically liberal stands, such as tax cuts and privatization of the public sector, which the Social Democrats themselves—no innocents in this process—had in fact initiated and pushed in the 1990s, the most basic tenets of the welfare system remain firmly intact. Health care, education, parental leave, unemployment insurance, pensions—all of these, while modified by the Moderates along liberal dimensions when they have been in power, still undergird the process of everyday life in Sweden. The *folkhem* metaphor may have disappeared as an explicit constituent of public political discourse, but the political structure that it helped support remains largely operational.

In the preface to her book *Nation and Family: The Swedish Experiment in Democratic Family and Population Policy* (Myrdal 1945), an English-language reworking of the *Kris i Befolkningsfrågan* material, Alva Myrdal spelled out what she feared might be her last description of the work she and her fellow Social Democrats had achieved in Sweden. Sitting in Stockholm in 1940, as the Nazi war machine marched across Europe, she wrote:

> It may be that before this book is published our form of free and independent democratic government in the far North will have perished. This book, begun and in the main written during a time of peace and in a spirit of assurance, would then come to stand as an epitaph of a defunct society. Even if that should be the immediate fate of our Scandinavian democracy,

this essay will have been worth writing. Our house may be burned, but this will not prove that there were basic faults in its construction. The plan will still be worth studying. (Myrdal 1945:v)

Worth studying indeed. Of course Alva's fears that Sweden would be defeated never came to pass, and the Swedish welfare system that she helped conceive, the house she helped design and construct, survived the war. Not only did it survive, but its entrenchment in Swedish society only continued to deepen. As the dialectical relationship between home and welfare society seeped into the Swedish cultural consciousness, the prototypical model for how the social order ought to be aligned acquired an increasingly domestic sheen—stipulating, in short, that all human relations, no matter what form they take, should, as in the home, spring from a sense of *responsibility* for others and *care* for common basic needs. And just as in the home, it doesn't always work out as planned.

What is crucial to recognize here is how through the work of particular expert actors and the temporally durable webs of influence they were able to spin, the home has been mobilized in the Swedish cultural consciousness since the nineteenth century as an *ideological* construct with significant *material* contours and consequences. Despite their emphasis on remaking social relations, the original architects of the SAP's program did not use a metaphor of *family* to characterize the welfare state, but instead chose the much more complex concept of *home*. The resonance of "family" as metaphor is restricted to a narrow, mostly inflexible understanding of social relations inhering between particular social roles. But by invoking the "home," explicit parallels between private, family relationships and public, social ones become subjected to the material contexts in which they dynamically subsist, accounting for a wider range of relevant phenomena without abandoning the significance of the social. The home is necessarily *emplaced*, a spatialized mixture of materials operating as a physical manifestation of social relations. It is also an *achievement*, a temporally regulated symbiosis greater than the individual elements that compose it. As such, the symbolic composition of the home—both materially and ideally—is comparatively malleable, while its core remains largely consistent and intact.

While the SAP exploited the *conceptual* flexibility of the home in constructing the *folkhem*, Ellen Key, Alva and Gunnar Myrdal, and the *acceptera* authors (with the unwitting assistance of Carl and Karin Larsson) seized on the *tangible* flexibility involved in beautifying real homes as a way to improve and standardize the material state of everyday life. As the political became the home, the home became the political—a strong chiasmic overlap with a popular appeal that is now all but fully absorbed into the cultural imaginary of everyday life in Sweden. And while the *folkhem* may be but a memory, Key's original association of beauty with functionality, simplicity, and affordability, re-rendered by the *acceptera* authors to suffuse the entirety of the material world, continues to thrive among taste professionals (see Auslander 1996) tasked with designing the objects of everyday life. The claim that "design is political," that social democratic ideology inheres in particular objects, that the everyday material world is a material rendering of welfare politics—all of that begins here, in this narrative and the rich semiotic traces it has left behind. But while the diagram of Swedish design may start here, and may thrive here, it certainly doesn't end here.

3

In the Design World

On a cold February evening, near downtown Stockholm, my friend Helena and I got lost. I had been invited to an independent furniture exhibition near Östermalmstorg, which is not an especially complicated part of town to navigate, but the Nybrogatan address I had been given seemed entirely inappropriate. It was an upscale hotel, not an exhibition space, and when Helena and I walked into the lobby we saw nothing but a few hotel guests quietly sipping drinks at the bar. Confused, we retreated back into the cold night. Standing there on the sidewalk, checking building numbers, we noticed a sign in the hotel window directing visitors around the corner toward something called *We Are Going Underground*. Peering into the alley, we found what we'd been looking for.

Outside the entrance to the hotel's parking garage stood a few fashionable men and women standing in small groups, some speaking English, some Swedish. Most were smoking cigarettes, and a few held plastic cups presumably filled with alcohol. Helena and I squeezed past into a dark, slippery tunnel steeply inclined under the hotel building. Music, light, and humid air awaited us at the bottom. Inside, the space was packed with a mixture of young designers and middle-aged men in khakis and polo shirts—furniture industry representatives intently examining the pieces on display. Loud electronic music echoed off the concrete walls, making conversation difficult. The place was lit almost entirely with white floor lamps crafted in the style of theater lights, most of them directed at the displays placed throughout the impromptu gallery. Thick white lines were painted on the floor, and numbers were spray-painted on the walls above them, markers of the individual parking spots that ordinarily filled the garage at any other time of the year. Throughout the tight, L-shaped space, seventeen separate displays were mounted on thick, white foam bases, each with a designer's name printed in simple black letters on the left edge. The exhibition was remarkably sophisticated and aesthetically coordinated. And despite its regular identity as a mundane parking garage, the space came alive as a showroom. The chairs, lamps, clocks, textiles, and graphics on display—some meant for production, others more conceptual pieces—all felt natural in this restructured artificial environment.

This was the opening of the second *We Are Going Underground* exhibition, an independent temporary gallery show organized by a small group of designers as a satellite event in conjunction with the annual Stockholm Furniture Fair (see chapter 5), the largest furniture trade show in northern Europe, that was taking place in another part of town. Here, in the basement garage of a downtown hotel, designers were free to display whichever pieces they wished, unrestricted by the corporate dominance of the Furniture Fair. Graphic designers showed off their experimental sides, and product designers proudly displayed both their production pieces and their most conceptual work. Indeed, while many of the furniture designers presenting at *We Are Going Underground*, like Peter Andersson and Thomas Bernstrand, were represented by established manufacturers at the fair and had objects on display there, most of the designers here at this show were working for themselves. The objects they presented were not primarily geared toward mass production or commercial consumption, but rather were offered as demonstrations of each designer's technical and aesthetic capabilities—a collective expression of the sheer artistry of design. The move underground was strategic—what they were showing in that subterranean garage was, in a way, too raw for the world above.

The *We Are Going Underground* exhibition neatly captures the ambivalent position—and dual loyalties—that designers are faced with operating within both aesthetic and economic markets. On the one hand, they are creative individuals working with aesthetic forms that "express" conceptual matter in ways similar to the symbolic labor of more traditional kinds of art. On the other hand, unlike artists working in the fine arts tradition, their daily worklife predominantly concerns crafting objects for mass production and widescale consumption, the mechanics of which require more attention to the minutiae of mundane *business* practices than to the semiotic force of forms. But perhaps even more so than a work of art, a design piece is always "a two-faced reality, a commodity and a symbolic object" (Bourdieu 1993b:113) whose double facade is always on prominent, simultaneous display. While the economic value of an artwork can be comfortably subsumed to its symbolic value in the art world, the two value forms are always in an uncomfortable relationship for objects in the design world. This is because the structure of the design world itself is constituted as two interconnected fields that in theory run anxiously parallel to one another—an economic field that trades on aesthetics, and an aesthetic field that resists economics. The task for designers, then, is to learn how to take advantage of this relationship by constructing roles that allow them to float between the two fields, and carefully manage their positions within them. While this fundamentally split disposition of design work can at times be problematic for some designers, it can also, when managed skillfully, significantly enhance and shape the social role played by designers in Swedish society—a twenty-first-century rendition of the vision of Ellen Key, Uno Åhrén, and Gregor Paulsson.

In what follows in this chapter I have two overriding, interlaced ends. In order to understand the wider social contexts in which on-the-ground design work is situated, in which the diagram of Swedish design is reproduced, I delineate and analyze the contours of the contemporary Stockholm design world. I consider the most instrumental players—designers, institutions, media—who propel the continued development of design as a profession, a community, and a consequential cultural practice in Sweden, primarily from the point of view of the expert designers who reside at the design world's center. Because I rely on their particular positionality in this network, the picture I present is necessarily skewed toward the concerns, activities, anxieties, and relations that preoccupy designers themselves, as opposed to firms, manufacturers, critics, politicians, and others. My second objective is to account for how designers, despite their explicit demurral concerning a manifest politics in their work, nonetheless continuously reproduce the conditions by which the objects they design are able to tolerate the final vocabulary of Swedish design—regardless of the pointed fact that designers rarely use it. As I argue, the careful movement between art and commerce, between aesthetics and business, between the exalted and the everyday, may allow designers to manipulate their positions with the design world for greater personal and professional gain—both economic and symbolic—but this traversal also renders their work semiotically unstable, creating what I call "heteroglossic artifacts," objects with multiple, often conflicting culturally elaborated meanings ascribed to their forms. It is because design objects tend to thrive in such states of instability, of symbolic equivocation, that they are so readily subject to ideological redescription—the suturing of statements to geometries—quite separate from the wills and desires of their original creators, which in turn contributes to the ongoing cultural enregisterment of Swedish design.

Heteroglossic Artifacts

Mikhail Bakhtin (1981) introduced the concept of "heteroglossia" both as a rejoinder to analytic models that focus exclusively on either the "formal" or the "ideological" aspects of a text (where for Bakhtin the ideological was more concerned with a generalized worldview than with politics), and to help explain the seemingly unique formal-semantic composition of the novel as a literary genre. The structure of a novel is necessarily comprised of multiple characters espousing multiple viewpoints through multiple utterances, utterances that sequentially align, build on one another, and often contradict one another in consequential ways. While the novel might, from a certain viewpoint, appear to project a singular, stable form, its internal anatomy is always imbued with a potentially infinite array of variegated meanings and associations. But this hybrid composition is not restricted to novels. Bakhtin argues that any utterance, in a novel or spoken aloud, even any single word, "is half someone else's" (Bakhtin 1981:293), already replete with multiple voices and the residue of past use. "Language," he continues, "is not a neutral medium that passes freely and easily into the private property of the speaker's intentions; it is populated—overpopulated—with the intentions of others" (294; cf. Duranti 2011). Language often appears to maintain forms and meanings across individual speakers, such that two different speakers can be considered to be using "the same" language, but Bakhtin argues that any given instance of language use, any utterance, because it is shaped by social context, a speaker's intentions, a hearer's interpretation, and other factors, is always a deviation from common forms and meanings, even if just a small one. Thus while a speaker may assume that her words are her own and express the meanings she intends, their shape and semantic tenor are as much, or perhaps even more, conditioned by the external social flows in which those words continuously reappear, as they are by her own intentions.

At its core Bakhtin's analysis is a treatment of relations between forms, meanings, and the forces that link them. Operating as the "parallel or simultaneous use of different signs and images belonging to partly opposed or conflicting spheres" (Ivanov 2000:101), heteroglossia is manifest in all sorts of situations in which seemingly stable forms—of words, of things, of behaviors—can accommodate and absorb multiple credible meanings at one and the same time. But this is not a kind of infinite and unrestrained polysemy. Instead, because forms and meanings are subject to particular forces exerted within particular contexts that are regulated by particular social conditions, the multiplicity of potential meanings ascribable to given forms is always regimented and controlled.

Most designers do not see their work as overtly political, though most do subscribe to a general sort of politics of "care" in their own lives that they would prefer their work to reflect. Nonetheless their work is "heard" as political, even if only in echoes, as it passes through certain institutions. In the context of the Swedish design world, then, commonplace things—chairs, lamps, tables—are transfigured from general commodities into heteroglossic artifacts reflecting multiple kinds of voicings, form-signs occupying several spheres at once—that of everyday objects, that of artistic works, and that of political instruments. In other words, one of the primary functions of the design world, in addition to generating economic value for designers through the financial valuation of their work, is to oversee the procedures through which certain classes of objects are made culturally meaningful, and to monitor the social terrain within which those meanings are delimited, elaborated, and contained.

Disaffiliating with Swedish Design

I sat with Björn P., a furniture designer, in his shared studio, one of the first and neatest that I visited in Stockholm (fig. 4). It was also one of the least centrally located, tucked away on the wooded grounds of Alfred Nobel's old dynamite factory, which the city of Stockholm, unable to devise a better plan, converted into a creative work space for artists and designers in the 1990s, complete with a sizable gallery and modest cafe. Björn's studio occupies part of the factory's old cafeteria. As we sat there, drinking coffee at one of his drafting tables and discussing his work and the work of his peers, the topic of politics emerged. "I cannot see my furniture in a political way," he said after a pause, when I asked him about the politics—or lack of politics—of his designs. The statement was surprisingly final. Surprising, because Björn had just insisted that design, either the Swedish kind or in general, is always *potentially* political, whether deliberately, as in the case of designing specifically for environmental causes,

Figure 4. The studio of designer Björn P., inside the renovated Nobel dynamite factory, on the outskirts of Stockholm. Photograph by the author.

or less intentionally, through the knock-on effects of the choices designers make, such as the materials they use in their objects.

This attitude—that design can be political, but that a designer's own work is decidedly not—is utterly pervasive in the Stockholm design world. Very few designers will uncritically voice their work through the final vocabulary of Swedish design. "I know some design is basically just made for political purposes," another designer named Stig A. told me. "But I'm not the kind of designer who likes to mix politics and design. . . . I think people who'd like to work with politics, they should be, like, politicians." As Mats H. put it,

> Dealing with people is a unique matter, and we're not experts in that. We're, like, experts in plastic, or steel beams, or, like, these things. And you're trying to do something socially by being social, and you realize that maybe that's wrong, you know? Maybe we're not social at all.

This is not to say that designers lack a political ethic in how they view what they do. While many are uncomfortable with the idea that their own designs are overtly political or can enact large-scale social effects, there is nonetheless a steady stream of reformist thinking in the Stockholm design world that frames the work of designers as at least minimally useful for improving society, even if only one person at a time. Annika T. told me, "I'm not interested in making yet another chair if it's not a chair that will make you sit better, or make you have less pain in your back or make you happy when you come to work or something." Peter expressed a similar point of view:

> I think the difference I can contribute is to make people see things in a different kind of way. From a different kind of perspective. Leaving the traditional way of looking at the world and things. So that way I have something to work with and make people discover new angles of life, by illustrating it in products.

Far removed from the contentious machinations of party politicians, the kind of social responsibility that most designers articulate manifests more as a micropolitics of everyday life, like a moral governance of how people interact with the material world.

In addition to avoiding any strong political associations in their work, few designers in the Stockholm design world will even admit to the existence of Swedish design as a recognizable category, preferring instead to frame what they make as somehow "just like" what designers from other countries create. Referring to a coat rack produced by the Swedish company Swedese, designer Måns S. once remarked to me in his studio, "I think that could be, like, an icon for Swedish design, and it's not—it's from Iceland or London or something" (the piece in question was actually designed jointly by a Briton and an Icelander). Instead of straightforwardly embracing the lines of enunciation of Swedish design, all of the designers I worked with—all of them—made sure to acknowledge the widespread existence of those discourses in Sweden and abroad, but only to then disavow any direct affiliation with them. There are many reasons why designers do this, not the least of which is a general tendency in Sweden to downplay individual uniqueness, and an aversion, especially among younger generations, to anything that too closely resembles overt nationalism (with the occasional exception of international competitions, like the World Cup and the Eurovision Song Contest).[1] There is also a strong if often implicit desire to connect their own work to global design trends and situate themselves among a much broader class of international design professionals. The phrase "Sweden is such a small country" recurred repeatedly in interviews and casual conversations as both an explanation for why Swedish design has supposedly had so little influence on design outside of Scandinavia and a justification for why Swedish designers should expand their professional imaginary more globally.

While most of the designers I spoke to are reluctant to intentionally release the objects they make into the semiotic flows of explicit political ideology, they do recognize that their work does have the potential to be *something more* than bare objects, to capture values and reflect voicings that extend far beyond the utilitarian. Designing widgets, objects without meaning to be used in uncontemplated ways and tossed out when no longer needed, is certainly one way to make money. But it is a way to make money that is resoundingly dispreferred. Designers are, after all, creative people who chose to attend design school to learn how to make things that they can show to the world, hoping to receive recognition for their efforts. They want what they design to have both *meaning* and *meanings*, to adopt an ontological status that exceeds its basest existence. In order to do this, to transcend the persistent threat that abject baublery might consume their work, designers require a system that supplies meaning to what they do, a system of learning, earning, and showing.

The Stockholm Design World from the Inside Out

Gustav drifted over to me as the others slowly trudged out from the building onto the wet sidewalk: it was just starting to rain, if only very slightly. We were emerging from a public lecture, sponsored by Sveriges Arkitekter, the Swedish Architecture Association, at which two of the collective's members had presented some of their latest work to a group of thirty or so attendees. After the talk ended a small group had gathered on the mezzanine outside the hall, but someone decided that moving to a bar was a better idea. The lot of us—four of the collective's many members and some of their friends—meandered down the narrow streets in pairs, drifting between cars from the sidewalk to the street and back again. We were ostensibly looking for a place to settle, but everyone seemed more interested in their conversations. "How do you measure if you're a success?" I asked Gustav, triggered by something he'd said. He considered the question carefully. It's not about money he replied, though money is certainly welcome. "If I can work doing what I love, living a comfortable life, then I think that's success to me. And probably to everyone else here." I chuckled, and he chuckled too, because he could tell what the "capitalist" American was thinking.

Few designers choose their careers early in life or envision themselves as designers from a young age. Almost everyone I interviewed first received training in fine arts, handicraft, or some technical field, like carpentry or stitching, and it was only after gaining preliminary experience with these skills that a career path in design became apparent. One reason this general pattern of "discovering" design by means of other technical or aesthetic fields is so common in Sweden is because it is carefully reinforced by the Swedish educational system (see Stenholm 1984). As a rule the system allows students to register for a wide variety of courses at approved educational institutions. The courses themselves, unless run by a private institution, are tuition-free, and students are guaranteed some amount of stipend or a loan by CSN (Centrala Studiestödsnämden), the Central Committee

for Student Support, a state-run institution that funds educational endeavors for all Swedish citizens. Beyond the level of *gymnasiet*, the equivalent
of an American high school, the Swedish schooling network consists of
universities, colleges, adult education courses (*komvux*), and *folkhögskolor*,
schools tasked with providing deep exposure to certain topics rather than
academic advancement—though they often serve as stepping stones to
higher-level university education.

Many designers, like many typical Swedish high schoolers, are not certain about what they want to do with their lives after leaving *gymnasiet*.
Because the state allows them, in effect, to sample their interests by en-
rolling free of charge in different courses at *folkhögskolor* or *komvux*, designers tend to gravitate toward design through a series of consistently
refined choices. An interest in painting, say, might lead to experiments in
sculpture, which in turn leads to a course in furniture design. While art is
generally conceived as a field in which it is difficult for most young people
to make a decent living, design seems more amenable to that goal, and
despite a strong rhetoric of unfettered creativity, designers do not attempt
to hide the fact that earning a steady income is a central motivation to what
they do. Design, then, especially for the practically minded young creative,
is a solid compromise between "pure" aesthetic achievement and the realities of economic survival.

Students can learn design at many different institutions throughout the
country, though only a small percentage of those offer official degrees. A
handful of small arts colleges scattered throughout the country special-
ize in more craft-oriented design, like ceramics and textiles. For technical
training in industrial design and interaction design—that is, the design of
high-tech objects and IT interfaces—Umeå University in northern Sweden is increasingly the destination of choice for many young Swedes and
students from abroad. In Gothenburg HDK (Högskolan för Design och
Konsthantverk), the College of Design and Crafts, which is part of the University of Gothenburg, offers a broad-based education in design and feeds
much of the west coast design world, while Chalmers University of Technology specializes in engineering, architecture, and business management.

Stockholm, however, is the center of design education in Sweden and
certainly a magnet for students who have graduated from programs in
other parts of the country looking to kick-start their careers. The country's
premier school of architecture is KTH (Kungliga Tekniska Högskolan),

the Royal Institute of Technology, which also houses interaction designers and other researchers and educators interested in IT and engineering. In contrast, fine arts and the specialized design disciplines—for example fashion, graphic, and furniture design—are primarily the domain of two dominant schools in Stockholm, Konstfack and Beckmans. These two schools, and especially Konstfack, produce the highest number of professional designers working in Stockholm today.

Konstfack was founded by artist and folk historian Nils Månsson Mandelgren in 1844 as Söndagsritskola för Hantverkare, the Sunday Drawing School for Craftsmen. A century later (and after two other names) the school was rechristened as Konstfack (literally, "art trade") in 1945. Today the institution offers programs in graphic design and illustration, interior architecture and furniture design, industrial design, fine arts, ceramics and glass, textiles, metal design, and interdisciplinary studies, a mixture of art and design disciplines that mirrors the eclectic interests of the student body. Students also complete courses in the history and theory of both art and design while working toward either a three-year bachelor's degree or a two-year master's degree. In 2004 the school relocated to Telefonplan, an area just outside the city of Stockholm, taking over the old factory of Swedish telephone manufacturer L. M. Ericsson, which still maintains a presence in parts of the building. Most of the designers I worked with in Stockholm received at least part of their education at Konstfack, and most did so during the 1990s, before the school moved to its current location.

While nearly all the designers who attended Konstfack cite their experience at the school as an influential force in their creative work, few saw the influence stemming from the institution itself or from their particular teachers. In fact many felt their teachers were too conservative in their views of design, and that they often tried to hold the students back in exploring their ideas. As Peppe B. put it,

> We were told not to work with furniture design because that's not a real job. They educated us to be interior architects. Then we had to work in an architecture studio and get a real job. And I guess we reacted towards that. And that reaction has shown up in what I do.

Reaction against what they were taught at Konstfack is a common sentiment expressed by students trained there during the 1990s. Despite

the fact that Swedish furniture design has had a long and storied history, many designers feel the integrity of the field of furniture design was
steadily undermined by the very institution teaching them their designing
skills—especially given the fact that furniture design and interior architecture are grouped in the same department—and so they transformed this
discouragement into a motivation for reinvigorating the field itself. Because students at Konstfack tend to interact with peers within their same
discipline and within their same cohort, there was a spirit of camaraderie
buttressing their efforts. Workshops, classes, and public critiques all served
as the foundation for acquiring the basic *skills* for doing design in the real
world, but the *relationships* they developed in those contexts were ultimately much more important to them. One designer, Torsten N., fondly
recounted the moment during school in which he met Per, one of his current collaborators:

> I remember one instance in school where I made this fantastic project
> [laughter]. And the teacher was like, "This sucks!" And I almost—maybe
> I even started to cry, I don't know. But then Per came up and [said], "That
> was, like, great!" And I said, "They didn't like it!" And he said, "Well it's
> like *student power!*"

Indeed, most designers contend that the most significant element of their
Konstfack education was the friendships and collaborations they developed with their classmates and the inspiration they derived from each
other's work.

In contrast to Konstfack, student life at Beckmans College of Design
is perhaps more subdued. Overall Beckmans is less prestigious than Konstfack and has a shorter history of influence in the Swedish design world.
Fewer of the designers I encountered received their entire education at
Beckmans. Unlike Konstfack, Beckmans was a private school—less culturally valued than public educational institutions in Sweden—and when
I was living in Stockholm had only recently begun the process of transforming into an official college that falls under the bureaucratic umbrella
of the state. The school was founded in 1939 by Anders Beckman, an illus-
trator and graphic designer best known for his design work on the Swedish pavilion of the 1939 World's Fair in New York, and the H55 exposition
in Helsingborg in 1955 (see chapter 5). The school's pedagogy is narrowly

focused on the explicitly commercial aspects of aesthetic production, offering only three distinct programs in advertising and graphic design, fashion design, and product design. To be sure, Konstfack is the more influential of the two design schools, but Beckmans students are making an increasingly stronger and deeper impact on the contemporary design world.

Design as an Art World

Again, I was lost, but quickly found. The Greenhouse is an area of the annual Stockholm Furniture Fair reserved for students and young designers to showcase their work alongside more established professionals and the manufacturers producing their pieces. The atmosphere inside is usually buzzy, colorful, and bright, with a looser feeling from the rest of the fair, but still quite polished. On that day in 2006 there was a makeshift amphitheater in a corner of the Greenhouse space, and on the stage at the foot of the carpeted risers four young women were preparing for a public interview. This was a homecoming of sorts, as the women of design group Front had first shown together at the Greenhouse three years earlier, in 2003, while they were still students at Konstfack. After that first show the group met with almost instantaneous fame, both in Sweden and abroad. Their highly conceptual work was featured in small and large gallery exhibitions, including the *konceptdesign* show at the prestigious National Museum of Art in Stockholm, and a gallery show in Amsterdam curated by world-renowned Dutch collective Droog Design, both in 2005. In September of that same year the group appeared on the cover of British design magazine *Icon* and in countless features in Swedish and international design publications. All this, despite never having designed one item that was put into mass production, or even limited production. The project that brought the group the most early recognition, "Design By Animals"— originally shown at the Greenhouse in 2003—was in fact almost impossible to produce on a large scale: wallpaper with patterns chewed into being by hungry rats; coat hooks formed by the twisting of a snake around a lump of clay; lamps shaped from casts poured from rabbit holes. The motivating idea behind these works, according to Front, was to introduce new kinds of "designers" into the creative process, to see how their activities affected the emergence of form and functionality. The ingenuity of their approach, combined with the surprisingly palatable results left by their animal collaborators, immediately caught the attention of the design world and landed Front at the center of a new generation of critically and conceptually engaged designers in Sweden and abroad. Now, back at the Greenhouse after three years of gallery shows and press coverage, Front was unveiling for the first time several new pieces produced for the consuming public.

The Stockholm design world, with its entangled latticework of schools, museums, galleries, trade shows, manufacturers, journalists, and others, is an imperfect analogue of what is typically described as an "art world." First identified by philosopher Arthur Danto (1964) as a means for explaining how certain objects become "works of art," the concept of the art world is a central analytic precept in the sociological analysis of aesthetic value (see, e.g., Becker 1982; Smith and Smith 1977; Bydler 2004; Ericson 1981; cf. Castañeda 2004; Marcus and Myers 1995; cf. Gell 1998). The chief characteristic of the art world is its structure, comprised of a network of different social actors and institutions with distinct social roles, intentions, and economic bases,[2] all of whom work cooperatively—though not necessarily in concert—to select and promote what counts as "art" and produce artistic value from those selections. From this perspective the value of a work of art does not solely originate either from the particular genius of a given artist or from the object itself, but instead is generated in the textured material interactions performed by a range of interested agents, including artists, art teachers, curators, dealers, art buyers, museums, critics, and art historians. The broad social and historical contexts in which these actions take place are intimately interpolated with the production of artistic value. Locating artistic value in the ebbs and flows of various art world paradigms has demonstrated that "pure" aesthetic worth is in fact subject to historical, social, and institutional processes that naturalize and conventionalize aesthetic judgments that would otherwise be unstable and contested in everyday experience (Sclafani 1973; Jones 2000). Working against a Kantian legacy that equates "value" with "beauty," and "beauty" with universal, disinterested judgments of taste that endure regardless of context or individual proclivities, the art world model posits that value is created and applied to objects rather than inherent in their features, and that their beauty is ultimately negotiable. In other words, because of its focus on people, their actions, and the institutions those actions stipulate, the dominant effect of art world processes is to render the sublime a purely social phenomenon.

Another of the art world's distinguishing qualities is its ostensible separation from what is often simply referred to as "reality." The uniqueness of art in relation to the everyday world has a long tradition in the philosophy of aesthetics and art history. As Susanne Langer (1953:46) phrases it, "Every real work of art has a tendency to appear thus dissociated from its mundane environment. The most immediate impression it creates is one of 'otherness' from reality—the impression of an illusion enfolding the thing, action, statement, or flow of sound that constitutes the work." Danto framed the art world along similar lines, characterizing it as set apart, if anxiously so, from the "real": "The artworld stands to the real world in something like the relationship in which the City of God stands to the Earthly City. Certain objects, like certain individuals, enjoy a double citizenship, but there remains . . . a fundamental contrast between artworks and real objects" (Danto 1964:582). The artifacts that circulate in the art world—that is to say, art pieces—are the very materials on which the art world is built, distinct from ordinary objects not because they possess an inherently different constitution, but precisely because they function peculiarly within specific social networks. The power to communicate or express ideas within a community, a power often directly compared to that of language (e.g., Danto 1974; Wollheim 1980; Dewey 1934; Langer 1957), is one of art's most commonly identified distinctive features. Yet as Danto maintains, many art objects are also "real objects"—that is, they are generally made of the same sorts of materials that nonart objects are made of. One of the central functions of the art world is to grant otherwise ordinary, unremarkable materials a distinct power to act on the world in particular ways, a version of Barthes's (1986) "reality effect" that succeeds more at holding "reality at a distance" (Danto 1974:145) than at calling it into being. Locating the materiality of art outside the realm of the ordinary bestows on artworks an ability to exert different effects on those who interact with them, and consequently, on the ways in which aesthetic markets are organized. In other words, exploring aesthetic value from the point of view of the art world requires less attention to the supposed inherent exceptionality of art objects than to the specific processes though which the *bare* objects of reality are transformed into the *symbolic* objects of the art world—the creation of heteroglossic artifacts, or what Danto (1974, 1981) refers to as "the transfiguration of the commonplace."

This distinction between "art" and "reality" must be employed with caution, of course. As unique as art may be in terms of its symbolic valence, such a perspective has the unfortunate tendency to reinstantiate the very ideologies it was designed to overcome. Art is always necessarily situated, as Pierre Bourdieu (1993c) points out, in a socially organized system of beliefs that itself constitutes reality. While Bourdieu (1993a:35) maintains that "the work of art is an object which exists as such only by virtue of the (collective) belief which knows and acknowledges it as a work of art," he rightly would not admit that some obdurate "reality" exists independent of the same kinds of processes that underpin the construction of the art world. That is to say, contrary to Danto's formulation, the art world as a social system is not some mutated version of "normal" social reality, but is in fact one variation among a range of actual market forms, each of which traffics in different currencies, and each of which constitutes its own strand of a wider, symbolically textured social world.

In the reality of the art world the public display of cooperation and contestation between artists and gallery owners, critics and dealers, museums and their visitors, and publishers and their readers produces a patina of high cultural value that adheres to select heteroglossic artifacts. This in turn renders the objects "priceless" and "invaluable," an irony that art dealers and curators exploit to increase the economic value of artworks in contexts in which they are bought and sold as commodities. Nonetheless, the most rudimentary kind of currency in the art world is still symbolic, though it always exists in a relation of interdependence with economic capital. Inasmuch as the art world supports "a trade in things that have no price" (Bourdieu 1993c:74), the economic value of art objects primarily stems from and relies on the symbolic capital they generate within the art world's aesthetic markets.

The Stockholm design world at first blush presents both structurally and functionally much like a prototypical art world. While artists occupy the center of the art world, designers, too, constitute the core of a design world network that also includes schools like Konstfack, Beckmans, and others, museums, stores, manufacturers, books, journalists, newspapers, and various professional organizations. In 2002, the last year for which data are available, there were just over eleven thousand design firms operating in Sweden, employing an equal number of men and women. This figure includes specializations like architecture, graphic design, industrial design, and furniture design—although furniture design and interior design are the smallest design professions, and accurate numbers are not available for those particular fields (Power, Lindström, and Hallencreutz 2004).

Design, like art, is fundamentally concerned with the creation of aesthetic products. Design objects can express ideas and communicate messages through their forms, and like art pieces they can acquire special symbolic significance within particular historical and social contexts. Design objects are also subject to collective beliefs about what officially counts as "design," insofar as they are recognized as such, and their symbolic value stems from the their positions and social utilities within the flows of design world interactions. Moreover, this symbolic value, as with art, is inextricably linked to the metrics by which design objects are economically valued in commercial markets. Design objects are, in other words, typical heteroglossic artifacts.

Yet the degree to which the Stockholm design world operates parallel to a typical art world is limited. The aesthetic markets of the art world are fundamentally driven by certain kinds of symbolic capital. While symbolic capital is used to generate economic capital, which then funds the machinery of the community's complex social system, the operational dynamics of the art world still display a fronted preference for symbolic value over market price—at least outside of the segments controlled by art dealers. That is to say, while the art world is powered by the kinesic vibrations of value converting back and forth between symbolic and economic forms, symbolic capital nonetheless remains the art world's primary currency of trade. Moreover, if in the art world what Bourdieu (1993c:76) refers to as "the ideology of creation" obscures the complex network of sites from which the value of art originates, in the design world it merely complements a transparent system of market pricing. Design objects are, after all, first and foremost *commodities* fabricated by companies working to turn a profit. In the corners of the design world concerned with manufacturing, economic value is foregrounded, theorized, and embraced, and symbolic value is positioned as a supplement to it. And if art places "reality at a distance," as Danto claims, design directly situates it in everyday life. Design objects, like chairs, tables, and lamps, are the stuff of the built environment, the basic building blocks for constructing a material reality. Given these divergences, the modes of production in art worlds and design worlds tend to operate in noticeably distinct ways.

But this gap, this space where art and design resemble one another but not quite, where processes that produce value overlap, or seem to overlap but never quite touch, in between these two semiotic markets is where designers in Sweden most often find themselves operating. It is neither a comfortable space nor a stable one, but there is pleasure there, and opportunities for success. Learning to exploit this ambiguous position between art and commerce is an absolute requirement for designers, but their peripatetic movement between these domains, between the City of God and the Earthly City, ultimately transfigures the objects they create into heteroglossic artifacts, unmoored from both and, thus, semiotically suggestive.

Gaining Confidence

Front began its presentation at the Greenhouse by describing some of its newest pieces, some examples of which were carefully scattered around the stage. The first was a simple trash bin with an exterior made of thin vertical metal slats, and an internal canister attached to a spring (fig. 5). The more refuse placed into the bin, the more the inner canister weighs down on the spring, which in turn causes the metal strips on the outside to bulge, indicating the receptacle's relative fullness. The second piece was a rigid, upright room divider made of translucent red plastic, shaped to resemble the free-flowing feel of an actual textile screen. While these two pieces were by no means standard in their construction, both displaying a playful commentary on traditional forms, compared to the highly conceptual work that had made Front famous—rat-chewed wallpaper, chairs cast from the voids produced by explosions—these objects seemed downright straightforward. They also exhibited lines of visibility quite common to many other pieces of Swedish design: monochromatic coloring, proportional construction, straight angles, and simple curves. After their presentation the moderator noted that the jury that had originally selected Front for inclusion in the 2003 Greenhouse competition did not think that the group would be able to design pieces capable of being produced at some larger than one-off scale. As he spoke, the women all adopted rather bored looks on their faces: it seemed they'd heard this comment quite often. They insisted that they don't much think about whether their pieces are fit for manufacturing. It's the process that matters to Front, and a principled attention to exploring what the process can generate. And besides, their very

Figure 5. The "Bin" trashcans designed by Front for Swedish furniture producer Materia, on display at the Stockholm Furniture Fair, in 2006. Photograph by the author.

presence at this forum, sitting among their production pieces, was proof that the jury was wrong.

Once design students leave school to become professional designers working in the real world, they are confronted with an often intractable tension. They tend to be *idealistic*, devoted to their craft with a stubborn tenacity toward their views of their work and the world. At the same time, because their education contained few lessons in fiscal management, they are almost entirely *unprepared* for entering an economic market in which they are forced to deal with the complex mechanics of establishing and running their own businesses. This includes a resonant apprehension that comes with toiling in environments in which their work is evaluated not only on its aesthetic merits, but also on its salability. Maneuvering through such environments is a skill that consequently must be learned on the job. As Matti explains,

> When I ended college I wasn't a *good* designer. I mean in that sense, to run a project, make logical decisions about things, I didn't know much about

manufacturing. But now I think I do, I mean especially if I work with furniture or lighting, then I know quite a lot about how things will work and how they can be put together and these kinds of things.

Starting out is in many ways an anxious event. For those not seeking jobs in larger design firms, the basic tasks—finding clients, building networks, procuring studio space, filling out the paperwork for establishing a small business, among numerous other requirements—are, at minimum, daunting prospects, and often quite complex to figure out. Learning to accept criticism from people other than peers and instructors—especially from people who provide work and money—can be equally as difficult to those accustomed to toiling away in the relatively nurturing sphere of design school.

One of the best ways to adjust to the judgmental climate of the professional world is by presenting in the graduation *vårutställningar*, the spring exhibitions hosted by both Konstfack and Beckmans at the end of every school year (see fig. 6). In the halls of each school's respective buildings

Figure 6. The Konstfack *vårutställning* (spring exhibition) 2006, in which design students present their final projects to the public. Photograph by the author.

seniors display their exam work for the general public to view over a week-long period. Journalists and manufacturers mingle with proud parents and alumni, all eager to discuss the aesthetic and conceptual dimensions of the objects nervously presented by their creators. Both major Stockholm newspapers, *Dagens Nyheter* and *Svenska Dagbladet*, carry articles covering the exhibitions, sometimes prominently featuring the work of the most promising up-and-coming designers. Even the national radio covers these events, broadcasting interviews with the young designers all across the country.

A successful exhibition inspires confidence in novice designers that their work is good enough for the open market, while an unsuccessful exhibition not only forces them to rethink how they approach both their work itself and how they represent it, but reminds them that success is not always easily attained. The feedback that they receive at these first public displays of their creative output is a useful gauge for estimating their prospects for designing in the real world, hopefully providing welcomed encouragement for continuing along the creative paths they have already begun laying out.

Starting a Company

After the moderator finished with his questions for Front, he opened the floor up to those of us sitting on the risers. Much of the highly conceptual work that Front had just described was still projected on the large screen hanging above the stage. "But how have you supported yourself?" asked a woman from the audience, with an underlying incredulous tone. With polite smiles, the members of Front assured her that they've had plenty of support, from scholarships and awards to other institutions interested in commissioning their work.

Different design fields have different patterns of employment. Industrial designers, graphic designers, and interaction designers tend to seek jobs in medium-sized companies with many employees. Many of these, like No Picnic, SandellSandberg, Stockholm Design Lab, and Propeller, offer a range of different design services, including product design, graphic design, and interior architecture, while others, like Ergonomi Design, operate as more traditional industrial design shops. Students leaving Konstfack and Beckmans often apply to work at design firms like these, or sometimes even in architecture firms or Internet start-ups, because they seem like reliable sources of a steady income stream. These jobs often work out, of course, but many designers feel that once they have experienced that type of work environment, it does not suit them well, especially since they do not move up the social hierarchy of the company quickly enough. Young designers also tend to possess a strong desire to release their creativity on the world, a desire left largely unfulfilled when performing the grunt work as a low-ranking team member in an architecture office. Ultimately these jobs are *money-oriented work*, good for paying the bills and maintaining a decent standard of living, but not necessarily adequate as lifelong pursuits. Consequently many designers drawn to *creativity-oriented work* are seduced by the independence and ostensible freedom afforded by running their own small businesses, which is reflected in the overall composition of the design industry—over 80 percent of design-oriented companies in Sweden have just one employee (Power, Lindström, and Hallencreutz 2004).

Despite the practical hurdles they face, like finding studio space and securing some preliminary financing, many designers, especially furniture designers, end up establishing their own companies not too long after leaving design school. Often, as was the case with Front, this is a natural extension of the work they were doing while in school, with some businesses having started while their founders were still students.

One of the most common ways of overcoming some of the initial pitfalls of self-employment is to collaborate with a group of like-minded colleagues, a tactic that began in earnest in the 1960s. This can mean forming a unified design group, like Front or another called Uglycute, whose joint work is consistently branded with the group's name, or it can mean establishing a collective, like OUR (see chapter 4) or many similar unlabeled groups, whose members share work space and other resources, but each of whom runs her or his own independent company. This, too, is often an extension of collaborations initiated in school, and many of these collectives are comprised not only of work colleagues, but also of close friends. There is a certain sense of safety in numbers at work in motivating the formation of these groups early on, and pragmatically it makes sense. Splitting the studio rental costs, sharing contacts, collaborating on projects, and just having another voice around are all invaluable benefits to novice designers making a start in their careers.

The most difficult aspect of launching a new design business is securing money to finance it. Many designers do end up taking entry-level jobs
at architecture firms or other companies in order to start saving money,
but this leaves very little time to actually develop one's own portfolio. It
is also possible to turn to the state for help. Through Konstnärsnämnden,
the Arts Grants Committee, the government provides stipends to Swedes
working within a widely defined art world sphere, including traditional
fine arts, design, theater, film, and dance. Many designers are successful
in seeking funding from Konstnärsnämnden early in their careers, which
provides them an income for several months and thereby allows them to
begin setting up contacts, working on new projects, and launching their
small businesses. Another funding source for young designers is IASPIS,
International Artists Studio Program in Sweden, which falls under the
purview of Konstnärsnämnden but is geared toward facilitating international exposure for Swedish artists. Often this takes the form of a grant
for designers to travel abroad to learn from other designers working in
countries outside Scandinavia. London, Holland, France, Japan, and New
York are popular destinations.

A little bit of luck also has its place in founding a small design business.
Connections made through teachers during school or during the spring
exhibitions can prove to be invaluable when the time comes to find paying
work. Stefan A., who was not trained at either Konstfack or Beckmans, set
up shop in Stockholm largely by happenstance:

> At the end of my last year I had a meeting with a designer from Stockholm
> who worked very much with screen printing and ceramics, and he asked
> me if I wanted to work for him. At that point I didn't feel at all like going to
> Stockholm to work with ceramics and stuff. No. But he was smart enough
> to call me two days after I finished school, when you're like lying in bed and
> you don't know what to do with your life. So I went up here and I thought,
> "Maybe I can work for him for a summer or so." So I went up here and took,
> like, a month or two and decided, like, "I got nothing to go back to in Norr-
> köping [a small city south of Stockholm]. I don't know why—" I really
> liked Stockholm. So I've been here since then, actually.

Such seemingly serendipitous connections, often involving a chance meeting or phone call, are a common feature of how designers rationalize
their professional biographies. Rarely do they describe early success as a

consequence of their own efforts and determination, but instead they tend to highlight a "falling into it" aspect of their narratives. This is not to say that they disavow hard work or their own unique talents and skills. Rather, designers prefer to background their own role in their success in favor of a spun story that foregrounds circumstances over abilities, at least when recounting the early stages of their careers.

Svensk Form and the Year of Design

If Ikea is the most powerful and recognizable force for promoting Swedish design on a global scale, Svensk Form, the Swedish Society of Crafts and Design, is its domestic counterpart. Svensk Form was founded by Nils Månsson Mandelgren in 1845 as Svenska Slöjdföreningen, the Swedish Society of Arts and Crafts (the name was changed in 1976), an offshoot of Söndagsritskola för Hantverkare (later Konstfack), which he had established the previous year. The original intent of the organization was to preserve traditional handicraft techniques from the perceived threat posed by mass production, a preoccupation that would steer the group's mission for several decades (Frick 1978). At the start of the twentieth century, however, the organization's attitude toward mass production began to shift, especially under the influence of its spokesman Gregor Paulsson, who published a tract in 1919 called *Vackrare Vardagsvara* (More Beautiful Everyday Things), which forcefully advocated the integration of artisanal quality and mass production techniques. Having begun as an organization charged with protecting the interests of artisans and craftspeople, by the first quarter of the twentieth century the association's custodial scope had expanded to cover even the people for whom objects were crafted. Nearly ten years after the publication of *More Beautiful Everyday Things*, Gregor Paulsson, recounting the social impact of the publication, and especially its title, to an audience at the Metropolitan Museum of Art in New York, remarked: "It was on everybody's lips. People became conscious that they must make their homes more dignified. The homes which were set up by the young people were to a quite astonishing degree built with that slogan in mind" (Paulsson 1927:4). In the years that followed, Svenska Slöjdföreningen, founded by an artist to safeguard the work of other artists against nineteenth-century modernity creep, became the most potent proponent of modern design for the Swedish public, and the most vocal champion of both Swedish design and Swedish designers.

Today Svensk Form operates under a government mandate to promote design in Sweden and abroad. Advocating *Bättre liv genom god design* (Better life through good design)—a slogan it prominently displays on its website—the organization frames its mission as one of responsibility to the needs of designers, businesses, and society as a whole. Along with numerous public talks, it funds several exhibitions each year, in its own gallery space in Stockholm, in other locations around Sweden, and through traveling exhibitions abroad. From 2009 through 2011, for instance, Svensk Form sponsored an exhibition called *17 Swedish Designers*, a collection of works by young women designers, including Front, that toured eight locations across the United States. It also publishes a popular magazine called *Form*, which has existed in several iterations since 1905, and houses an extensive archive of diverse materials related to design in Sweden, much of which has been digitized and uploaded to the Web. From the point of view of designers themselves, Svensk Form is particularly instrumental in supporting design projects financially with scholarships and stipends, and recognizing examples of innovative design work though awards like Ung Svensk Form, established in 1998 for young Swedish designers; the Design S award, given out biannually since 2006; and the now-defunct Utmärkt Svensk Form award, which helped raise the profile of many designers throughout the 1980s and 1990s.

Svensk Form was also, along with the Swedish Industrial Design Foundation (SVID), the National Museum, and several other institutions, responsible for implementing and steering the government's Designåret (Year of Design) initiative in 2005, a yearlong, country-wide campaign devised to publicly promote the necessity of design in everyday life, and, perhaps more importantly, reposition its role in the Swedish industrial and public sectors. Across the country over 1,600 activities were organized—workshops, exhibits, contests, publications, television programs—backed by almost 64 million kronor (about 9 million dollars) from the government, along with smaller donations from dozens of private companies. Stickers and signs bearing the red-and-white "Designåret 2005" logo were ubiquitous in Stockholm in 2005, Designåret events were scheduled all over the city in multiple venues, and SVT, the national television corporation, broadcast a different thirty-second design-oriented clip every night over the entire year. While Leif Pagrotsky, the minister of culture, declared Designåret 2005 a success as early as September of that year, most of the designers I spoke with had a very different assessment.

"I don't know if I can talk about it," laughed Björn when I asked his thoughts on Designåret. Like many of his peers, designers not working for large global companies like Volvo, Ericsson, and Electrolux, he felt that Designåret was overblown and misdirected. From its inception in 2002 the campaign was explicitly organized to increase the profile of design in Sweden by targeting three particular areas: business, the public sector, and everyday life. It quickly became apparent to many designers, however, that the needs and desires of business interests were considered far more important to the campaign's agenda than those of self-employed designers, who constitute the vast majority of designers in Sweden. Even before Designåret started, organizers faced criticism in the press over lack of financing and poor allocation of funds (Ohlsson 2004), a criticism many designers repeated to me often in late 2005. While the campaign made strong public pronouncements supporting the work of designers, there was very little funding available to help most independent designers participate in Designåret events and showcase their work. Anna Lindgren, one of the Front designers, told daily national newspaper *Dagens Nyheter* in late 2005: "As designers [Designåret] hasn't influenced us. We get our assignments by showing internationally at different fairs and exhibitions. It's too bad that there hasn't been any money to apply for making our own projects, that maybe would have changed things." In the same article designer Zandra Ahl echoed Lindgren's sentiment, adding a rebuke of the campaign's promoters: "There wasn't any money for practicing designers while the [Designåret] brand gives a lot of cred to those who stand behind it" (Hernadi 2005). A young independent curator named Petra D. framed the problem in historical-political terms:

> I think maybe because the Design Year [organizers] themselves weren't very clear about exactly what the purpose of the Design Year was. I guess the social demo—state commissioned buildings and hospitals and city planning was once upon a time a very close collaboration between the state commissioners and the designers. Today you have the state is just—because of the de-centralization trend, where a big percentage of things has to be—what's it called, private and not state-run, the state has much less control over how

commissions employ designers or not. So things are loose, and state-control, standardizations and stuff are also losing validity and currency in current political agendas. So it's a practical way to force commissioners, both private and state and communal[3] to work more closely with designers. And then also to try and educate industry how they can win, how they can cut production costs and stuff through working with designers. So it's definitely, it's trying to make Sweden a more competitive country industrially, but you know, it just seems like they weren't very good at presenting their real agenda about it. And also to actually document that work. I mean that would have been really cool, if they could have illustrated those aspects.

From the perspective of design professionals working outside corporate institutions, Designåret focused too much attention on the business and marketing aspects of design and not enough attention on the creative efforts of the actual individuals employed though design work. The dominant rhetorical thrust of the campaign, and more importantly, its financial model, treated design not as considered aesthetic concerns, but as a blunt tool that companies could use to delineate new market segments in Sweden and abroad. Amid the hundreds of events organized around the country, and the hundreds of publications that were circulated in conjunction with them, there was little celebration of the art or skill of the designer, and little recognition of the challenges that young designers face in building their careers. Instead many felt like the organizers, and by extension the government, were cynically using designers as props in an argument for economic development that they themselves were not allowed to contribute to. In other words, the designers felt themselves to be "useful idiots" in a state-sponsored scheme that cared little about their particular needs and little about the details of designing. So many of them—most of them, probably—simply ignored Designåret entirely.

Almost entirely, anyway. Alongside their disappointment that Designåret offered little economic help to practitioners, many designers conceded that the campaign's goal to push public awareness of design was laudable, and possibly even effective. "It's really popular among designers and architects to complain about the Design Year," Måns S. told me as we sat in his shared studio. Someone else mentioned the nightly television clips. "You can be critical and you can—about the content and stuff like that but still, it's, you know, three hundred sixty five, almost three hundred sixty five designers and products on TV." His partner Johanna G. immediately jumped in: "I mean that's a very good thing, I think." Indeed, while few designers felt any direct effects from Designåret, either in the form of government funds or in new assignments from paying clients, there was a general sense in the Stockholm design world that Designåret 2005 at worst still functioned as a useful, if inchoate, public endorsement of the worth of design to Swedish society.

On Navigating Fields

Lars and I were walking back to his apartment after lunch at a nearby mall. As we passed a small cell-phone shop, he paused, then moved toward the store's inviting front window. "I just want to see some of the new phones," he said as I followed him up to the glass.

Lars is an industrial designer. To be more precise, Lars was one of the first industrial designers in Sweden, and to be even more precise, Lars turned stereos black. His original training at Konstfack was in silversmithing, since there was no such thing as industrial design before he helped clear a space for it, partly through his own work, and partly though savvy institution-building—he helped establish industrial design as an official discipline at Konstfack in 1976. Early in his career Lars developed a particular interest in sound machines, like speakers, radio tuners, and telephones—an interest he would sustain over his entire career. His first major projects were for a stereo equipment manufacturer, and one of his assignments there—he was given many over the years he worked for the company—was to design a smaller stereo receiver. In the 1970s, stereo components were generally heavy silver metal boxes trimmed in wood or fake-wood veneer. They were also quite large, but necessarily so, given the sizes and shapes of all the internal parts required for the stereo to work properly. Given the engineering constraints, designing a smaller receiver was next to impossible. So Lars did the next best thing—he made the box look smaller. Retaining the same basic dimensions as the legacy receivers, and cutting down the weight, he replaced obtrusive wood and silver metal with the most minimal of rectangular forms crafted from black metal, employing what amounts to an optical illusion to shrink the receiver down in size. And it worked. Bulky wooden receivers and cassette decks soon disappeared not just in Sweden, but the whole world over, and even though stereo components have indeed gotten smaller over the years, the black metal box remains the standard form for stereo equipment design today. Of course turning stereos black isn't Lars's most significant contribution to design, nor is it his favorite. But there is something rather elegant about it nonetheless—a manipulation of form and material to change the experience of an object, rather than modifications requiring a complex re-engineering of technical parts.

We stood outside the cell-phone shop, foreheads pressed against the glass, pointing to different phones resting on their small displays. I was curious what Lars thought of these cutting-edge devices, since he'd been instrumental in advancing mobile-phone design during the earliest days of cellular telephony, but none of them really moved him. He did finally admit, though, that a phone dubbed the Chocolate, a small dark slab of solid plastic just released by the Korean company LG, looked like it might be worthwhile. We stood there for a few more beats in silence, then turned away from the window, in the direction of his apartment.

As significant as establishing one's own business—finding studio space, making connections, and securing paying assignments—is for a young designer, there is also a need for recognition, which motivates what a designer does. This recognition is not simply an acknowledgment of a designer's economic success, but more a recognition of his or her creative abilities and talents. There are practical reasons for this, of course, since getting your name out in the design world—and with some luck, beyond—increases the chances that manufacturers will contract you to design new products. But the practical effects of recognition are only partially responsible for pushing designers to seek out opportunities for presenting their objects in ways that symbolically redound to their reputations as creative people.

For many designers the business side of what they do is viewed as a necessary evil that facilitates their more creative endeavors. Managing a small design firm, even if the firm consists of only one designer, is fundamentally a matter of keeping a business afloat, and to that end much of the daily work designers do revolves around menial housekeeping. Organizing paperwork, paying bills, responding to e-mails, making phone calls, researching materials for future projects, these tasks regularly keep designers away from actual drafting. Managing a small firm also involves a fair amount of self-promotion, which almost every young designer I worked with expressed reluctance toward. Rather than soliciting manufacturers for a pitch, which is a completely legitimate custom in the field, most prefer to wait for the phone calls and e-mails to come to them, even if it means less revenue in the meantime. It is quite common to view self-promotion as a practice that designers are "bad at," or, as Erika G. describes it, as her "worst side as a designer."

Of course most of these issues are either differently organized or non-existent for designers working in the context of larger design firms with more substantial staff and more institutional support. Yet most designers choose to strike out on their own and start small businesses despite their anxieties around the management aspects of doing so, in large part because the recognition they receive from the design world when running their own firms is considered a worthwhile trade-off.

To most designers the drawings they create and the products that stem from those drawings are not simply things replaceable and exchangeable for similar others—they are *works*, not merely work. Designers view themselves as engaged in a deeply aesthetic craft, more intimately connected to the currents of the art world than to the shuddering assembly lines on which their objects are fabricated. Their labor is fundamentally technical in nature, but it is also fundamentally aesthetic, creative, and beyond what they perceive as problem solving or "office work." As Peter phrases it, "That's the tricky thing with this profession, to mix it, to find the poetry in the engineering." Artists adrift in a sea of merchants, designers work hard to uncover that poetry, to give what they do meaning and to receive recognition for it, by turning to the art world for inspiration.

And this makes some sense, as recognition for artists is one of the art world's core features. A work of art is almost always intimately connected to the artist herself. This is true both in a literal, graphic sense, as with signed paintings and gallery placards, and more figuratively, as when the mention of an artist's name—Diane Arbus, Pablo Picasso—evokes images of specific works or kinds of art. Of course this holds for some designers, too—Frank Gehry, Philippe Starck—but only because their work has been subjected to the same treatment that works of art tend to undergo. Generally speaking, most designed objects do not acquire the status of art objects and are not primarily evaluated according to aesthetic criteria; nor are most designers treated like artists. The overwhelming majority of designed things that populate the world—chairs, paper shredders, cars, mugs, gears, watchbands, door stoppers, lampposts, and so on—do not have their designers' names attached to them and are usually not evaluated in any consequential way according to their aesthetics. They simply exist as things. Thus for designers in Sweden creating mundane, usable commodities that more "naturally" thrive in anonymity, attaching their names to their objects and receiving recognition for their creativity require exploiting social processes that transform those things into something more meaningful with values that exceed their utilitarian functions. This means participating in design exhibitions, in both small galleries and museums, and submitting their work for evaluation by design critics. This means giving public lectures presenting their work and explaining their philosophies of design and their design process. And this means appearing in glossy design magazines and sitting for interviews with design-oriented websites. Designers engage in all of these practices and more, structured almost exactly like the practices that propel the art world, not only because they fetch designers new assignments that bring them money, but because the recognition that these processes provide gives meaning to what they do.

There are several strategies that designers use for productively walking this line between art and commerce, most of which involve developing and cultivating a dual identity. The pattern of dividing one's efforts into *money-oriented jobs* and *creativity-oriented jobs*, where income from the former supports the ability to do the latter, which may have been necessary upon graduation, can take on a different kind of significance over time. Some designers, like the members of the design collective Muungano, hold steady employment working in architecture firms or other "regular" jobs even many years after leaving design school, and they use their spare time to develop their design work with the group. In such cases design work, usually without recompense, remains the central passion of the designers, but the steady income of a regular job is a lure that is hard to resist. Other designers are able to supplement their incomes from design work by teaching at one of the local design schools. While teaching jobs still fall within the general sphere of design work, the specifics of what is involved are different enough that designers are able to partition their roles quite cleanly.

This is, of course, a rather common necessity for many aesthetic practitioners with technical skills. Graham Jones (2011), for instance, stresses that for magicians working in Paris, performing tricks is not just a practiced skill aimed at entertainment, but rather a highly developed productive craft gleaned from years of guided apprenticeship. Yet in order to continue developing their technical skills, skills much more valuable to their membership in the magic community, magicians are often forced to work for money performing simple tricks for nonmagicians at restaurants and parties. The split identity that Swedish designers often possess is most commonly manifest in the different kinds of *products* they create and what they do with those heteroglossic artifacts—at once both art pieces and putatively "everyday objects"—rather than in the different jobs they may work. For many designers, gallery pieces and production pieces are two distinct categories. Some of what they make is for show, some is for sale. Erika G. explains it best:

> You can see it from two angles, maybe. Because I'm working in two tracks, parallel. One track is the things you see on my webpage, which are more, maybe, conceptual products. I'm working more towards art maybe. People say. I don't know if I design it like that. I work from my inside. . . . Anyway, and the other track is pure industrial design. And this track, industrial design, gives me money to live. The other track [involves] exhibitions, the Milan furniture fair. The bicycle basket [a more conceptual product she has designed] will soon come out, next year. It took three years to get that product out. They haven't started to get me money, because all that is royalty money, and it takes a while. So at that track [the more conceptual track], no money—yet. So I need the other track to survive.

One of the most appealing aspects of creating artistic objects is that working in a more conceptual mind-set allows a designer to achieve a more authentic sense of *freedom* in her labor. Typical commercial design work, because it is plugged into economic markets, business cycles, and the exchange of money, is viewed as *constraining* the creative process. By crafting pieces for exhibitions, or a one-off prototype that appears in a magazine, designers can express themselves in more satisfying ways than they can in purely commercial pieces. As Matti explains,

> A couple of years ago I did, like, a lot of exhibitions, more work for free. But now I have so many commissions, and that takes all my time, and I also need the money, of course, from them. So it's been kind of, you know, office-like,

for a while, which is kind of nice. But now it feels like one would like to break. Sort of work more—more freely.

An understated goal for many designers is precisely to create heteroglossic artifacts, for their artistic pieces and their production pieces to be one and the same, and indeed this is possible in many cases. Much of the material on display at the *We Are Going Underground* show was already in limited production, and indeed various prominent venues, like the Stockholm Furniture Fair, the National Museum, and even retail outlets like Ikea and DesignTorget, blur this distinction between aesthetic artifacts and objects for purchase in the presentation tactics they employ (see chapter 5).

There is, of course, a danger for designers in this plying of commodities as aesthetic objects. Because the structure of the design world—inasmuch as it resembles an art world, but is more overtly beholden to the dynamics of market forces—compels designers to maintain dual allegiances to selling and showing, it is sometimes difficult to determine the correct balance between the two. If a designer's work is considered not "artistic" enough, or too commercial or boring or unoriginal, then it becomes quite difficult to receive the kinds of recognition that designers seek out. Curators will not select their pieces for inclusion in exhibitions, nor will critics profile and evaluate their works in newspapers, or editors feature their designs in magazines and books. Without these tokens of recognition, designers are forced to hustle more actively to find paying work, since manufacturers are unlikely to seek them out, but they are also left structurally positioned more firmly in the field of commerce, rendered nameless and faceless makers of mere *things* rather than known creators of aesthetic *works*.

At the same time, if designers are perceived by manufacturers as residing too comfortably in the art world, as designing things that have no utilitarian function or potential mass appeal, then their identities as makers of sellable everyday objects, and thus their main source of income, begin to fade away. While many designers discovered the profession of design through art, and they see themselves as working within and alongside the art world, the ability to create useful objects that ordinary people interact with is a significant reason for choosing design as a profession over fine arts. Thus projecting the identity of designer, rather than artist, is an important goal for many in the design world.

In the early years of the twenty-first century the freely expressive and artistic sides of Swedish designers gained greater and greater exposure in Sweden, largely through a movement dubbed *konceptdesign*, or conceptual design. Pieces that fall under this rubric blend many aspects of the traditional modernist Swedish cultural geometry with more openly artistic formal experimentation and highly conceptual, often critical messages. In 2005 the National Museum in Stockholm curated an acclaimed exhibition on *konceptdesign* that introduced dozens of these objects to the general public, considered by some design critics as "the most important exhibition" that the National Museum had put up for quite some time (Cornell 2005).

As popular and potentially significant as the *konceptdesign* movement was, however, there is also a sense that it pushed design too close to—or even over—the fragile border between art and design. For the public to perceive contemporary design not as simply *related to art*, but *as art itself*, as something beyond the realm of everyday life, might weaken its commercial appeal. After all, design must sell to be effective. As one letter to the editor of *Form* magazine put it, in reaction to the *konceptdesign* show, "Making a sellable product that many people can like and buy is a thousand times harder than simply making a unique radio with roses on it" (Madestrand 2005). While this was not a common attitude among the designers I interviewed, the sentiment was still lurking just below the surface:

> I get quite tired of all these photos in design magazines of all these impossible, strange concept design things. I mean, they are so colorful and so strange in the shapes and everything, so the photographers for all the design magazines prefer to take photos of these funny-strange-design-artwork-things, instead of some furniture that really works in reality. So in the long run nobody can BUY these kinds of products, they're never coming into production, nobody can buy them. (Stig A.)

To be sure, *konceptdesign* marked an apotheosis of design-as-art in Sweden, explicitly challenging the relationship between the two semiotic domains. However, most of the critical response that emerged around this exhibition focused on the objects themselves—like Mats Theselius's carrot holder—questioning the new forms and (non)functions of objects supposedly labeled "design" in the exhibition. "Is it reasonable to design gadgets that nobody needs?" asked Finnish reporter Nina Weckström (2006), reviewing the *konceptdesign* exhibition. "Can anyone live without a carrot holder?" While much of the debate centered on the objects themselves, and whether they could be more neatly described as either art or design—a division that the exhibition was intended to overcome—what few participants in these public debates were able to see was that the design world itself was *already* structured as an art world analogue, complete with an analogous evaluative infrastructure of critics, galleries, studios, magazines, and educational institutions. From this point of view the "Is it art or design?" question was irrelevant. By highlighting the anxious parallels between art and design, the *konceptdesign* exhibit only called attention to a reality that designers themselves had been maneuvering for decades. For them the overlap between art and design is not just about the objects—it is about the social formations that undergird the entire design world, of which the objects are only one part.

But of course the objects *are* important. They are, after all, the core of what designing is about. The picture of the Stockholm design world I have presented has focused mostly on what designers do to become professional designers, the pressures they face and the resources they have at their disposal to build careers and gain recognition and integrate themselves into the fabric of the existing design world. Aside from a shared conviction that designers can, perhaps even should, consider the social effects of their work on the world, overt politics are practically nowhere to be found in the ordinary practices of Swedish designers. And yet their objects—still, and for a long time—continue to be popularly designated political. As it turns out, designers do actively participate in this process, though rarely do they do so intentionally. Ironically, the things that they do primarily as a means of *achieving success* are the very same practices that help redraw their work into the diagram of Swedish design and bestow it with its distinctive ideological patina.

Meaningful Oscillations

What I am arguing is that the circulation of design objects through all of these various design world domains, and in various modes, is precisely what affords their appropriation as political objects, even if their creators do not directly affiliate with such voicings. In their role as businesspeople, designers meet with manufacturers, cultivate relationships with vendors, and occasionally visit factories. They research construction techniques, order samples of new materials, build their websites, and clean up the workshop when it gets too dirty. In their role as artisans they submit their work to juried competitions, organize their own gallery shows, and give interviews to journalists for local and national publications. They also sometimes present public lectures or write pieces for edited books. As designers move between and among these different practices and events, their designs—the heteroglossic artifacts that travel alongside them—endure the effects of forces that both mold them into utilitarian everyday objects and refashion them as something more akin to a work of art, as objects open to specific kinds of expert evaluation. In the process of moving back and forth through these domains, these heteroglossic artifacts accrue the attendant "voices" indigenous to each, such that each "utterance"—or each "appearance," in a store, in a home, in a magazine, in a museum, or even in a trash bin—is always suffused with the whole range of associations, including those that match the final vocabulary of Swedish design.

Given the semiotic dynamism that circumscribes design objects, derived from the basic operations of professional design practices, these objects, rendered heteroglossic artifacts as they move through the design world, are left disposed to appropriation and redescription, including those unanticipated or unintended by their designers. To a certain extent designers can maintain some control over how their work is presented, for instance, by organizing their own exhibitions or writing the catalog copy for their pieces themselves. But in other situations, for instance, showing a piece in a curated exhibition (like the *konceptdesign* show or the design exhibition in the National Museum), designers cede some of their ability to control the messages expressed by their work to other actors in the design world, like the curators assembling the exhibition, the critics reviewing it, and the attendees who come to see it, and it is here, in these corners of the design world, that the lines of enunciation of political design are most strongly delineated. While designers resist, sometimes stringently, the dominant discursive climate that treats Swedish design as overtly ideological, because of the ways in which the design world is organized, especially the mechanisms that accord recognition, they have little choice but to engage in practices that often work to stitch together lines of visibility and lines of enunciation in their designs, even if they disprefer doing so.

One of the most significant ways in which ideology is first pressed onto design objects is through *glossing procedures*, practices in which design world experts, drawing from the final vocabulary, offer descriptions and elaborations of a given piece of design. They raise associations—with ideas, other names, other objects—and provide context for interpreting the significance of a piece. Some glossing procedures are principally devoted to promoting the category of Swedish design by identifying emblematic tokens and describing, sometimes inexactly and sometimes in great detail, the specific features that confer on it membership in the class. Such glosses usually trade in matters like tradition, modernity, Swedishness, minimalism, and the like, without delving too deeply into overtly political language. Other glosses, though, are more centrally concerned with describing design in ideological tones, sometimes delivered as suggestions, and sometimes framed more as decrees. The dominant structuring of these glossing procedures positions visual images with textual elaborations, sometimes short and pithy, other times long and narrative, in formats that highlight the *alignment* of form and meaning. In galleries, objects are placed on podiums with small cards noting the designer's name and a short curatorial description of the piece, an arrangement that is replicated and expanded in the exhibition's catalog. In published books on Swedish or Scandinavian design, photographs of objects illustrate chapters about specific designers or specific traditions, often amid text stressing how minute material qualities—lines, curves, mass—are the object's distinctive features. Even in some stores, like DesignTorget, Ikea, Nordiska Kompaniet, and Design House Stockholm, the names and faces of designers are sometimes placed alongside their objects for sale, linking Swedish identities to specific commodities by highlighting local talent. All of these glossing procedures, consistently and steadily applied to both new and old objects in a range of different contexts (see chapter 5), contribute collectively to the ongoing redrawing of Swedish design.

But there are, of course, limits placed on the kinds of descriptions that heteroglossic artifacts afford, along with limits on the kinds of objects that fit certain descriptions. Some forms are unable to fit the Swedish design designation. Not just any chair can be credibly described in political terms, nor will any table take on the Swedish label comfortably. And while a carrot holder manufactured for sale may appear both in museum catalogs and on store shelves—it was produced and sold in 1996—its seemingly purposeless function might not appeal to many consumers. Bakhtin recognized the limits of heteroglossia. Words and utterances cannot simply assume any meaning a speaker chooses. There must be some socially acknowledged and accountable connection between a given word-form and its associated meanings in order for communication to take place. Words cannot be easily redefined, nor can the rules of appropriate usage be ignored. Any lexical reappropriations must be relatively small scale, and also somehow believable, or else they face the likelihood of failure. And some words and utterances simply cannot be easily recontextualized:

> And not all words for just anyone submit equally easily to this appropriation, to this seizure and transformation into private property: many words stubbornly resist, others remain alien, sound foreign in the mouth of the one who appropriated them and who now speaks them; they cannot be assimilated into his context and fall out of it; it is as if they put themselves in quotation marks against the will of the speaker. (Bakhtin 1981:294)

The same holds true for heteroglossic artifacts. Since the 1930s only certain objects—those crafted with the Swedish cultural geometry—afford redescription and appropriation with political formulations in the Swedish design world, while pieces not made from these forms "stubbornly resist" the final vocabulary. In cases where acclaimed works created by Swedish designers do explicitly reject the Swedish cultural geometry and its attendant associations, for example Front's rat-chewed wallpaper, they will most likely be labeled as "art" and thus removed from the world of functional everyday goods, decreasing any damage they might do to the brand. When such works do receive critical attention, the glossing procedures they undergo will usually indicate their deviations, thereby reflexively reentrenching the specific qualities that officially count as normative Swedish design. Not all deviations are excluded, of course, and even some intense departures are incorporated, if uneasily, into the canon. But in consequential moments of evaluation, in the glossing procedures that confer both aesthetic values and political ideologies, design objects endure a second set of forces that push and pull some kinds of objects toward Swedish design while simultaneously pushing others away.

What this means, then, is that the generalized glossing of design objects as political in Sweden is directly facilitated, and in some ways unexpectedly cultivated, by the actions of designers who express little interest in describing their objects so bluntly—work that is otherwise left up to journalists, authors, government officials, and ordinary Swedes. Most designers focus on practicing and honing their creative skills. They want to run a business and be successful at it. They want to collaborate with friends, for shared economic security, enhanced creativity, and fun. And they want to be recognized for their work. While most designers are politically oriented in the way that members of a welfare society are usually socialized to be, and while they would prefer the objects they create "do good"—or be at least neutral—rather than bringing some harm to the world, they maintain virtually no direct connection to the specific statements forwarded by Key, Paulsson, and others. To most contemporary designers, the lines of enunciation are easily recognized but left largely unarticulated in how they conceive and describe their work.

But not the lines of visibility. These lines persist, and designers are quite involved in their reproduction.

4

In the Studio

Peter is heading into the workshop. It's time to make a foam prototype of the candleholder he and Matti have been tinkering with for the past several days. As the printer slowly coughs out a digital rendering of the candleholder, an ongoing process marked by clunky whirs and a droning buzz that loudly fills the studio's open space, Matti, who had originally sent the digital file over to the printer from his computer, stops Peter and calls him back to their worktable—it seems as if the file that's printing is not quite right. "Hey," Matti says, looking down at a hand sketch he's made in a small spiral-bound notebook (see fig. 7). "Actually, there's something with the geometry that you'd have with what I've done," he says, alluding to a difficulty he's discovered: how to evoke the sense of softness they desire from the foam block that the prototype will be carved from. "I thought that it should be like this." As Peter walks back to the table, Matti begins to explain how the lines and surfaces that appear on the printout—the document that would guide Peter's manual labor on the foam—should be longer and smoother than originally rendered on the computer. However,

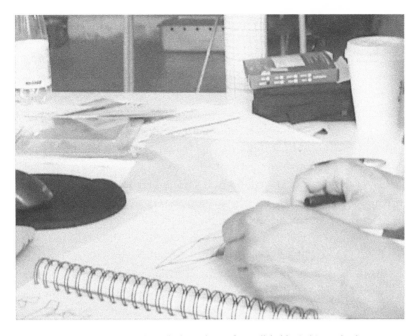

Figure 7. Matti sketching the basic shape of a candleholder in his notebook.
Photograph by the author.

he does not say this in any explicit way. As Peter stands over him, Matti
uses his pen to trace and retrace and retrace again the new shapes he had
been sketching in his notebook. As he slowly moves his pen over the blocky
lines on the notebook page, moving from one edge to another and across
the object's surfaces, the lines begin to take on a more curved appearance.
"So I made one surface"—he then draws for two seconds in silence—"like
this," he says, "and then up; then it goes diagonally here a little bit." His
pen is in constant motion, drawing Peter through this new iteration of the
candleholder's form. As Matti's strokes slow to a halt the designers' talk
shifts toward more practical issues, like how to cut the block and sand the
foam. Peter then walks back to the printer to fetch the printout, grabs a
marker from the table, and quickly augments the digital drawing with his
own handmade guidelines based on the conversation he had just had with
Matti. He then takes the sheet of paper in his hand, along with the marker,
and resumes his trip back to the workshop.

In one sense there is nothing remarkable about this short interaction, a
common kind of exchange between designers that occurs multiple times a

day in almost any design studio. But in a very real sense it is in these very small motions and language games—putting pen to paper, talking while drawing, submitting ideas for evaluation—that the actual work of design is carried out, that the *giving of forms* unfolds. As part of their everyday "phenomenology of expertise" (Boyer 2005b) designers engage in all sorts of work that directly and indirectly relates to designing, a mixture of hand sketching, computer drawing, Internet research, and manual labor, along with all the basic and necessary managerial tasks underlying the business side of running a small company. And on top of that, the work that goes on inside the walls of the studio is always tethered to the wider worlds in which designers operate—the manufacturers who contract them, the factories that produce their objects, the design schools they attended (and may now teach at), the critics who assess their work, the consumers who buy it, and so on. All of this matters for doing design, and for reproducing the diagram of Swedish design. But what I want to isolate in this chapter is a very significant, and often overlooked, aspect of what goes on in the studio—the seemingly minor motions involving computers, paper, pens, prototypes, and most crucially, other designers—and the specific kinds of effects that these actions have on reproducing, in a very literal way, Swedish design's normative lines of visibility.

Of course in its barest form the argument that specific practices undergird design in consequential ways is self-evidently uncontroversial. But the difference here is that my analysis attends closely to language use within language games—that is, the way designers talk to each other as they design—as a primary force that structures how forms are worked on, out, and through, and how they are given to objects. Ethnographic accounts of professionals in action have demonstrated that expertise is often distributed within the sociomaterial worlds in which experts are embedded (e.g., Harper 1987; Orr 1996), and the nature of professional expertise as a specifically embodied phenomenon has been argued from a number of different angles (e.g., Boyer 2001, 2005a; Grasseni 2009; Herzfeld 2004; Sudnow 2001), including specific attention to the collaborative interactional dynamics that facilitate expert action (e.g., Murphy 2005; Reeves, Brown, and Laurier 2009). Following from these traditions, I explore design expertise in the studio not only as materially situated and embodied, but also as highly mediated by particular linguistic formations that structure designing in face-to-face interaction. In other words, I lay flesh on what might otherwise seem abstract "practices" and "processes" sequentially culminating in an eventual design, treating the interactions that designers engage in with each other not as vectors for communicating design ideas, but as sets of conditions whose own intrinsic dynamics facilitate the reemergence of the cultural geometry in designers' collaborative work.

In his exploration of architectural education Donald Schön (1984, 1985) has argued that what he calls "the language of designing"—that is, simultaneously talking and drawing and manipulating the tools of the trade as one works through a design—sits at the very core of how design expertise is learned, and indeed, as Peter and Matti show, how designing is fundamentally accomplished in the studio. Under the guidance of more experienced instructors, students are socialized to continuously reconceive and reconsider their emergent designs according to the structuring feedback, both verbal and visual, that they receive. This pedagogical arrangement is not so much a matter of a master *determining* the outcome of the student's actions; it's rather a constant engagement with the tools of the trade as well as a training regime oriented explicitly to knowledge practices that posit collaboration and reflexivity as fundamental elements of designing in action. To know an unfolding design is to talk it out, to draw it out, to submit it to evaluation by others, to allow it to be redescribed, reappropriated, and redrawn in unexpected terms all in the service of improving it. It is in this nexus of interactional conditions spun by designers in the studio, I argue, that the cultural geometry materializes—even when designers do not see it as such.

Note that for Schön (1984, 1985) the language of designing is not a strictly linguistic phenomenon. Form giving in design interactions is always mediated by different sorts of tools, some of which are material (computers, paper, pens, foam, sheet of plastic), some of which are embodied (gestures, manipulations, enactments), and others that are indeed linguistic (ways of talking, habits of reasoning, even features of grammar). Crucial to my analysis is the notion that form giving in the studio is inherently collaborative, the collective outcome of many minds, many artifacts, and many utterances all brought together in consequential actions that together continuously shape the conditions within which objects are brought into being, even down to the smallest details of the work designers do.[1] Of course not every action in the studio is directly socially mediated. Individual designers do often sit alone at their computers undisturbed by the

hubbub that surrounds them. But in a studio environment in which multiple creative people share space and work together on the same or similar
projects, even the drawings one makes alone will at some point be "put
to the social," brought into a context where they are examined, critiqued,
described, accepted, or transformed.

While this analytical approach at first blush seems to decenter the will
and creativity of individual designers, that is not my intention. What I am
attempting to do instead is to locate the thrust of creative action not necessarily within individual designers, but in their patterns of talking, habits
of thought, and sociomaterially situated communicative techniques, all of
which operate in the studio with a causal pressure all their own. Guiding
this argument is the assumption that the small-scale interactional contexts
within which design objects are given form are "endogenously generated
within the talk of participants and, indeed, as something created in and
through that talk" (Heritage 1984:283) rather than in the midst of it. In
other words, the ingenuity responsible for creating objects, for giving them
forms—for giving them Swedish forms—is actively produced in the materially mediated communicative activities in which designers participate
while drafting and crafting their objects.

During my stay in Sweden I spent time at over ten different studios,
ranging from formal, corporate design firms to more informal spaces
shared by loosely organized design collectives. In nearly all of them the
same basic activity dominated everyday design work, an activity that Mag-
nus, half of the design duo Ons, described most succinctly: "We go to the
computer and stay there." While this commonly articulated self-reflection
is not entirely inaccurate, it does tend to obfuscate the complex patterns
of talk and task that together operate as the giving of forms to objects. In
what follows I present a snapshot of life in a studio I am calling Kontoret,
the studio run and managed by Peter and Matti (fig. 8). I use Kontoret as a
case study of how the quotidian social textures of on-the-ground designing
play out in Stockholm, and how from those textures—and I am selecting
only a few from the nearly infinite number of actions designers perform
in their work—the Swedish cultural geometry is instantiated in objects.
Different studios work differently, of course, and the specifics of how design interactions unfold in the Kontoret studio are not shared among all
designers in Sweden. But in conducting this deep dive case study I am
not forwarding a claim about the relationship between particular studio

Figure 8. Designers Matti (*left*) and Peter (*right*) in the studio, discussing and evaluating one of their designs. Photograph by the author.

dynamics and particular features of the Swedish cultural geometry. What I *am* doing is making the case that giving forms in design—refining, deliberating, changing, and preserving them—is not simply a matter of "choice" on the part of expert designers who may or may not "like" certain qualities over others, but is itself fundamentally shaped and conditioned by unrecognized and habituated patterns of interaction that in turn, beyond the wills of designers, result in a privileging of certain forms—in this case, those that match the cultural geometry—over many others. In this way the continued material reproduction of the cultural geometry need not be inextricably linked to the distinct tastes and proclivities of individual designers, but to the interactive work they do *with each other* as they actively create their objects.

Inside Kontoret

Upon my first visit to the Kontoret studio I was quite surprised to discover that it was, in fact, not my first visit there. During a pilot study I had undertaken two summers before, I had conducted my very first interview in this same space with Gunnar B., a friend and former colleague of the two designers, Peter and Matti, who now occupied the studio's central room. Since I had come into contact with Peter and Matti through completely different channels than I had with Gunnar, and since their work situation had changed since my last trip there—Gunnar and almost everyone else who once worked in the Kontoret space had moved out—I had not made the connection that this was the same place I had already been.

Little had changed outside the Kontoret studio, which occupied part of the basement of an apartment building near the edge of Södermalm. Like many of the studios I visited in Stockholm, Kontoret is not prominently marked. There are no signs anywhere indicating its location, and most residents in the neighborhood are probably unaware that there is a design studio in the building. To enter the place one opens a gate and squeezes past two Volvos almost always parked in the driveway in front of the building's gravel courtyard. After punching in a security code at the door—a ubiquitous practice for entering apartment buildings and offices in Sweden—one walks down a short, stone staircase and through a light blue metal door into the studio itself.

Inside, the air smells like coffee and soot. The walls are stark white cinder blocks, perfect for enhancing the sunlight that penetrates the basement through north- and south-facing windows, but the floor is newly refinished concrete; the space is clean but also clearly crafted for labor. The open room is arranged and decorated quite differently from the last time I had been there. In some ways it looks more professional than before, and in others it looks more bedraggled, with dust covering many surfaces, and signs of both remodeling and ongoing design work readily apparent. Still, it quite obviously remains a space for creativity. Contrary to the indistinct open plan I had seen on my previous visit, the studio is now divided into four separate work spaces plus a few other common areas and a workshop.

Directly to the left of the entrance lies a very simple green chaise lounge, in front of which sit a table and chairs designed by Peter. This area is intended for holding meetings or eating lunch, though I never saw anyone use the table for anything other than storage. Behind the table is a clean work area, in fact the cleanest work area in the place, which belongs to a textile designer who sublets some space in the studio. Because rents are high in Stockholm, designers are usually forced to pool resources and share studio space with other creative people, many of whom are not always working in the same specific industry sector. The space to the right of this area, cluttered with books, desks, chairs, and computer equipment, is occupied by a group of interior architects called Red, while a video artist named Jonas keeps a small work space in the back of the studio.

The central area of the Kontoret space belongs to Peter and Matti (fig. 9). The studio's main open area holds a long worktable shared by the two designers, which on first impression gives an inaccurate sense that they control the room as a whole. Each of them sits at one end. The table's surface is strewn with prototype lamps, scattered papers and catalogs, and some used and unused computer equipment. Small bookshelves hang on a nearby wall, filled with books as varied as *The Da Vinci Code* and design school catalogs, and bar-coded cardboard boxes and stacks of paper that probably have not been looked at in months, if not years. Two old keyboards, with no computers attached, rest on a shelf below, carefully positioned as if waiting for someone to use them, but long abandoned for more up-to-date equipment. Around the corner another set of bookshelves, full of art books and technical manuals, is mounted on the wall of a hallway

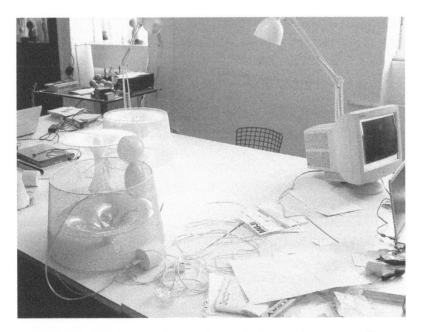

Figure 9. The central work space shared by Peter and Matti in the Kontoret studio.
Photograph by the author.

that leads to the bathroom and the workshop beyond. Some old stereo components, CDs, and still more computer equipment also rest on these shelves.

Behind Peter's end of the table is a small sitting area, with several pieces of furniture designed by the designers themselves, including chairs, a few lamps, a bench, and a table. This space looks the most complete and remodeled, and while it is more formal than any other area in the studio, during my time at Kontoret it was rarely used for more than watching World Cup soccer on a nearby TV brought out specifically for that purpose. The workshop sits in the very back of the studio. This is where prototypes are made and tools are stored. A large table saw looms against one wall, and random scraps of wood lie around in various corners. The room is dark, because it has no windows, and the air inside feels quite stale. A large pane of dark glass remains propped on its side in the rear of the workshop, untouched, waiting to be installed.

Finally, in the studio proper, floating between the entrance area and the space used by Peter and Matti, is a small kitchen that was slowly under construction during my time at Kontoret. Calling it a kitchen is generous, actually, as it is more of a tabletop hung between two load-bearing columns, but as a kitchen it serves its purpose well enough. The tabletop holds a small sink with a drainage pipe that empties into an open drain in the floor, while a coffeemaker—the most important piece of equipment in any Swedish workplace—and cups, plates, and bags of ground coffee are scattered next to the sink. The kitchen's exposed electrical wiring is more improvised than elegant—high above, a power strip dangles over a set of tubes that stretch across the ceiling, its cord draping over the counter and down to a second, larger orange industrial power source whose much thicker cable reaches over to one of the studio's properly installed electrical outlets. Functional, but not quite aesthetically pleasing.

Peter and Matti, the Designers of Kontoret Studio

In many ways Peter and Matti are typical examples of successful, independent furniture designers in Sweden. They do not work directly for a large company like Ikea. As freelancers they manage and run their own small businesses (*egna företag* in Swedish), creating new designs on a contract basis for various furniture and lighting producers, and they often share various assignments by collaborating with other designers, especially each other. They are well known within the world of Swedish furniture design, and they even have a reputation in Japan, but neither is a national or international superstar.

As with most designers, success did not immediately greet Peter and Matti, and it took them several years to get their reputations off the ground and their businesses functioning to the degree that they could in fact make a living off the products they design. Indeed, for many designers the years following college graduation involve working some other job, either for an architecture or design firm or outside the design field entirely, in order to support their own design endeavors (see chapter 3). But the hard work pays off, and both Peter and Matti have been recognized multiple times with different prestigious awards for their design work. Moreover, in addition to appearing in temporary design exhibits in Scandinavia and beyond, some of their pieces are now part of the permanent collections of major art museums in Sweden.

Peter has lived in Stockholm since the mid-1990s. He originally comes from Skåne, in southern Sweden, and while his accent has dulled during his time in the capital, his Skånska dialect is still detectable when he speaks. After five years at Konstfack Peter graduated with a master's degree in 1999, having studied in the Department of Interior Architecture and Furniture Design. Upon graduation he established the OUR design studio on Södermalm, along with several of his Konstfack colleagues, including Matti. While this group of designers all worked in the same studio, and they often collaborated with one another on projects, each designer operated as an independent freelancer. The reputations of OUR's members grew simultaneously within the Stockholm design world, and in 2002 Svensk Form, the organization charged by the state to promote design in Sweden, put up an exhibition of some of the work done by the OUR collective. The group continued working independently and collaboratively until 2005, when, after ten years together, including their time at Konstfack, the collective dissolved, soon after moving to a new location on Södermalm. By all accounts the split was friendly and ultimately necessary. "We needed some change in our lives," said Peter. "No hard feelings at all." Several of the designers began working from home, and Peter and Matti stayed in the second Södermalm studio, which today houses Kontoret.

Peter has won many awards for his work. In 2005 a chair he designed called Tilt, whose rear legs are rockers to facilitate leaning back and balancing, won Product of the Year from *Sköna Hem*, one of Sweden's largest popular home-decorating magazines. Before graduating from Konstfack he twice won Svensk Form's Ung Svensk Form (Young Swedish Design) award for designers still early in their career, and soon after took their Utmärkt Svensk Form (Excellent Swedish Design) award. Thanks in part to the skills that helped him achieve this acclaim, he was asked to share the position of head of the Form Department at Beckmans Design College from 2003 to 2006, and in 2006 became a senior lecturer at Konstfack.

Peter specializes in chairs, sofas, and lighting, but also designs tables and small household items, and he has occasionally worked on some retail interiors. Almost all of Peter's designs reflect a "typical" Swedish cultural geometry, including shapes, colors, and materials. Wooden chairs and tables are often colored in single, basic shades, and their lines are generally straight—and when they are not, they are simple, organic curves. The most unique quality of Peter's work is a single playful element, "a twist towards the unordinary and the unexpected," as he himself proclaims, that is immediately apparent when one looks at or uses the object. When I first saw the Tilt chair, for instance, the residual child inside me was almost magnetically drawn to it, craving to sit in it, lean back, and prop my feet up on a nearby table. Similarly his Solidarity chair, otherwise ordinary but for the extrawide seat that can accommodate a sitting partner, inviting a sitter to grab a friend and take a rest together. Both of these chairs draw from a long tradition of design in Sweden in that they are simply designed, uncluttered, and functional, though they also offer a comment on that very tradition, a contemporary attitude built into the form itself.

Like Peter, Matti has lived in Stockholm since the 1990s. Born in Gothenburg, he graduated from Konstfack in the same class as Peter in 1999, also having studied furniture design and interior architecture. Immediately after finishing he started working at an architecture firm, which gave him a taste of how it feels to work as one employee among many in a large company. Because he had studied furniture making, he was often tasked with working on the interiors of buildings, which entailed more graphics work than actual designing, and he sketched his own products only in whatever free time he could find, collaborating with Peter when he could. In 2000 the head of Beckmans College of Design asked him to chair the

Form Department there, a position he later shared with Peter, which then freed up time for Matti to concentrate on establishing his own studio. This position was quite ideal. It came prepackaged with important contacts in the furniture industry, and because the job commitments were not strictly set as with most full-time jobs, Matti could use his more flexible schedule to begin growing his business, largely funded by the money he earned by teaching. Indeed, by supplementing his studio work, the income he earned over the six years he served as department head at Beckmans crucially helped him to attain a level of exposure within the design field at which he can now live comfortably from his designs.

Like Peter, Matti has also won many awards for his work. His lighting designs have been especially successful, including his Droplight and his Kampoor lamp, which was awarded best product at the Stockholm Furniture Fair in 2003 by *Forum*, one of Sweden's biggest architecture and design magazines. In addition to some work grants, he was, like Peter, awarded the Ung Svensk Form and Utmärkt Svensk Form awards early in his career.

Matti primarily designs lamps, chairs, and sofas, but also works with tables and glass pieces. His products are in many ways quite traditionally Scandinavian. Their colors are stark and solid, and their forms are dominated by the Swedish cultural geometry. Most of his lamps and chairs are unadorned and functional, often with a playful element, though not in the same way as Peter's products. The two designers do possess a similar style, no doubt cultivated through years of collaboration, and some of the products they design together are often difficult to distinguish from those each designs on his own.

The Social Life and Work inside the Studio

Overall the topography of Kontoret is a mixture of creative chaos and high design chic. Prototypes of the lamps and chairs that the designers have made are scattered throughout the studio, neatly arranged in the sitting area or leaning upright against a wall, even hunched stranded in a corner under a pile of forgotten plastic wrap or sheets of paper. These design objects themselves lend an air of sophistication to the place. In contrast, though, the tools of the trade used in the reality of everyday designing leave a small tornado's worth of minor storm damage to the sections of the studio most used for working. This is not to say that the designers of Kontoret are messy, but that the studio, unlike the pristine shops and galleries that the general public is usually exposed to when confronted with design, is fundamentally a place for labor, not for display.

Activity in the Kontoret studio wavers between frenetic momentum and near-absolute silence punctuated only by the sound of mouse clicks and unconsciously tapping feet. Peter and Matti tend to work alone at their own ends of the table, but they also often interrupt each other's isolation with questions or comments about particular projects, sometimes twisting a monitor or laptop around so the other can evaluate a sketch. At any given time they are working on multiple assignments at once, some of which are collaborations, and others that are projects all their own, and the work of each day is often split among tasks related to various projects, each of which is at a different stage of development. They make phone calls, some personal and others professional, and scan the Internet for information about materials and inspiration for new projects. When they are working on prototypes, the designers may move back and forth between their desks and the workshop, occasionally asking for advice or evaluation as the prototype is formed. They may even leave the studio for long periods of time to run personal errands or purchase necessities for the job.

Much of the interaction that goes on in the studio is highly social. Joking around and gossiping about mutual acquaintances are common. When I first started to interact with designers at the beginning of my project, everyone stressed that the vast majority of the workday for a designer is spent doing very boring things like checking e-mail, drinking coffee, making phone calls, and chitchatting with colleagues. Very little time is spent actually *designing* things, they insisted. I was warned over and over again that, contrary to my expectations of a day full of deep and intellectual meetings about the objects being created, the everyday life of a designer is in fact quite prosaic and dull. While I would probably use a different set of words to describe what most designers do, it is indeed true that most of the time the Kontoret studio is a calm and quiet place.

Long periods of time can go by without a word uttered. This does not mean that the studio operates in complete silence, however. Aside from the professional and personal conversations that regularly puncture the workday tranquility, the sounds of Kontoret are mostly artificial—the pitter-patter of a computer mouse moving across the table, the syncopated push of a document through a printer, the tinny clink of teaspoons on ceramic mugs, and the rubbery squeak of sneakers on concrete. Sometimes music plays over the studio's stereo system, primarily controlled through Matti's computer, usually current popular independent rock bands from Sweden and abroad. And every once in a while a woman from a cleaning service shows up and without a word begins vacuuming the floor and straightening up the space.

The Micro-Mechanics of Designing in Action

When designers come into contact with one another, sitting or standing in front of a computer monitor or sketch, confronting what they see as *a design to be dealt with*, they are faced with a compulsion either to accept or change, or at the very least comment on, the current state of a design, even if just for the time being. There are many different kinds of assessment points: sometimes designers ask for advice directly, sometimes they simply turn a laptop or monitor around for others to see—an implicit request for evaluation—and sometimes they offer one another unsolicited advice. They may grab a pen and start tracing their own ideas, either in another designer's notebook or on a nearby piece of scrap paper, or point to a particular feature on the screen and identify it as "nice" and worth keeping. In such minor motions, when designers come into the most immediate contact with an emergent design—with various representations, materials, and technologies that together call a design into being—is where form giving thrives most comfortably. Amid this conversational push and pull, where certain ideas and forms are highlighted and others are ignored, where one designer's preferences and tastes are matched with another's, and where sketches and visions can live or die, lines of visibility precariously emerge, always skimming the surface of design interactions regardless of the objects under consideration. In other words, forms are not necessarily always *given* by designers in a strict sense, but are often coaxed, prodded, and nudged into existence by a performative force that sustains the social-technical and communicative organization of studio design work itself.

Order-Words

Working from John Austin's (1962) theory of performativity, Deleuze and Guattari (1987) offer a framework for understanding how the dynamics of social interaction underwrite particular form-giving practices in the studio. Like Austin they center their theory of pragmatics on a notion of force, arguing that the natural state of language—all language, not just overtly "performative" utterances—is suffused with the capacity to move people, to simultaneously bring them together and push them apart, and "to claim and ascribe places in a power game" (Lecercle 2002:169). From this perspective meaning is subordinate to the impulse of language to exact effects on the social world. Force here has a double sense: it is both an underlying causal influence, as in physics, and a kind of violence produced as a function of social power. From Deleuze and Guattari's perspective, the syntactic and semantic aspects of language, while undoubtedly significant, have been accorded too much authority in linguistic theory. Their model, in contrast, rather than focusing on *language-in-use*, is more deeply concerned with the *use-of-language*, with the ways in which speakers manipulate social conditions, intentionally or unintentionally, in their acts of speaking. The difference between what they propose and other pragmatic theories is subtle, but important: various structural relations that adhere in language are not strictly system-internal but immanently and causally subsist in the world of social relations, and the composition of those relations is always one of emergence and transformation rather than stasis (indeed, the manifestation of seemingly stable forms and relations is a result of machinic processes that render them as such). From this point of view, language is not so much an "instrument" that speakers use "in" the world—though it is very difficult to avoid this sort of spatialized utilitarian phrasing—but is instead a kind of fibrous connective tissue continuously pushing and pulling, shaping and reshaping, the social body. Language is not an independent system brought into the social, but is instead always vitally embedded within it, a channel of forces that helps give shape to its emergent form and propel that form, indiscriminately, along.

For Deleuze and Guattari (1987) all language is comprised of elementary units that they call "order-words." The double meaning of "order" in this phrasing is intentional: these are words that *order* in the sense of "arrange" as well as *order* in the sense of "command" (in French the term is *mots d'ordre*, which carries the same double sense as in English, though the phrase also has the colloquial meaning of "slogan" or "motto"). Order-words—which again are the elemental building blocks of all language—in their uttering exert a force that both organizes relations between subjects, positioning various parties against, around, or alongside one another, and compels subjects to fashion their subsequent thoughts and actions in particular ways. They are in some aspects akin to Austin's (1962) performative speech acts, but not as restrictive:

> We call *order-words*, not a particular category of explicit statements (for example, in the imperative), but the relation of every word or every statement to implicit presuppositions, in other words, to speech acts that are, and can only be, accomplished in the statement. Order-words do not concern commands only, but every act that is linked to statements by a "social obligation." Every statement displays this link, directly or indirectly. Questions, promises, are order-words. The only possible definition of language is the set of all order-words, implicit presuppositions, or speech acts current in a language at a given moment. (Deleuze and Guattari 1987:79)

Deleuze and Guattari concur with Austin that "illocutionary" utterances exert a force that leaves certain consequential effects on the world. Where they differ from speech act theory, however, is in their understanding of the nature and location of the illocutionary. For them the illocutionary is immanent in all utterances. It is what "constitutes the nondiscursive" (77), calling forth "implicit presuppositions" about the social world and linking them to current circumstances. All utterances are specific social acts that ensnare speakers in configurations of obligation—even if that obligation is simply to somehow respond, though often it is much more—while at the same time transforming the social terrain by specifying how subjects and "subjectification proceedings" are distributed. The very act of speaking—not just certain kinds of utterances in certain situations—is to engage in ordering procedures that both position subjects (and other things) in relation to one another and the rest of the social world and compel those subjects (and other things) to comport themselves in particular ways. This positioning and control can take many forms and intensities, ranging from the minute and relatively innocuous give-and-take of everyday conversation to the politically charged repercussions of targeted hate speech, but in all cases the ordering force of language is its most critical feature.

The force of order-words operates in at least two "tones," what Therese Grisham (1991) recasts as their "limitative" and "expansive" modes. The limitative tone of "the order-word is a death sentence; it always implies a death sentence, even if it has been considerably softened, becoming symbolic, initiatory, temporary, etc." (Deleuze and Guattari 1987:107). This mode of force tends to *prevent* progression and *impede* agency. It slows kinetic movement to a crawl, or stops it altogether. It is a force that says, "Halt." The expansive tone, in contrast, "is like a warning cry or a message to flee" (107). This mode of force incites *flight* and movement away or forward or onward. It is a force that is immanent in what Deleuze and Guattari (110) call "pass-words," "words that pass, words that are components of passage" rather than "stoppages or organized, stratified compositions." It is a force that says, "Proceed."

When the force of order-words (and pass-words) is exerted, it produces particular effects that Deleuze and Guattari call "incorporeal transformations." Order-words do not necessarily impact bodies in any way when they are uttered (though of course they can); however, they do transform relations, conditions, attitudes, orientations, and lines of power. These transformations are incorporeal but nonetheless materially consequential to the textures of relations between subjects, circumstances, and the surrounding world. As Deleuze and Guattari (1987:80–81) explain, an instantaneous proclamation by a judge "transforms the accused into a convict" without in any way affecting the bodies of the parties involved (unlike the original transgression, the arrest, the eventual imprisonment, etc.). Similarly they argue that passengers on a commercial airliner undergo incorporeal transformations into "hostages" (and the jet into a "prison") when a hijacker first brandishes a weapon. To be sure, participants may also undergo embodied transformations—sweat, blood, and so on—but the becoming of a new kind of subject is produced and effected without the need of any physical changes of state.

Design interactions in which objects are given forms by their designers are largely organized as overlapping sequences of order-words and pass-words—that is, as interactively arrayed utterances that structure form giving through an intricate meshwork of communicative pushes, pulls, and positionings that continuously result in an emergent design. As order-words, some utterances exert a force that pushes a design in a certain direction and limits its trajectory—a suggestion to make a line longer, for instance, or to think about an object's functionality in a new way. Order-words also help lay bare relations between designers as they work, compelling particular configurations of their work, and even their bodies, within the studio space. As pass-words, some utterances exert a force that pushes potentially competing design ideas aside, which allows for others to survive, persist, and proceed—for instance, a simple comment that a designer "likes" a curved surface or color choice, or even simply *not objecting* to some new idea.

Inscriptions

While order-words and pass-words entail particular incorporeal transformations of the abstract overall design of an object—an object that does not yet possess a coherent and cohesive material form of its own—they also create specific corporeal transformations of both the technical media used to fabricate a design, and the designers who control the process. Everyday design work is largely comprised of interlocking practices that produce and are mediated by different kinds of inscriptions. This, of course, includes the kinds of marks left behind that one would expect to find in a design studio: leaded lines traced with pencils on white paper, and printouts of objects first rendered on the computer, sometimes upgraded with their own hand-drawn markings. But there are also others. Most sketching and drawing today is done onscreen with computer-aided design (CAD) software—a suite called Rhinoceros 3D, or Rhino, was the program of choice for most designers I worked with, including the designers of Kontoret—the use of which in some ways overlaps with, and in other ways diverges sharply from, traditional hand-sketching. Lines and shapes can be drawn on the computer with Rhino in ways that mimic the ease of hand sketching, but drawings in Rhino also offer their own affordances. For instance, they are infinitely and instantly manipulable. A designer can duplicate, stretch, shrink, or delete a shape with a single mouse click, and because such programs render drawings in three dimensions, the objects designers create are virtually viewable from any angle, even as they are emerging.

But I would also like to add more kinds of inscriptions to the mix. Sketches on paper and lines digitally rendered on a computer monitor do not subsist in the studio as independent artifacts, as the most obvious visible evidence of designerly knowledge. Alongside these inscriptions designers use other sorts of inscriptions, embodied movements and gestures that not only act as "a mode of critical testimony," in Boyer's (2005a:260) terms, displaying and enacting particular kinds of designerly knowledge, but also critically push designs along—an extended index finger circling a well-regarded detail, hands held aloft to model the proportions of a lamp shade, or prototype forms carved from foam or shaped in flexible plastic. Even casual verbal descriptions of possible design solutions leave their marks on design trajectories. While such actions might not fit a traditional notion of inscription that stems from writing, they nonetheless retain some similar evocative qualities. In many instances inscription addresses what Ricoeur (1976:26) calls the "problem of fixation," the need to make permanent otherwise ephemeral phenomena. As such, it bears an ontological status directly opposed to the fleeting nature of uncontrolled speech and other kinds of action, a form that perdures across moments of time. But the permanence of inscription is in some ways its least interesting aspect, and certainly cannot be its defining characteristic. After all, a child's name quickly drawn in the sand is no less an inscription because an incoming wave immediately washes it away. What is more critical to inscription is the capacity to leave marks itself, regardless of how permanent those marks may be, and the repercussions they might bring. Inscriptions such as lines drawn in ink or even on a computer screen are marks left behind in some medium, the residue of actions that preceded their existence. But they also serve socially meaningful purposes for designers looking to perform ongoing action, constituting some of the most basic tools of production available to them. As such, inscriptions operate as sociotechnical instruments not simply because they preserve traces of action and knowledge, but because they at the same time incite further action and generate further knowledge.

While hand gestures, embodied enactments, and certainly verbal utterances tend not to leave marks in some material medium, that does not mean they do not leave marks. I am calling these actions, along with their more traditional counterparts, *perlocutionary inscriptions*, to highlight the implications of this capacity. In Austin's (1962:101) terms, *perlocutionary* refers to the "consequential effects upon feelings, thoughts, or actions of the audience, or of the speaker, or of other persons." In other words, perlocutionary effects are changes and revisions in the social world, potentially both small scale and broad, that result directly or indirectly from the use of talk in context.[2] Typically scholars have treated perlocutionary effects as predominantly immaterial (or incorporeal, in Deleuze and Guattari's words), impacting thoughts or emotions more than the things of the world. However the effects of talk—all kinds of talk—can indeed be quite material and visible when language is systematically treated not simply as words, but as Schön (1984, 1985) has argued in the context of designing, as a materially mediated social interplay between speakers, material objects, speech, and moving bodies.

Hand gestures and utterances do leave marks on the incorporeal abstraction of an emergent design. If only by degree, they influence the conception of a design that designers share by calling attention to a given element and describing it or redescribing it in a particular way. Every time a designer utters the phrase "It could be . . ." or "Let's try . . . ," the horizon of possibilities expands; every time he shakes his head at a suggestion, or draws a line through a sketch and turns the notebook page, the horizon of possibilities contracts. But these fleeting gestures and casual utterances do indeed leave material marks, too, though not always in obvious or immediate ways. Indeed form giving is fundamentally centered on the asymmetrical accumulation of all sorts of perlocutionary inscriptions made by designers—and for each other—in the studio, the outcome of various ordering practices that produce the gradual fixation of forms in various media, culminating in a final object.

"What do snowmen look like?" Matti asked the room one day, laughing as he posed his question. The candleholder that he and Peter were designing, the one mentioned at the start of the chapter, was supposed to look like a winter landscape scene filled with gently rolling hills and small mounds of snow. One of the features they had considered including was a small snowman figure, which could potentially be used to extinguish the candles. At the start of the project—several days before Peter would make the foam prototype—Matti decided to try his hand at drawing a snowman on the computer. But there was a problem: he could not remember what a snowman looks like. Upon hearing Matti's question Peter immediately reacted with laughter of his own and dismissed his partner with a loud "Naah," apparently not believing that Matti could forget such a familiar form. The two designers, the intern, and the anthropologist then sat without words for several seconds, while Matti stared pensively out the window. Perhaps moved by the silence to speak, Peter finally responded, "It can, you know, look another way." But still unable to escape his disbelief, he then quickly uttered the tautology, "It can, you know, look like a snowman. It's just like this." He then held his two hands up in the air, and with his index fingers extended, he slowly traced out the shape of a traditional snowman, each finger taking on a vertical half: one small circle with a larger circle underneath and a third even larger circle under that. A gestural trace. But Matti was not impressed with what he saw. "But it isn't as fun," he said, "or it isn't as nice." Nonetheless, later that day when I glanced over at his screen again, a small traditional snowman mostly matching what Peter had inscribed in the air stood, lonely, in the corner of Matti's drawing.

Of course Peter's snowman gesture did not compel Matti in any direct sense to draw a similar form in Rhino. But his gestural inscription, and its placement in time, did exert a real ordering effect on the slow progress of the unfolding candleholder. The designers had already settled on experimenting with the snowman figure, but this was an abstract choice: the figure still required a form. Matti's query, then, was the initiation of a form-giving sequence, a request for raw formal materials to work, manipulate, and tinker with in pursuit of fabricating a "nice" design feature, and the snowman traced by Peter temporarily sufficed. In fact it remained in digital form as part of the design for several days, always visible on the Rhino file, drawn near the candleholder but placed just outside the frame. The designers eventually abandoned the snowman in the final version of the candleholder, but even after doing so they still made a small figure for the prototype, an homage to an old idea.

This is embodied designing in its barest guise. It is performative form giving through the progressive accretion of stepwise suggestions and ideas proffered by designers interactionally engaged with their tools and, crucially, with each other. Over time iterative, punctuated utterances and inscriptions culminate as a cohesive series of outcomes that together grant forms to a designed object. A single sentence, gesture, or click may in itself seem inconsequential in isolation, but embedded within a context in which each serves to impact the trajectory of a larger process, even if only by degree, they all become significant for the doing of design. The inscriptions that underlie this process do enact a kind of agency, but this agency is not embedded in the inscriptions themselves, or their constitutive materials. Rather it subsists in the specific linguistically mediated courses of action in which designers put inscriptions to use. In other words, the capacity of order-words and perlocutionary inscriptions to produce knowledge and motivate design work is entirely predicated by the particularities of their conditions of use—the ways they are talked about, looked at, and gestured toward; the ways they are reappropriated, redescribed, and reevaluated; the sequentially ordered points in time they are taken up; the larger social flows in which they operate; and even the ways in which they become entangled with grammatical structures and patterns of talk.

If the diagram of Swedish design is redrawn and cultivated by multiple forces independently operating on its various elements, one of the most critical for preserving lines of visibility is precisely the performative force that routinely keeps the cultural geometry in play through the order-words and perlocutionary inscriptions that organize design in action. What I will do now is turn to three interactional frameworks, three patterned ways of talking through and embodying emerging designs in the studio. These frameworks—and again, these are just a few among many—are unrecognized by designers but nonetheless pervasively organize and motivate the work they do through particular order-words, pass-words, and perlocutionary inscriptions that contribute to the ongoing reproduction and conservation of the cultural geometry in the very barest moments of form giving.

Selecting and Preserving: The Formal Calculus

As the formal features of designed objects move from ideas to drawings to material objects in the design process, they face some significant inherent constraints. A chair, for instance, must possess a surface for sitting in order to fulfill its primary function, whereas a knife should be able to cut, and a bed should offer a plane—hopefully a comfortable one—on which a body can recline. Whereas designers who create objects that explicitly challenge conventional functions and traditional forms might be able to eschew some of these constraints, most designers drafting market objects for popular consumption are compelled to work within them.

Beyond basic limitations entailed in the nature of an object's function, however, the forms a new object can take are, in theory, infinitely open for innovation and experimentation. This of course assumes that an assignment given to the designers by a manufacturer does not specify any formal requirements. While some design briefs are very precise, most are not, and while a client's aesthetic preferences may come out during casual conversations, designers are generally granted a tremendous amount of freedom in creating and refining the look and feel of their objects. That is, after all, what they are paid for. I say this freedom exists "in theory," though, because despite the abstract sense of utter autonomy engendered by the creativity that motivates the design profession, designers are in fact faced with very real regulatory structures constraining and channeling the work they do, even at the smallest level of detail.

The routine ways in which particular forms are verbally and gesturally inscribed in design interactions, and the ways they are evaluated and those evaluations are applied to drawings, are one of the strongest forces selecting and preserving the cultural geometry in mundane design work. Amid their casual discussion of a drawing or proposals for new ideas, the Kontoret designers regularly invoke a kind of formal calculus, a logical-rhetorical structure realized verbally and nonverbally, as an instrument for reckoning the physical qualities, like size and shape, of an object. This formal calculus is arranged as a set of order-words and pass-words that delimits a range of possible stylistic choices, which then allows the designers to set the basic forms of their objects, which themselves in turn serve as the foundation of all subsequent design choices.

The prominent formal calculus at play in the Kontoret studio relies on an opposition between squares and angles on the one hand, and roundness—and its surrogate quality, softness—on the other. These qualities are routinely rhetorically positioned as self-evidently opposite formal categories, though in theory this need not always be the case, since other forms could also act as the "opposite" of either squares or curves. In some objects the two properties may be combined, but in most cases they usually cancel one another out. In practice, if a designer does not want a design to reflect one of these qualities, the formal calculus, patterned in a contrapuntal configuration, has the practical effect of projecting the opposite quality—and only the opposite quality—into the design. In other words, the logic works as follows: if not square, then rounded; if not rounded, then square; and all other variables are left out of the equation.

On one occasion Peter was instructing Fredrik, the Kontoret intern, how to go about designing a soap dish and a jewelry bowl, both of which would be part of a matching set of items for the bathroom. At this point in their conversation, Peter was concerned in particular with the shape of the jewelry bowl:[3]

Peter.   Det—det skulle i princep—princip
            It—it would in thea—theory
            kunna va som tvålkoppen.
            be able to be like the soap dish.
Fredrik.   Mm.
            Uh huh.
Peter.   Fast (.) kanske tvålkoppen skulle ha
            Although (.) maybe the soap dish would have
            en (.) rektangulär form,
            a (.) rectangular shape,
Fredrik.   Mm.
            Uh huh.
Peter.   som en tvål. Och den smyckeskålen skulle va rund.
            like a bar of soap. And the jewelry bowl would be round.
Fredrik.   Mm.
            Uh huh.

Peter had not yet decided on the shape of either the soap dish or the jewelry bowl, so he was talking through his ideas with Fredrik. He claimed that the jewelry bowl could look like the soap dish, which would have a rectangular shape inspired by a bar of soap, but its overall shape, in contrast to the soap dish, would be round. Within this framework the two objects would "be like" one another, with the main distinguishing characteristic being their different overall forms—one rectangular, and the other round. Peter used the formal calculus, which opposes square shapes with round shapes, as the very basis for visually differentiating two objects that are, in large part, functionally similar, in that they both *contain* material. In setting up this opposition, Peter's formulation precluded other potential shapes—a triangular bowl, for instance, or a heptagonal soap dish—from making their way into Fredrik's sketches.

On another day Matti and Peter were evaluating one portion of a computer drawing of a diaper-changing table they were designing, and trying to decide how exactly to sculpt the table's edges. Matti did not particularly

like the idea of rounding the edges, which he had drawn for one version
of the table, both at the request of the company and in order to make more
room for accompanying features:

> Matti.   Jag vill inte att den ska va rund där uppe.
>   *I don't want it to be round up there.*
>   Jag tycker den är rätt fint att den är fyrkantig. Men—
>   *I think it's quite nice that it's square. But—*
> Peter.   Ah ja.
>   *That's right.*

Matti here used the formal calculus as a framework for simultaneously expressing and explaining his preference for this design detail. He counter-
posed his lack of desire for rounded edges with his opinion that the square
shape is "quite nice." While Matti does, in fact, use square shapes in his
work regularly, he is by no means antagonistic to using roundness in the
objects he designs. Indeed, when pushing for roundness in a design detail he often employs the formal calculus to counteract an object's square-
ness. By continuously pitting squares against curves, the formal calculus
provides a ready-made alternative to both qualities—if the designer does
not like the way a square object looks, he makes it round; and if it does not
look good round, he makes it square.

This metric is indeed very conservative and reductionist. At the same
time it is itself quite efficient and free of noise, and its simplicity affords
the designers closer attention to other, more complex facets of the larger
design scheme. As useful as the formal calculus might be, however, op-
erationalizing it in design activities has the effect of perpetuating two core
components of the Swedish cultural geometry and hindering formal innovation on a very basic level. This is not to say that the designers are
compelled to use either squares or curves in their designs, but rather that
the virtual interchangeability of these two categories has the practical effect of limiting alternative formal solutions in the progression of the design *when the formal calculus is invoked*. Given the relative frequency with
which the formal calculus is indeed invoked in design interactions, these
two forms—squares and curves—end up as the core aesthetic norms reflected in the objects produced at Kontoret.

One correlate to how the formal calculus is used in design interactions is the implication or assumption that the physical quality of roundness functions as a proxy for the expression of *softness* in an object (see Murphy 2012). When the designers discuss drafting round design elements, or transforming square ones into round ones, it is often explicitly in the service of "softening" features that would otherwise express harshness—though they never explicitly treat squares and angles as harsh.

Matti was showing Peter his latest version of the changing table. He swiveled his monitor around for Peter to see, and he manipulated the changing table image as he spoke:

Matti. Jag har mjukat upp allting.
       I've softened everything up.
Peter. Mmm.
       Mmhm.
Matti. Det var lätt.
       It was easy.
       (1.0)
Peter. Ah det var inte fel.
       Yeah, that wasn't wrong.
       (2.0)
Matti. De snackar ju mycket om att allt ska va sådär rundat.
       They talk a lot about how everything should be rounded like that.
Peter. Ja::. (2.0) Det känns som Leksam.
       Yes::. (2.0) It feels like Leksam.

Matti had "softened" the edges of the changing table, which he was showing to Peter, because Leksam,[4] the company they were designing the table for, talked "a lot about how everything should be rounded." In this exchange Matti drew a practical equivalence between rounding the edges of the table and softening it up, working on the assumption that rounding the edges produces a self-evidently "soft" expression. Softness is treated by the designers as a comfortable attribute, one that evokes a more humanistic connection between the user and the object. Leksam is well known in Sweden for producing high-quality toys and furniture for children. For Peter and Matti to design the table with more organic, comfortable contours is one way for the company to demonstrate that their product cares for the user—first and foremost, a small child, but of course parents, too—since the ostensibly harsh edges of a square design would, in theory, hurt more in accidental situations. By attributing softness to the curved surfaces, the designers make their object more inviting to delicate users.

On another day Matti was working on the legs of a coffee table that, as a sparse rectangle, he suspected might be a little "too simple." Peter suggested that Matti angle the legs more to give the table more character. After about twenty minutes toiling away redrawing the legs, which could only be reangled slightly for structural reasons, Matti suggested making the angle a curve to give the table more softness.

> ((As Matti speaks, he moves his hands up and down in the air in front of him, tracing the contours of the kinds of curved legs he is envisioning.))
>
> Matti. Om det är en sån liten vinkel, det kan ju va att
> *If it's such a small angle, it can be that*
> man bara gör dem riktigt mjuka böjarna,
> *you just make them really soft curves,*
> så det verkligen [släpar så.
> *so it actually [trails like this.*
> Peter.   [Mm. ((nodding))
>   *[Yeah.*
> Matti. Det kan ju va rätt fint (.) att det blir mer (.) sån (.) mjukhet i det.
> *It can be quite nice (.) if it gets more (.) of that (.) softness in it.*
> Peter. Mm.
> *Yeah.*

Matti explained to Peter that the newly positioned legs would have only a "small angle," which, after having sketched several options, he would like to replace with "really soft curves." He repeatedly demonstrated to Peter what he meant by using his hands to inscribe in the air the curve of the legs he was drawing. This solution would be "quite nice" according to Matti because it contributes "softness" to the design.

Here again squares are rhetorically positioned as opposite candidate solutions to roundness, or in this instance, curves. The legs of the original sketch hit the tabletop at right angles, which Matti assessed as "too simple" (not transcribed here). This prompted Peter to suggest "angling" the legs, though how exactly that should be done was left up to Matti, and Matti instead turned to designing curved bends in the legs precisely because it evokes softness. While Peter's suggestion to angle the legs deviated from the formal calculus by pushing for nonright angles in the design, Matti nonetheless gravitated toward roundness as the formal alternative to his initial rectangular design.

The initial ideas designers come up with and sketch out in a notebook or on a computer screen are filtered through embodied design interactions that all in various ways serve as regulatory checks that monitor the flow of an idea from its origins to its end point in a final drawing or prototype. Within most design interactions there is little, if any, explicit debate about breaking free of the formal calculus by which the typical physical aspects of Swedish design are reckoned. Instead, discussions largely circulate around which features to upgrade and which ones to downgrade in any given object. During the design process the cultural geometry is treated as taken-for-granted fact—not as one portion of an infinitely expansive realm of formal possibilities, but as actually constituting the entirety of the field itself. I am not arguing that designers do not think about formal alternatives to the cultural geometry as they design their objects, but rather that how the formal calculus is operationalized in design interactions affords a dominant preference for squares and simple roundness—configured together or as "either/or" alternatives—and this practical opposition has the effect of preventing other solutions from entering the discussion. The implication of this is that linguistically mediated design interactions significantly order the reproduction of the cultural geometry by publicly displaying—and simultaneously rendering participants accountable to—the formal calculus as a taken-for-granted system used for explaining, justifying, and understanding design choices.

Assessing and Approving: The Evaluative Matrix

Much of the work accomplished in form giving in the Kontoret studio hinges on making assessments of one's own designs or, more often, of the sketches produced by the other designers. While these assessments can take many forms and can focus on a range of qualities displayed in the drawing—from its overall look or feeling all the way down to the pitch of a curved edge—the designers often frame their broad evaluations with a small set of generalized positive and negative assessors, which together constitute a dominant evaluative matrix. This matrix consists of four quadrants, each concerned with an object's (or feature's) positive or negative valuation in either its aesthetic (material) or expressive (affective) qualities. Take, for instance, the following exchange in which Matti presented a sketch of a table to Peter for evaluation:

Matti.	Peppe?
	Pete?
Peter.	Ja?
	Yes?
	(3.0)
	((Matti turns his screen toward Peter.))
	((Peter and Matti stare at the screen, as Matti turns the image for 10 secs.))
Matti.	Lite roligt!
	A little fun!
Peter.	Ja visst.
	It sure is.

After turning his monitor around so that Peter could see the sketch he had made, which included several versions of the table in different colors, Matti manipulated the image on the screen so that Peter could see the objects rendered from multiple perspectives. After doing this Matti offered an evaluation of his own sketch, "Lite roligt" (A little fun), and Peter immediately agreed. The word Matti used to describe the table, *roligt* (fun, pleasant), is very common in Swedish. It is not typically used to make aesthetic evaluations specifically, but rather most often describes a feeling of amusement or entertainment evoked by a person, an object, a story, or a situation. Similarly, the word *kul*, (fun) is also typically used to characterize a range of phenomena as interesting or amusing, and the designers frequently use it when talking about their designs. When Peter and Matti finished the prototype of the candleholder shaped like a snowy landscape, Peter suggested including footprints in the snow: "Can't we have footprints?" he asked. "Just because it's fun."

These two adjectives, *roligt* and *kul*, both of which cast their accompanying nouns as somehow "fun," form one positive quadrant in the designers' evaluative matrix, a logical-rhetorical structure they often use to link simple, positive expressive qualities to positive aesthetic evaluations, often without directly commenting on the aesthetics themselves. Notice that these assessments do not specifically concern aesthetic qualities. Rather they characterize the design in a generalized framework of affect, what the design evokes in the viewer or the user.

This positive quadrant is structurally opposed to another pair of adjectives frequently invoked to negatively evaluate the expressive qualities of a design—*tråkigt* (boring) and *dumt* (dumb). Thus, when Matti attempted to persuade Peter and Fredrik that a small table he had drawn was not very good, he repeatedly described it as "boring," using the descriptor *tråkigt* three times within four turns at talk to frame the table's form as explicitly not fun, not *roligt*. Similarly the designers will also describe an idea or design as "dumb" when they observe a problem with an object's form or function. For the changing table they were designing, Matti and Peter decided to integrate the tabletop with storage boxes and the table's legs in some innovative way, but that proved to be somewhat complicated. Just as Matti was about to propose a new solution, he cut himself off, described his idea as "dumb," and said they "really ought to" stick with their original arrangement:

Matti.   Jag kan ju tänka mig, fast—nä, det är ju dumt.
         I can imagine, but—nah, it's dumb.
         Egentligen skulle man kunna göra skötbordet och (benen ihop) med annan låda.
         One really ought to make the table and (the legs together) with another box.
         (2.0)
Peter.   Ah.
         Yeah.

Together *tråkigt* (boring) and *dumt* (dumb) form the negative expressive quadrant of the designers' evaluative matrix. These terms stand in clear, though rarely directly verbalized, opposition to the commonly invoked positive expressive qualities *kul* and *roligt*. While these qualities are rarely explicitly opposed to one another in interaction, it does sometimes occur. In the following example Fredrik was working on some bathroom cabinetry, and was trying to construct the doors in an unorthodox fashion—not by attaching them to the frame at right angles, as is typically the case, but at acute angles. Faced with some initial skepticism from Peter, Fredrik admitted the idea might be *dumt* (dumb), but possibly *kul* (fun):

Fredrik.	Du.
	Hey.
	((Fredrik turns his laptop toward Peter.))
	E::m, den där—den sidan, och den där
	U::m, that side, and that ((pointing to drawing on the screen))
Peter.	Mm.
	Yeah.
Fredrik.	var liksom som en vinkel de satt ihop.
	were, like, an angle, they sat together.
	((Fredrik demonstrates the angle with his hands.))
	Gångjärnen hade början där och där.
	The hinge had the start there and there.
	((Points to screen again))
	De liksom öppnades,
	They, like, opened,
Peter.	Dörr?
	The doors?
	((As Peter talks, Fredrik mimes opening the doors of the cabinet.))
Fredrik.	Ja heheh. Lite dumt men (.) kanske kul.
	Yes hehehe. A little dumb, but (.) maybe fun.
Peter.	Ja. Det är frågan om (1.0) det är dummare än vad det—det är kul.
	Yes. The question is if (1.0) it's dumber than what it—it is fun.
	(3.0)
Peter.	För att det är en belastning på gångjärnen där.
	Because it's a load on the hinge there.
	(2.0)
Peter.	Kör.
	Go for it.
Fredrik.	Heheheh.
	((Turns computer back))

After getting Peter's attention and turning his laptop around to display the sketch, Fredrik explained what he had done with the door and gesturally inscribed its structure and function with his hands by "opening" the imaginary doors, which he depicted as hanging at an angle in front of him. When Peter asked for clarification, Fredrik laughed and said, "A little dumb, but maybe fun." Peter agreed, but cautioned that the issue was whether the idea was "dumber than it is fun," since the structure might put unnecessary stress on the hinges. Nevertheless he encouraged Fredrik to continue.

This exchange makes explicit the contrast between "dumb" and "fun" that guides many evaluative sequences in design interactions at Kontoret. The embedded implication in this formulation is that "fun" ideas are "smart" ideas, and that "dumb" ideas are intrinsically not fun and not pleasant—regardless of how innovative the idea might be. Of course in colloquial speech "dumb" and "boring" ideas are typically treated as "not fun," though that may not always be the case. However, the significance of this distinction in design interactions at Kontoret stems from its position in the overall evaluative matrix.

The most basic positive assessment one can make of an object's aesthetics is that it is *fint*. This adjective, a cognate of the English word "fine," can best be translated as "nice," although when applied to objects it has much stronger aesthetic connotations than "nice" does. Designers constantly describe their own work and the work of their colleagues as *fint*—a shorthand way to express that they like or approve of the design, especially in its overt aesthetic dimensions.

The following example illustrates this clearly. Peter, who was working on the same set of bathroom cabinets that Fredrik presented in the previous example, showed a sketch of one of his cabinets to Fredrik, who, after looking at the form closely, evaluated the sketch as "nice":

Peter.	Du?
	Hey.
	((Turns his laptop toward Fredrik))
	(2.0)
Peter.	Här har du den.
	Here you have it.
Fredrik.	Fint.
	Nice.
Peter.	Mm.
	Yeah.
Fredrik.	Hur ser den ut brevid den andra?
	How does it look next to the other one?

Peter.   Vet inte. Heh.
           Don't know. Heh.
           ((For 11 secs., Peter adjusts and re-renders the drawing with two cabi-
           nets side by side.))
           ((Peter rolls his chair back, and stares silently at the screen for 8 secs.))
Fredrik.   Det är fint.
           It's nice.
           (4.0)
Fredrik.   Jag gillar verkligen denna.
           I really like that.

Peter first turned his computer so that the intern could see the drawing, which Fredrik soon described as "nice." He then asked what this cabinet looked like next to another one they had been working on, and Peter spent a few seconds re-rendering the drawing so they stand side by side on the monitor. When he was done, Peter and Fredrik looked at the drawing, now showing two cabinets, and after two long pauses Fredrik said that "it's nice" and that he "really likes" the cabinet.

This particular assessment is dominantly focused on form. There is no discussion about how the doors will work or the materials that will be used in its construction. Instead the sequence centers on the physical, aesthetic form of the object, and how it "looks" next to another similar object. More-over, the "nice" assessment follows a long (practically required) period of silent visual assessment, as the designers position their bodies to observe and absorb the image. The long pauses during which the designers stare at the sketch from afar are constituted as consequential actions—in looking they take in the aesthetic form presented before them, a necessary precur-sor to levying judgment. This action not only prepares them for passing reasonable judgment, but also publicly displays that their judgment is con-sidered and thoughtful, not rash and spurious. Thus Fredrik's assessment of the sketch as "nice" is produced in an act of looking focused on the formal qualities of the object, an act that displays that one possesses an authentic "professional vision" (Goodwin 1994) attuned to aesthetic detail.

What gives the evaluative matrix its particular force in design interac-tions is the way in which "nice" qualities are rhetorically equated with "fun" qualities, which is to say, how aesthetic forms are directly linked with more expressive qualities in design activities. Objects that are "nice" are "fun," and those that are "fun" are "nice." In the following exchange

Matti was working on an armchair, which he was presenting to Peter for the first time. As Matti talked, Peter looked intently at the drawing from across the table:

Matti. Den blir faktiskt väldigt fin den här fåtöljen.
       It's actually getting pretty nice, this armchair.
       ((Matti swivels monitor to Peter.))
Peter. Heheh, verkligen mycket sympatisk.
       Heheh, really very attractive.
       (3.0)
Matti. Om den är bekväm, vilket man förstår om man tittar på nu—
       If it's comfortable, which one understands if one now looks at—
Peter. Naj heheh [(. . .).
       Nah heheh [
Matti.   [är en helt annan.
                   [is totally another thing.
       ((Peter stares silently at the sketch for 10 secs.))
Matti. Mycket rolig.
       Very fun.
       ((Matti swivels monitor back around.))

As Matti prepared to reveal his sketch to Peter, he claimed that the chair is "actually getting pretty nice." As Peter silently stared at the drawing, Matti described his chair as "very attractive"—another term focusing on the object's form. After more silence from Peter, Matti noted that though it might look nice, it was "totally another (thing)" if the chair was comfortable. Peter stared at the sketch for another ten seconds, after which Matti turned his monitor back around, referring to it as "very fun."

Matti focused specifically on the aesthetics of the chair he was showing to Peter. He characterized it as *fin* and *sympatisk*—both words that draw attention to its form, which he directly contrasted to its function by questioning whether it would be comfortable in the real world—a quality unknowable and only imaginable from just looking at the computer drawing. As he closed the assessment activity he called the chair "fun," drawing a parallel between the aesthetic form he had indirectly asked Peter to examine and the expressive qualities the chair gave off. Both terms, *fin* and *rolig*, are used to positively assess the chair, though each hits a slightly different target. By rhetorically placing them in parallel positions, Matti made explicit the connection between aesthetic and ex-pressive qualities.

In the final example we return to the legs of the changing table Peter and Matti were designing, as we saw earlier:

Matti. Jag tyker i och för sig att den där bortre ben(stapeln) är lite roligare
        I think, actually, that that leg(-stem) farther back is a little more fun
        än den där nya (.) eller den jag har gjort nu.
        than the new one (.) or the one I've done now.
        ((5.5 secs. of silence, as the designers stare at the screen))
Peter. Finare. (2.5) Fast jag gillar den där nya ändå.
        Nicer. (2.5) But I still like the new one.

After Matti pointed out that the older version of the leg was "more fun," Peter agreed by characterizing it as *finare*, "nicer." Here the parallel be-tween *roligt* and *fint* is strengthened by the recycled comparative construc-tion first used by Matti (*roligare*), and then used by Peter (*finare*). Both descriptors compared the new version of the leg to the old version of the leg, but did so in different ways. By picking up on Matti's use of *rolig-are* and transforming it into *finare* in his next turn, Peter made the rough equivalence of these categories explicit and relevant to the progress of the design.

In appraising an object's expressive qualities—the overall feeling evoked by the object—the designers tend to use *roligt/kul* for positive assessments and *tråkigt/dumt* for negative assessments. When specifically focused on an object's aesthetic features—how it looks—they typically use *fint* as a positive assessor. However, there is no corresponding negative as-sessor for aesthetic qualities in the evaluative matrix. I have never observed the designers referring to their own or each other's work as *ful*, "ugly," or some other equivalent descriptor relating to the object's aesthetic qualities. Indeed, the designers' negative assessments almost always explicitly refer to their work as *tråkigt* or *dumt*.

I would argue that the lack of a negative aesthetic descriptor in the eval-uative matrix is highly functional in design activities. Directly referring to the creative work of a designer as being "ugly" is a potentially highly offensive act. After all, most designers—including Matti and Peter—have devoted their careers to crafting "beautiful" objects. Referring to their own

work or the work of their peers as "ugly" concretely undermines the very
endeavor in which they are engaged. To avoid this dilemma the designers
find other, less direct means for signaling displeasure with an object's aesthetics. Given the rough equivalence interactionally drawn between "fun"
objects and "nice" objects—objects that are "fun" are rendered as "nice,"
sometimes explicitly, sometimes implicitly—the characterization of an object as "boring" or "dumb" implies that the object is simultaneously "ugly,"
or at the very least "not nice," without having to state it directly. In other
words, by coordinating the force of the terms *roligt* and *fint* in design interactions, the designers imbue the terms with a practical correspondence
whereby *roligt/kul* becomes a proxy for positive aesthetic assessment, and
the logical implication of this is that their opposite, *tråkigt/dumt*, through
semiotic associations, thereby becomes a proxy for negative aesthetic assessment. This allows the designers to offer negative aesthetic evaluations
without facing the consequences of directly challenging the artistic abilities
of their colleagues.

Stitching Emergent to Extant: Designing through Abduction

As we saw earlier, Peter and Matti were designing a changing table for a
well-known Swedish company. It was a wooden piece of furniture for a
child's room, and Matti had taken the first crack at working through the
table's overall form. As the two designers sat behind their own screens
at opposite ends of their worktable, Matti swiveled his monitor around
to show Peter the drawing he had been working on. "I don't want it to
be round up there," he said, as he swept his cursor over the structure's
straight-lined tabletop, highlighting the area he wanted Peter to see. "I
think it's quite nice that it's square." Peter agreed quickly. "That's right,"
he said. Matti then smiled and looked at Peter: "You know, I'm Ando," he
laughed, grabbing the monitor and turning it back around.

Matti is of course not Ando. Tadao Ando is perhaps Japan's most famous contemporary architect, a world-renowned disciple of the straight
line, and Matti's invocation of his name in this exchange was not innocent.
Earlier in the day there had been some debate as to whether the tabletop
should be rounded or square in its overall form, and in a previous iteration
of the drawing Matti had experimented with rounded edges. When he

displayed the update to Peter, the one with square edges, he stated outright that he preferred this new version. And by jokingly calling himself Ando, he directly called forth an entire world of forms and structures associated with the name, which not only described the forms he had given the table within a particular idiom, but also justified the choice he had made.

This linking of emergent form choices to previously existing objects, styles, and names is *designing through abduction*. Charles Sanders Peirce (1955) described the concept of "abduction" as a kind of analogical reasoning whereby certain features of one object are made at least contingently comparable to those of a second (see also Bateson 1979; Tannen 2010; Gell 1998; Kolko 2010). For Peirce abduction works by holding distinct entities against one another to verify their potential similarities, as a "proposition added to observed facts, tending to make them applicable in any way to other circumstances than those under which they were observed" (Peirce 1955:151). Moreover, abduction is not solely concerned with a feature-by-feature comparison between objects, but also with the implications that those few shared features might project, for, as Peirce noted, "where we find that in certain respects two objects have a strong resemblance, [we can] infer that they resemble one another strongly in other respects" (Peirce 1992:189), even if the overall resemblance is not quite perfect.

Peter and Matti use abductive comparisons in their work in many different contexts and for many different purposes. In so doing, they performatively inscribe indexical links between emergent forms and real-world objects, embedding their unfolding designs within a particular formal framework and ordering the potential trajectories the design might take. Sometimes the comparisons are only partially specific, invoking general objects for some specific comparative reason. For example, earlier in the process of drawing the changing table, Matti invoked the image of a car to frame the forms he has been drawing:

Matti.   Finns det några argument för att ett skötbord
         Are there any arguments for how a changing table
         ska ha liksom (.) designreferenser till en bil?
         can have like (.) design references to a car?
         (3.0)
Peter.   Naj.
         No.

Matti.   Fartig och hastighet och heheh.
          Fast and speedy and hehehe.
Peter.   Ska ju kännas snabbt och enkelt (. . .).
          [It] will feel quick and simple (. . .).

While Matti delivered this imagined comparison in a joking frame, there
are nonetheless real features of his sketch that have prompted him to suggest
that the changing table has "design references" to a car. Peter curtly rejected
the comparison, but after Matti continued with the idea, jokingly describing the table as "fast and speedy," Peter joined in, adding that the table "will
feel quick and simple." The irony present in the joking frame in which
the imagined comparison was made reveals that the changing table should
not resemble a car, lest it express car-like qualities (like speed) that are presumably unbefitting a table designed for changing dirty diapers. Since the
form that Matti had been drawing for the table was reminiscent of a car,
he claimed, Matti turned back to his drawing to reduce its car-like details.

On a different day, Matti was instructing Fredrik, the intern, how to
create a prototype for a hanging lamp they were designing together. The
computer drawing of the lamp was almost done, but neither designer was
exactly sure what the size of the prototype should be:

Matti.   Jag vet inte hur stor den ska va, så där kanske?
            I don't know how big it should be, like that, maybe?
            ((Matti holds his arms in a triangle shape in front of his face, until
            he specifies the size below.))
Fredrik.   Mmhm.
            Mmhm.
Matti.   En köksbords (.) lampa stor, liksom.
            Like (.) a kitchen table lamp big.
Fredrik.   Ah.
            Yeah.
Matti.   Fyrti centimeter i diameter kanske.
            Forty centimeters in diameter maybe.
            ((Matti holds his hands out in front of him, about 40 cm apart.))
Fredrik.   Mm.
            Yeah.

With both designers sitting at the worktable, Matti first produced a
quick visual model of the lamp shade by forming a triangle shape with

his arms, approximating the size of the lamp Fredrik should make. He kept it held there as he talked, tying this visualization to an explicit invocation of a kitchen table lamp as an abductive reference for conceptualizing the prototype. This was then followed by a measuring gesture in which he attempted to demonstrate for Fredrik a forty-centimeter diameter for the bottom of the shade. In producing these gestural inscriptions alongside his mention of the kitchen table lamp, Matti marshaled specific embodied knowledge—knowledge that was at once both designerly and common—to provide Fredrik with a visible and conceptual point of departure for transforming his drawing into an accurate three-dimensional prototype. Generic comparisons to things like cars and lamps (or, typically, to examples of a type of object) are common in the Kontoret studio, and in all sorts of design work. They often function as loose guides for designers, allowing them to press nascent ideas and forms onto existing objects to evaluate an emergent design in some way. They help order forms as they come into being on the computer screen—and in prototypes—allowing certain design gambits to pass, and others to die quiet deaths.

But some abductive comparisons are more specific, and it is often the case that the more specific the comparison, the more it can restrict, contain, and categorize forms in different ways—often indirectly relating them to "Swedish" style. Matti was working on a small square table, drawing the simple rectilinear form on his computer. The table looked like a bare cube, a plain square top with plain legs as long as the top was wide. Clearly not satisfied with his design as it stood, Matti attempted to persuade Peter and Fredrik to commiserate with him over how "boring" the drawing was. "How boring is this?" he asked as he swiveled his monitor around for the others to see. The three designers stared at the screen as Matti rotated the drawing in three dimensions. "It's super boring," he reiterated, while the other designers looked on in silence. Peter then inquired about the legs—"They're just wooden legs," Matti replied—and Fredrik asked if the tabletop was wood, too. "And damn thick!" Matti answered, with a hint of derision in his voice. He clearly did not like the table that he himself had drawn. "It's like a chopping block," Peter then offered. "Yeah, it is," Matti replied. "It's super boring."

Matti then made a move implying that the table was so boring that he should probably abandon what he had drawn, but before he finished Fredrik interjected, "It's like those tables that are—that have, uh, square thingies." He then used his hands to trace in the air what appeared to be four square table legs. "By Ikea," he finished. Matti and Peter then looked at each other across the long table, directly in the eyes. They paused, before laughing together, loudly and forcefully. "But that's just what they want!" Matti replied, before turning the screen and getting back to work.

Peter's abductive comparison to a chopping block initially affirmed Matti's assessment of the table as boring by indexically linking it to an often-forgotten piece of material culture, one that usually does not receive much design attention. Most chopping blocks are, almost by nature, uninteresting in their formal composition. But Fredrik's comparison was a little different. He invoked a ubiquitous table made by Ikea, called Lack, a small square table with square legs. Like Peter's comparison this too affirmed a sense of boringness, since in their world the Lack table is an icon of uninteresting form. However, because the company Matti and Peter were designing the table for actually *wanted* for them to design just such a boring table, Fredrik's innocent comparison provided a rationale for why Matti should nevertheless carry on with the boring design as it stood. Thus by comparing the table that Matti had designed to a table by Ikea, Fredrik reminded Matti that in some sense he was expected to replicate "boring" shapes. Pushing boringness as a reason to drop the sketch turns out to have been a losing strategy, since in the end, it does not matter. Swedish companies like to produce these kinds of forms. The sketch continues on, eventually helping to bring another "boring" square table to market.

Several days later, in the midst of drawing a different set of small tables on his computer, Matti swung his monitor around to show Peter what he had done:

Matti. Så!
        There!
        ((For 5.5 secs., Peter stares across the table at the monitor as Matti manipulates the onscreen image to reveal the tables from multiple angles.))
Peter. Nu är de ju väldigt lika (.) fåtöljen.
        Now they're really like (.) the armchair.
Matti. Va?
        What?

Peter.   Nu är de ju väldigt lika den—
          Now they're really like the—
          ((Peter completes his sentence by pointing to the armchair sitting
          behind him, dark gray and low to the ground, straight lines and a
          prominent seat with a light curve and rounded edges.))

By pointing to the chair that was sitting in their immediate environment
and pulling it into his evaluation of Matti's drawing, Peter established a
visible and concrete formal common ground that he shared with Matti for
understanding the basic aesthetic contours of the emergent object. Peter
used the armchair to *explain* his vision of the table to his partner, to anchor
the new form in the familiar and thus associate it with one that had already
passed the test: after all, at least one manufacturer deemed the chair worth
producing, which boded well for the formally similar tables.

In Peter's assessment of Matti's drawing the armchair is an example
of what Charles Goodwin (2003) calls "local metrics," resources immediately available to speakers to elucidate through abduction the nonpre-
sent details of a topic under discussion. For example, in telling a story a
speaker may use features of the space in which the story is told to represent elements contained in the narrative itself ("The scene of the crime
was a little bigger than this room"). In this case Peter's use of the armchair
as a local metric instantly places Matti's table design within a framework
of viable forms. His assessment is not simply a neutral and dispassionate
noticing of formal similarities between the table and chair, but a tacit
acknowledgment that the course Matti has taken with the table's design
is a good one. By linking the drawing to a real-world object through their
shared aesthetic qualities, Peter unleashes an attractive force between
them, with the forms of the armchair gently pulling forth similar forms
in Matti's design.

Another strategy of abductive comparison is to fit a given design explicitly into some recognizable style. These kinds of comparisons in particular entail deep assumptions about specific cultural knowledge related to
what formally constitutes a given style or the work of a particular designer.
In the following example, Peter had walked over to Matti's computer to
evaluate the latest iteration of their changing table design. He stood behind
Matti, who sat at the desk manipulating the image on the screen. After

they both admitted to liking this new version, Matti focused his attention on one small detail, the legs of the table.

Matti.   Jag tyker i och för sig att den där bortre ben(stapeln) är lite roligare
I think, actually, that that leg(-stem) farther back is a little more fun
än den där nya (.) eller den jag har gjort nu.
than the new one (.) or the one I've done now.
((5.5 secs. of silence, as the designers stare at the screen))

Peter.   Finare. (2.5) Fast jag gillar den där nya ändå.
Nicer. (2.5) But I still like the new one.
(2.5)

Peter.   Ännu bonnigare liksom.
Even more, like, simple ((lit. "peasanty"))

Matti.   Mmm. (1.0) Lite nationalsocialistiskt på nåt vis. (. . .).
Mmm. (1.0) A little National Socialist in some way. (. . .).

Peter.   Nä: (1.5) Nationalteatern.
Na:h. (1.5) Nationalteatern.

As the two designers stared at the drawing on Matti's monitor, Matti singled out the stem of one of the table's legs, which he had retained from an older version of the design, and claimed that it was "a little more fun" than the newer legs he had drawn. Peter agreed that the older leg was nicer, but claimed he also liked the newer leg, which was "even more simple," using the slang term *bonnigare*, which literally means something like "more rustic." Picking up on the formal simplicity implied in Peter's descriptor, Matti then joked that the newer leg was actually "a little National Socialist," comparing it to the stark design style of the Nazis, and using an overtly negative reference to characterize the version of the leg he dispreferred. Peter responded playfully by building off Matti's comparison and characterizing the leg contrastively as "a little Nationalteatern"—which refers to a famous Swedish rock band from the 1970s known for their extreme, leftist political leanings. While "Nationalteatern" does not represent a formal style in the way "National Socialist" can, because of the political imagery associated with the group it nonetheless indirectly evokes in this instance an echo of Soviet architecture—which itself shares formal similarities with both National Socialist architectural style and the lines of visibility common to Swedish design.

Abductive comparisons such as these, delivered in passing or even half-jokingly in the flows of workday activities, are replete with a highly charged creative force. In the context of design work they serve to link forms to forms, to align what is to come to what already exists, and to anchor the possible firmly in the realm of the actual. They constitute a hylomorphic action in which immaterial forms, temporarily inscribed in pixels and gestures and words, are granted an initial glimmer of material reality through indexical connections that designers draw between them and existing objects. In some cases because well-known design styles are often associated with particular forms, histories, and ideologies, when used as points of comparison they potentially convey much deeper significance than does a straightforward comparison of formal qualities. In other cases the comparison may not be used as a tactic of persuasion, but more as a means of explanation. In all of these examples of comparisons, speakers indexically specify particular items in the known world that already possess certain qualities deemed relevant to what is being worked out or evaluated. Sometimes these qualities are made explicit verbally—though the relevant features can also be shown with gestures—and sometimes the relevant features are unspecified and left for the hearer to decipher. Across the cases, however, comparisons function as formal checks on unfolding designs, ordering new ideas in the realm of immanence and channeling creativity through given forms and meanings.

I have been exploring in detail the work that takes place in Kontoret as a way to account for on-the-ground designing in action, for how form giving subsists within the minutiae of everyday design practice. In particular I have focused on how certain language games, patterns of linguistic and embodied action, set conditions for reproducing the Swedish cultural geometry, even without designers explicitly attending to the fact that they are doing so. What this approach reveals is that the language of designing, in all of its details, is as much a technical assemblage that shapes expert form-giving practices—and thus shapes forms themselves—as the technologies and skills that designers employ in the contemporary design studio. Indeed, the interactional frameworks that organize collective design work are themselves the primary means by which design knowledge is operationalized in collaborative practice, the best resource designers have for displaying, calibrating, and evaluating expert knowledge in real time. Through particular habits of talking, ways of moving, and mundane logics, designers create perlocutionary inscriptions of various kinds—order-words that resist certain forms in a design; pass-words that promote others, gestures that highlight the forms that matter and equate them with real-world objects—that, together with their incorporation alongside computer drawings and hand sketches, becomes the raw material for subsequent design work.

I have intentionally avoided addressing such things as designerly "preference" and "taste" in the analysis in favor of focusing instead on how these get realized in the flows of interaction—not primarily as some set of culturally determined value sets, but as strategic moves in series of iterative exchanges that accumulate to gradually shape forms and performatively create designed objects. The forms that count as the cultural geometry routinely "survive" the form-giving process not because the designers are explicitly intent on preserving straight lines and moderate curves in their designs, but because these forms receive a substantial amount of attention in the design process. By consistently highlighting straight lines, moderate curves, and right angles over other possible forms, and focusing consequential evaluative actions on them, the cultural geometry continuously passes through in the design process and is fixed into its objects. In other words, as a result of the ways in which working through design ideas in interaction tends to unfold, the details that render an object "Swedish" are often unreflexively coaxed out of designers rather than consciously selected by them, motivating an understated ordering of design trajectories toward familiar forms and qualities.

5

Displays of Force

Upon entering the Swedish pavilion at the 1939 World's Fair in Queens, New York, visitors were greeted by a simple photomontage composed of six faces—three women of various ages (only two of whom were smiling), two men, and a toddler. Alongside the mural the following text was inscribed:

> WE KNOW the home to be one of the most important factors in modern society. WE KNOW that good homes can be created only by sound people, in hygienic houses, through education and knowledge, with furnishings attuned to the times. WE KNOW that beauty and comfort should be provided to all. WE KNOW that beauty and high quality can only be achieved through the intimate cooperation of artist and manufacturer. This, in brief, is the meaning of the movement SWEDISH MODERN. (Stavenov et al. 1939:5)[1]

The phrase "Swedish Modern" had been coined two years earlier by an American journalist at the 1937 Paris Expo (Hagströmer 2001), but the organizers of the 1939 Swedish pavilion had decided to appropriate the term—adding the subtitle, "A Movement in Sanity" (Stavenov et al. 1939)—as a way to package the emergent functionalist style of Swedish design, along with its attendant ideologies, and deliver it to an international public. This was the first major introduction of twentieth-century Swedish design outside of Europe, and it would be the opening move in a series of exhibitional gambits organized outside of Sweden over the following decades—all of which collectively left lasting marks on the public imaginary of Swedish design both inside and outside Sweden. The traveling exhibition *Design in Scandinavia*, which was shown throughout the United States and Canada between 1954 and 1957, helped cement the very notion of a unified Nordic design (Guldberg 2011), and the term "Swedish Grace" had circulated in Sweden and abroad after several European exhibitions in the 1920s (see Remlov 1954).

The work these exhibitions did identifying, labeling, and glossing Swedish and Scandinavian design—creating the category and filling it with relevant exemplars—was an important international counterpoint to a trend that had started in Sweden long before 1939, springing forth, as was common throughout Europe, in the wake of the Great Exhibition of 1851. And today, while the grand expositions of the nineteenth and twentieth centuries have all but faded into obscurity, in Sweden there is still a robust and powerful exhibitionary complex (Bennett 1988) that fills the role once played by those expositions—ensuring the ongoing enregisterment of a politicized Swedish design.

I have been arguing in this book that design is a diagram, in Deleuze's (1988, 1992) sense, composed of both lines of visibility and lines of enunciation, of perceivable forms and particular concomitant discourses that describe and purposefully delimit interpretations of those forms. In previous chapters I explored just how those lines are wrought, from multiple points of view and at different scales, often without much direct relation to the work unfolding in other corners of the Swedish design world. In this final chapter I turn to the exhibitionary complex as one of the most critical domains in which these lines are brought together to form a more coherent whole, where the diagram of Swedish design is most explicitly delineated, and its image given shape, mass, and texture. The politics here are subtle. When the final vocabulary is used it is often quite basic and often linguistically subdued in single words and phrases. Yet in the curatorial display of

Swedish design in these sites politics emerge in a sensorially complicated visualization as the accoutrements of a "care-full" everyday life. Working with Foucault's (1998) complicated concept of "heterotopia"—complicated not necessarily in its content, but in the history of its use—I examine four different exhibitionary sites, each of which is a particular example of a more general kind, and all of which, though they exist for different purposes, serve as similar spaces of persuasion and directed semiosis that help suture together the lines of visibility and lines of enunciation, and in the process help materialize Swedish design for a consuming public, and anchor its cultural significance in direct experience.

Swedish Grace, Swedish Space: Civic Expositions and Social Reform

Turn-of-the-century Sweden, like much of the rest of Europe, was a place of tremendous social and material inequality (see chapter 2). As the economy rapidly transformed from predominantly agrarian to increasingly industrial, large numbers of rural families migrated to urban centers like Stockholm and Gothenburg looking for work. The existing housing stock was ill equipped to handle the influx of new inhabitants, and property owners were reluctant to renovate or rebuild their decrepit tenements. After years of steady urban population expansion the cities were soon in dire need of replanning (see Deland 2001); the small rented rooms in town were strained from the burden of accommodating many more people than was either comfortable or sanitary.

Sweden's final great exposition of the nineteenth century, and its first foray into hosting world's fairs, the Stockholm Art and Industry Exhibition (Stockholmsutställningen) of 1897, opened its gates amid this social turmoil. While trade fairs had been a staple of the Baltic region for centuries (Wurdak 1996), the tradition of the universal fair introduced by the first world's fair in London in 1851 had set a new standard for the patina of a publicly oriented exposition. The Art and Industry Exhibition was the greatest fair Sweden had seen up to that point. With over one-and-a-half million visitors, most of them from Sweden rather than abroad (Pred 1995:73), the exposition was intended not only to showcase the latest advancements in Swedish industry and technology (Hagströmer 2001)— of which many were on display, both at the fair and in concurrent media coverage—but also to celebrate the achievements the nation had made in transitioning into a capitalist economy (Ekström, Julich, and Snickars 2006). One effect of this was a push for the working class "to supplant old consumption practices with novel ones [and] to succumb to the latest 'tastes'" (Pred 1991:47). Indeed, the cheap, clean consumer goods on display, perhaps the most familiar results of capitalist production, were pitched as a decent means for escaping the horrid living conditions that plagued the city's laborers. The 1897 Stockholm Exhibition was the first major attempt in Sweden to crosscut class-based consumption patterns and encourage the lower classes, not just the bourgeoisie, to think and act more like modern consumers by buying mass-produced goods—*beautiful* mass-produced goods, as Ellen Key would argue two years later—to satisfy their material needs.

Hemutställningen 1917

In the years following the Art and Industry Exhibition the belief that harnessing the power of mass production to better the social position and material conditions of the working class gained fervid momentum in Sweden. It also continued to underpin the rationale for several planned civic expositions. In 1917 Hemutställningen, the Home Exhibition, opened its doors to forty thousand visitors at the newly constructed Liljevalchs Konsthall on Djurgården, one of Stockholm's central islands and the same area that had hosted the 1897 exhibition. The Home Exhibition had been conceived several years earlier by members of Svenska Slöjdföreningen, the Swedish Society of Arts and Crafts (see chapter 3), including Elsa Gullberg, a textile designer deeply influenced by the Deutscher Werkbund,[2] a precursor to the Bauhaus in Germany, and Gregor Paulsson, the Society's director. In collaboration with Centralförbundet för Socialt Arbete, the Central Association for Social Work (Hedqvist 2002; Lövgren 1993), the final plan for Hemutställningen was to initiate a contest for young designers to create simple utilitarian furniture in the hopes that industry would then produce the designs for low-income workers (Hagströmer 2001). Among the winners of this contest was Carl Malmsten, who later became a titan of early twentieth-century Swedish furniture design. Several noncompeting architects, including a young man named Gunnar Asplund, who would later go on to design the Stockholm City Library and lay important groundwork for modernist architecture in Sweden (see chapter 2), were also chosen to draft additional display rooms in which the furniture was presented. While the Svenska Slöjdföreningen team—who were, according to the exhibition's catalog, "convinced that the Swedish public's taste was better than its [bad] reputation" (quoted in Hedqvist 2002:34)—organized the broad strokes and low-level logistics of the Home Exhibition, the whole endeavor was financially supported by a number of Swedish companies (Wickman 1995a; Hedqvist 2002), some of which commissioned their own artists and designers to craft glassware, dinner services, and other domestic accoutrements to fill the exhibition's mock rooms. The 1917 exhibition instigated the first earnest attempts to forge close working relations between artists and industry in Sweden, with the explicit goal of social improvement through design.

The contestants were charged with designing and fully furnishing three types of rooms, each with a specific cost limitation (see Wickman 1995a:64): (1) a single room with a tile oven at 260kr (about $1080 in 2013 dollars); (b) a large kitchen and extra room at 600kr ($2,500); and (c) two rooms and a kitchen at 820kr ($3,400).

In all, twenty-three rooms were constructed, and the exhibition was met with general praise from the press and mostly bourgeois visitors. Unfortunately for the organizers, the tangible reformist results they had anticipated did not follow, at least not directly. While the 1897 Stockholm Exhibition was widely attended by Swedes from all class levels, the working classes for whom Hemutställningen was conceived did not show up to Liljevalchs. Besides that, those who did attend were not impressed with what they were offered: home goods styled somewhere between familiar, traditional handcrafted forms and modern machine-cut pieces. Yet the exhibition was still in many ways a success. Unlike the 1897 exhibition, this one was organized by activists interested in stimulating change in industrial practices and instigating national debate to further their mission. Hemutställningen prompted industry to integrate more artists into the still-nascent arena of mass-produced furniture (Lind 1970) and managed to instantiate a national discussion about the living conditions of the working poor (Hagströmer 2001). Importantly, this latter point was accomplished not merely through the rhetoric of *housing*, but largely through an experienceable presentation of the *good home* (see chapter 2). Despite the cool reception from the working classes to the exhibition, Svenska Slöjdföreningen persisted in its mission.

The Stockholm Exhibition of 1930: Modernity on Display

The outbreak of the First World War had put the planning of most civic expositions on hold in Sweden. Despite assuming a neutral position in the conflict, the nation still deeply felt the economic ramifications of the war. But by the mid-1920s fair planning was back on track, and Swedish exhibition organizers were eager to present innovations in the emerging field of functionalist design to the country's population.

Nowhere did modernism seem more viable, more revolutionary than at the Stockholm Exhibition of 1930.[3] While large-scale civic expositions in other countries had already introduced functionalist architecture and furniture to a world quite comfortable with the traditional order of things, the Stockholm Exhibition was different. The exposition's organizer, Gregor Paulsson of Svenska Slöjdföreningen, and his chief architect, Gunnar Asplund, one of the winners of the 1917 competition, explicitly envisioned the fair as a forum to advance social change (Pred 1995), a chance to present a new way of life, at worst; and at best, a mechanism for inciting a "bloodless revolution" in Swedish society (Johnson 1961, as quoted in Pred 1995:97). The functionalist style—dominated by clean, simple lines, solid colors, natural materials, a lack of ornamentation, and a sharp eye toward practicality, or in other words, what was to become the Swedish cultural geometry—was the great equalizer. *Funkis*, as functionalism was affectionately dubbed in Swedish, distilled taste into the simplest of forms; with straight, clean lines, these honest forms aspired to be nothing other than what they were designed for—for example, the legs of a chair do not decorate; they support human bodies. If the organizers had their way, this fair would present the emerging cultural geometry to the masses, raise the level of popular taste, and push for improved living conditions for the lower and working classes. Their hope was that the fair would help lead the country on a straight, clean line up from poverty and into modernity.

Over five hot months, about four million visitors—equal to two-thirds of the country's population at the time—trekked to the fairgrounds in Stockholm. The main thoroughfare at the exposition was called Corson—a Swedification of the Italian Il Corso, or "the course." It was a broad, straight promenade along which the main exhibition halls were scattered. At the end of Corson sat Paradiset (Paradise), an imposing glass and steel structure, designed by Asplund, which held the fair's central restaurant and served as its de facto hub. There were exhibition halls dedicated to almost every imaginable good, from traditional handicrafts to glassware, from lamps—or "electric light fittings" in the stilted language of *funkis*—to books, typography, and printing presses. There were even several halls devoted to high-end objects for the rich, but the fair's overall message of social reform was clear. For example, in the Hall for Non-Precious Metals and Musical Instruments, a visitor could find a wide assortment of pots, pans, and ultramodern kitchen equipment designed to help ease the stress of progressive living—note that these appliances were so new at the time that they were grouped according to material, rather than purpose (see fig. 10). A bit farther down the way was the Hall for Mass-Produced Furniture, within which stood the best inexpensive yet high-quality chairs, sofas, and tables that Swedish industry had to offer. Indeed, nearly all of the objects on display at the exposition were sponsored by Swedish companies poised to launch them into production. But it was still unclear whether the public was willing to buy them.

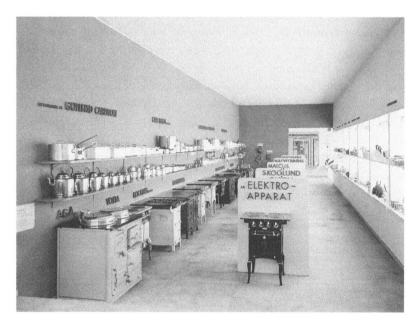

Figure 10. Hall 9, featuring contemporary kitchenware, including appliances, at the Stockholm Exhibition of 1930. Reproduced with permission of Svensk Form.

While the halls along Corson amassed large numbers of objects with a certain family resemblance, a taut simulacrum of the hegemonic presence of functionalist design hoped for by the exposition's organizers, the halls beyond Paradiset had a more didactic purpose. As with the 1917 Home Exhibition, these halls contained examples of large and small model apartments with standardized layouts—all fully furnished with machine-cut chairs, beds, and tables from the halls along Corson—showcasing simple, functional solutions to common domestic problems. This was the rhetoric of the place, the persuasion. Whereas the collections of curious objects were nice to look at, these rooms, which most visitors could afford to recreate at home, worked magic by laying bare the promises of a modern, democratic future and materializing them in intimately familiar spaces. They were "dream spaces," to use Kavanagh's (2000) phrase, though not for imagining a world of the past, but a more personal world still to come, just beyond the current temporal horizon. In these rooms, people could imagine a new life, a new mode of being (see fig. 11).

Figure 11. The living room of villa 49, a single-family home designed by Sven Markelius, on display at the Stockholm Exhibition of 1930. Reproduced with permission of Svensk Form.

One would be hard pressed to used the word "subtle" in describing the Stockholm Exhibition: a long, straight course lined with cutting-edge functionalist housewares, leading directly to Paradise, just beyond which the "home of the future" awaits. In addition, along the way stood a three-story pavilion, called Svea Rike, dedicated to the proud display of tokens of Swedish nationalism. It should be no surprise, then, that several years after the exposition, modernist design took root in Sweden with vigor, in large part because of the fair's deep impact on the Social Democrats. In developing the welfare state and constructing the *folkhem*, they drew heavily from the fair's message, especially in terms of housing policy, and encouraged industry to ramp up the manufacture of high-quality, inexpensive furniture, thus instantiating a tradition of more or less amicable cooperation between government, designers, and industry.

H55 and the Triumph of Functionalism

After a lull in production caused by the Second World War, the Swedish home arts industries took off in the late 1940s and 1950s. During World War II Svenska Slöjdföreningen began offering popular night courses around the country aimed at educating young people in how to best organize their homes. Ingvar Kamprad, the founder of furniture giant Ikea, was a diligent student in some of these courses. Meanwhile, simple mass-produced furniture was gaining popularity, and investigators from Hemmens Forskningsinstitut (HFI), the Home Research Institute, sat quietly in kitchens around the country, observing women as they cooked and cleaned, with the goal of improving their material working conditions by designing better appliances and kitchen tools (Parr 2002).[4]

The period immediately following the war saw several large-scale exhibitions along the lines of the Stockholm Exhibition of 1930, the most notable of which was H55, held in Helsingborg, in the southwest of Sweden, in 1955; it was an event that in many ways represented "the zenith of Swedish Modern" (Hagströmer 2001:49).[5] Whereas the Stockholm Exhibition of 1930 presented a snapshot of the possible, an imagined democracy of small things, H55 was much more concerned with achievements. As one of the exposition's architects put it (Silow 1995:178–179), "The period between 1930 and 1955 freed the development of Swedish functionalism from provocative slogan[s] to thoroughly worked out application[s]." At

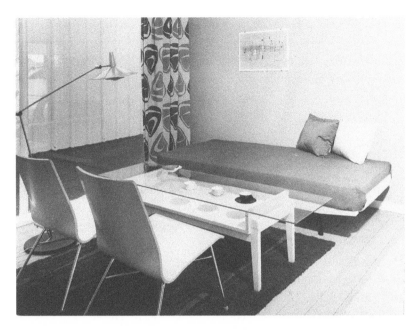

Figure 12. Living room interior, on display at the Helsingborg Exhibition of 1955 (H55). Reproduced with permission of Svensk Form.

H55, what were once possibilities were now displayed as realities, and through the halls stuffed with modernist furniture and ergonomic appliances (see fig. 12), the fair's ideology was unavoidably felt—we are not *trying* to change society for the better, we *are* changing it, and the results of that project are clear.

As the twentieth century trudged on, the popularity of civic expositions waned. Since the late nineteenth century, periodic large-scale design expositions had served a critical role in the modernization of Swedish society. By pushing the reform of common material needs, they inspired an understated class solidarity, and transformed the home from an intimate space into a site for political action in the collective consciousness. And they did it all with fun. It was social engineering through entertainment, or perhaps more precisely, a "social imagineering" that spread prevailing state ideology not through top-down imposition, but almost unnoticed, through the visceral textures of pleasurable experience. As spaces removed from the strictures of ordinary social relations and relying on the manipulation of individual experience to shift visitors' perceptions of the normal order of things—not in a spurious way, but to effect social change, loudly proclaiming, "You *can* have a better life!"—these expositions functioned not quite as utopias, but rather as "heterotopias," different spaces that, in this particular case, helped to entrench the idea that the design of everyday things is a moral endeavor in Sweden, and the way it is done there is special.

Heterotopias: Space, Difference, Experience, Effect

In a lecture delivered to the Architectural Studies Circle in Paris in 1967, Michel Foucault (1998) attempted to elaborate the basic operational principles common to a certain kind of cultural space in which the ordering of social relations is somehow skewed from its ordinary configurations. He called these spaces "heterotopias," borrowing a term from the medical sciences. Foucault had actually first introduced the concept in the preface to his book *The Order of Things*, published in France a year before the 1967 lecture, but left it almost entirely undeveloped in the body of his official published work. Nonetheless, the deep sketch of heterotopias he outlined in his lecture provides a constructive heuristic for understanding the role played by civic expositions, and the rest of the Swedish exhibitionary complex (Bennett 1988)—the network of institutions charged with *showing* design to the public—in the construction and reproduction of Swedish design.

Foucault contrasts heterotopias both to "the real space of society," the geographical/topological space of everyday social interaction, and to utopias, spaces that, like heterotopias, contain emplacements—arrangements of things in social space—that are distinct from those in real space, but that are, unlike heterotopias, fundamentally *not real*:

> Utopias are emplacements having no real place. They are emplacements that maintain a general relation of direct or inverse analogy with the real space of society. They are society perfected or the reverse of society, but in any case these utopias are spaces that are fundamentally and essentially unreal.
>
> There are also, and probably in every culture, in every civilization, real places, actual places, places that are designed into the very institution of society, which are sorts of actually realized utopias in which the real

emplacements, all the other real emplacements that can be found within the culture are, at the same time, represented, contested, and reversed, sorts of places that are outside all places, although they are actually localizable. Because they are utterly different from all the emplacements that they reflect or refer to, I shall call these places "heterotopias," as opposed to utopias. (Foucault 1998:178)

While heterotopias stand outside real space, they are at the same time undeniably real—spatial lacunae organized according to their own rules. Kevin Hetherington (1997:viii) refers to heterotopias as "spaces of alternate ordering [that] organize a bit of the social world in a way different to that which surrounds them." Foucault provides several clarifying examples, including cemeteries, ships, libraries, museums, colonies, prisons, hospitals, brothels, and other places, like large-scale expositions, that are always embedded within the structure of a society and serve some collectively acknowledged purpose, but also in so doing somehow significantly alter normative relations.

Foucault identifies six distinct principles that apply to all heterotopias. First, while the forms that heterotopias take are diverse, they are nonetheless universally present in all cultures. He points to menstrual huts and other taboo places as examples from traditional societies. Second, heterotopias serve very different purposes in very different contexts, and those purposes can change over time. A prison in Norway today does not occupy the same cultural position as a prison in Britain (Baer and Ravneberg 2008), nor does it operate like a Norwegian prison did two centuries earlier. Third, heterotopias can handle, if not reconcile, several incompatible emplacements at once that otherwise could not coincide in real space. Natural history museums are a prime example of this (see Kahn 1995), compressing vast swaths of space and time into one easily consumable building. Fourth, heterotopias are removed from the normal flow of time, both quotidian time and historical time, and display their own peculiar temporal proclivities. Cemeteries, for instance, stop the flow of time completely, freezing the moment of death—or at least the moment of burial—in one locatable spot and hiding the ravaging effects time has on the decedent's body (Heatherington 2011; Johnson 2008). Fifth, heterotopias "presuppose a system of opening and closing that isolates them and makes them penetrable at the same time" (Foucault 1998:183). That is to say, there is some "price" to pay to gain access, a real monetary price or some other symbolic cost. Heterotopias are spaces that require passings-in, -out, and -through and reject permanent inhabitance. Finally, heterotopias serve some purpose in relation to the real spaces they oppose. They are not simply alternatives, or assemblages of tokens of difference, but instead they work in tandem with real space and offer something to society as a whole, what Foucault (1986:27) describes as either "illusion" or "compensation."

Institutions serving exhibitionary functions, like museums and fairs, have been treated as prominent examples of heterotopic spaces, though, as both Bruce Owens (2002) and Arun Saldanha (2008) point out, the ways in which the concept has been employed have varied. In analyzing *museums as heterotopias* many scholars have slipped into a definitional game that instead reverses directions and casts *heterotopias as museums*, which is to say, a misrecognition that all heterotopias possess many uniquely museological qualities. Miriam Kahn (1995:324), for instance, in discussing how unrelated Pacific cultures are represented in several different museum exhibits, including at the American Museum of Natural History, takes the minimalist-literalist perspective on heterotopias, defining them as "combinations of different places as though they were one," a highly restrictive meaning. Gottfried Korff (2002:31), on the other hand, refrains from redefining heterotopias and instead uses the concept to define museums as "places in which juxtapositions . . . are made, arrangements which push together the near and the far, which create distance to the familiar and use the distant as a screen for projecting the familiar onto it, for the purpose of reflecting and reassuring." Beth Lord (2006) also focuses on difference within space and reads heterotopias not primarily as *spaces that are different*, but as *spaces made up of difference*, "in which the difference between words and things is put on display and made available for contestation" (Lord 2006:11). However, where Kahn sees difference *elided* in heterotopic space, Lord sees it pronounced and elaborated.

Peter Johnson (2006) notes that there is some confusion in how exactly "difference" matters in the idea of heterotopia as Foucault originally presented it.[6] One common reading, favored in applications to exhibitionary contexts, highlights the *containment* of difference in a given space, and indeed Foucault did note this as one aspect of heterotopia. However, as Johnson (2006) thoroughly demonstrates, there is evidence in Foucault's own writing that his view of heterotopias was not primarily concerned with the difference *within* heterotopic space, but the difference *between* heterotopic space and what comprised all other social space.

There is, of course, a problem in this formulation. To claim that certain spaces are separate from normative social space implies that normative social space is itself thoroughly homogeneous, which neglects the fundamental diversity of the social world. Moreover, as real spaces, heterotopias cannot plausibly be severed from society if they are already embedded within it. However, if we expand our focus to include not only the nature of the space itself but also the kinds of practices it can afford, we can see in Foucault's text an attempt to elaborate a concept of space and spatial difference based not necessarily on the *organization* of space, but on the *experiential effects* that movement into and through the space could enact. Crossing the boundary between space experienced as normative and heterotopic space involves an "outward clash," to borrow Peirce's (1992b) term, in the process of transition. One notices discrepancies from expectations, feels that things are somehow not "right," sees them arranged in unfamiliar patterns, and acts in uncommon ways. All heterotopias distill social relations, spatial relations, and object relations into a highly concentrated, easily consumable format. Regardless of the form the heterotopia takes, because it is a space "as meticulous, as well arranged as ours is messy, ill constructed, and jumbled" (Foucault 1986:27), maneuvering through it is unquestionably distinct from what is normally experienced in other domains of everyday life.

Beginning in the late nineteenth century and continuing on today, the design exhibitionary complex in Sweden has persisted as a network of interconnected heterotopic spaces that collectively construct the public imaginary of Swedish design through semiotic practices that attempt to shape individual experience in particular ways. Large-scale expositions are not very common these days, but trade shows, museums, and department stores are still quite popular. Each of these institutions serves its own immediate purpose, of course: trade shows, museums, and department stores capture different target audiences, have very different revenue streams, and hold quite different positions in various cultural and industrial fields. Yet they all function as *indexicalizing heterotopias*, relying on specific techniques of selecting, identifying, assembling, describing, and presenting certain kinds of objects alongside what Corrine Kratz (2011) calls "rhetorics of value" to enregister Swedish design in moments of direct experience.

An indexicalizing heterotopia is a space that is arranged to enhance specific indexical relations between particular entities, links that might otherwise seem tenuous, while simultaneously minimizing other potential indexical relations. Such heterotopias are filtering spaces, mapping this to that without clutter or noise, presenting a preferred understanding of how things are ordered and what they mean. Indexicalizing heterotopias are rhetorical spaces, spaces that highlight and suggest—and sometimes even insist—but still reluctantly admit that alternative interpretations are possible. They are spaces of continuous persuasion, of processes that tacitly recognize that their work is never finished. Visitors to these heterotopias may or may not believe in any settled way the messages expressed there: even if the persuasion fails to stick, the ongoing process of indexicalization that they facilitate serves as a next-best proxy for acceptance.

One of the most important indexicalizing functions of the exhibitionary complex is to *gather* Swedish design. In these spaces the impossibility of experiencing the totality of Swedish design is overcome by amassing many formal exemplars in one place and facilitating their easy consumption *as such*. The spread of material objects in the world, coupled with the limiting nature of human experience, allows us to take in only what we confront piecemeal, leading us to group similar but not copresent objects only after the fact and in our minds—this chair here and now is somehow *like* that chair there and then. To compensate for this, the exhibitionary complex does a lot of the cognitive heavy lifting by placing actual objects side by side, in relations and interpretive configurations that would not, or could not, exist in everyday sorts of spaces. One obvious outcome of this is the possibility for creating categories that otherwise might not be gleaned from everyday experience, like, for instance, that this chair here and now and that chair there and then, neither of which obviously proclaims where it was made or what it "means," are both tokens of Swedish design. Thus the components of the exhibitionary complex with an explicit focus on the national origins of objects, or even those organized with a current of implicit suggestiveness toward where the objects come from, provide viewers with a model for identifying which kinds of objects to "flag" (Billig 1995) as Swedish in everyday life, and which ones, by comparison, are left unmarked.

Simultaneous to gathering Swedish design and rendering it immediately experienceable, the exhibitionary complex works to adhere ideologies to forms and objects in direct and indirect ways. Text displayed on a placard placed next to a chair in a museum, or in an accompanying brochure at a trade show, that contains language like *enkla linjer, funktionell*, and *demokratisk* highlights the object's "simple lines" and describes it as "functional" and "democratic," explicitly drawing on some of the most prominent examples of the final vocabulary. This indexicalizing move is quite common across the exhibitionary complex. However, what is far more pervasive is the construction of showing environments suffused with an ambient semiosis that stresses indexical links between objects and ideologies in ways that are indirect, but still nonetheless controlled. In these spaces the "political economy of detail" (Foucault 1977:139), surging through markets of text and material form, is felt on the ground, diffuse and pervasive. Clean, straight lines, unburdened by the clutter of the past, do seem to lead to modernity. Everything is functional, which is to say, helpful, even if the function is not new: chairs are as much "machines for sitting," to paraphrase Le Corbusier's famous aphorism, as ergonomic scissors are machines for cutting. Light colors improve moods, plastic keeps prices low, and suddenly the white table on display hints at the promise of a better morning with more money to spend. Indirect indexicalization hints, maybe even insists, that these objects "fit" the ideological ambit most explicitly articulated in the final vocabulary, which may not be explicitly manifest in the space, but, because of further indirect indexical links between nodes in the exhibitionary complex, is never too far away. The serialized repetition of such themes throughout the exhibitionary complex is a force powerful enough to imprint such ideas on the experience of most visitors—even if some components of the exhibitionary complex are temporary and recursive, not entirely fixed or stable. When they leave the heterotopia, and return to the everyday world, there is, no doubt, some residue.

The Stockholm Furniture Fair: Art as Commerce

Early February in Stockholm is cold, gray, and wet. The first rays of light that mark the onset of spring are still too distant to inspire hope that the dark will soon subside. The comfort of the Christmas holidays has faded, replaced by a solemn recognition that three more months of snow and chill are largely unavoidable. Torpor prevails as the city slows down into a state of waking hibernation, biding time and conserving energy until summer. This is the peak—or perhaps the low point—of Swedish winter.

February is also the month in which Stockholm Design Week takes place. It is the most important time of year for the Nordic furniture industry, injecting a flash of activity into the Swedish design world and breathing new life into the city, if only briefly. All over Stockholm shops, showrooms, restaurants, and bars host events, held mostly during after-work hours, that feature particular designers, manufacturers, or products with which a design-interested public can interact. The keystone event of Design Week, the Stockholm Furniture Fair, is a core ritual in the sphere of Swedish furniture design, a place where names are made and careers are launched (see chapter 3). For young designers the five-day exposition is a crucial opportunity to unveil their designs, while for manufacturers the fair facilitates smooth sales of their products to builders, architects, and dealers. For the rest of the city, the fair is a distraction from the pressures of winter living, and if one is able to attend, a spectacle not to be missed.

The fairgrounds are in Älvsjö, a ten-minute train ride south of the central city. Outside the complex of exhibition halls, packs of visitors smoke quick cigarettes and rub their arms to stay warm, most speaking Swedish or English, but Italian, Finnish, Danish, and Japanese are also in the air. Inside, the main lobby is surprisingly small, staffed with a squadron of docents and cashiers who check credentials to ensure only trade professionals and journalists—and apparently anthropologists—are allowed through the turnstiles. The general public is able to attend, but only on the last day.

The Stockholm Furniture Fair, called Stockholms Möbelmässa in Swedish, but more commonly branded with its English name, is the leading furniture exhibition in the Nordic countries and the largest of Scandinavian furniture in the world. Each year over forty thousand people, including thousands from abroad, visit the fair to meet designers and survey the latest offerings from Scandinavian furniture manufacturers—or foreign manufacturers producing furniture in a Scandinavian style. According to designers, and journalists, and based on the palpable buzz that saturates the place, the Stockholm Furniture Fair is, at least domestically, ground zero for Swedish design.

Images of the great exhibitions of the twentieth century flashed through my mind as I wandered the place. The spectacle here was different of course, but the contours of the experience must have felt like this. The nerve center of the fair was Hall C, a massive hall that processed most of the heavy traffic circulating in the building. Once I squeezed past a line of guards I entered a humid and cavernous hall pulsating with colors and buzzing loudly with voices and excitement. Row upon row of display platforms held chairs, tables, and lamps aloft a few inches from the ground. The furniture was what had become familiar to me after about four months of living in Sweden, made of modern materials like plastic, with simple and colorful forms—somehow just Scandinavian-looking. Not everything fit the model, of course, but every one of the chairs and tables greeting visitors at the threshold of the hall could appear without protest on the cover of any book dedicated to Swedish design. The only problem was, so much of the stuff here looked so similar, and I had a difficult time anchoring myself within the exhibition's plan. I struggled to navigate the space, and cursed myself for not insisting that one of the designers I knew guide me through the event.

Hall C attracted not only lots of people, but also lots of *kinds* of people. The aisles crisscrossing between the displays were teeming with visitors of different ages and speaking various languages: hip design students, bored high schoolers traveling in packs, well-coiffed architects, crews of foreign television journalists, and of course scores of salespeople.

Each display was sponsored by a particular company. These were predominantly furniture producers presenting their latest catalog items for architects, builders, interior designers, and other tradespeople to experience up close. Fittingly, the displays often served as impromptu furnished meeting rooms for closing deals (see fig. 13). Many companies asked their products' designers—most of whom were independent contractors (see chapter 3)—to appear at scheduled times, as a bonus feature of the display. The names of internationally well-known designers, like Tom Dixon and Eero Koivisto, often prominently accompanied their products with distinct signage, but even the names of up-and-coming young Swedish designers, like Peter Andersson and Thomas Bernstrand, were lettered next to their creations. Most of my informants themselves kept a low profile during the fair and showed up only when needed by a manufacturer. Otherwise, their names and their products could speak for themselves.

The displays were of various complexities. Some contained a wall or two to separate them from their neighbors, and a few, like Vitra, contained elaborate mock living spaces and offices. Kinnarps, one of Sweden's

Figure 13. An impromptu business meeting on the floor of the Stockholm Furniture Fair, 2006. Photograph by the author.

largest furniture producers, built a two-floor building-within-a-building and served free beer inside. Most displays, though, were small and open, with items placed neatly on short, broad white podiums. Some allowed visitors to test out the furniture while others protected their goods like museum pieces to prevent wear and tear. The company Materia went so far as to place a beaded curtain around their entire display, adding an air of mystery to the activities inside. Overall, the flashiest, most central, and most colorful displays drew in the biggest crowds, regardless of what was on offer. And while this was a trade fair organized to facilitate business transactions, there was no physical signal of money values to be found, no prices marked on any display or in any catalog. This spectacle was strictly for show.

The fair's main material was a mixture of office and home furniture, though the boundary between products designed for public space, work space, and domestic space was particularly blurred. The products at Nola, for instance, were intended for outdoor use, yet gave off a distinct sense of indoor comfort. Some companies showed traditional office furniture, while Klaessons, a well-respected producer in Sweden, highlighted a large range of strict modernist office furniture and stackable chairs. As I toured the halls, passing each section several times, I was struck by how basically similar most of the products were, all using the same cultural geometry to derive the final look of the objects. Even companies from countries like Italy were showing products that fit the Scandinavian model—simple lines, familiar, organic shapes, single solid colors, and recognizable materials dominated.

While the Furniture Fair lacks any direct message of social reform, it nonetheless follows in the tradition of the twentieth-century civic expositions in Sweden. It is a spectacle, massive, temporary, and physically removed from the turbulence of the center city. Like those fairs it is hopelessly focused on aesthetic innovation, even if the innovations are not as radical as they once were. It quite literally defines "the new" in Scandinavian furniture design, offering a small sample of what is in store in the very near future for those who are willing and able to buy. Manufacturers eagerly show their goods with the promise of an aesthetically improved lifestyle, and potential buyers survey the selection in the hopes of securing a deal. These objects are unquestionably *wares*, goods on the market and ready to be sold. But they are also displayed like museum pieces, many of them not meant to be touched or used but only to be looked at from a safe distance. Thus visitors find themselves vacillating between playing the role of audience and playing the role of consumer, appreciating the object at one point for its formal qualities and at another point for what it might cost.

Also significant is the fact that the Furniture Fair not only defines "the new," but also resiliently defines what is "Swedish." Walking through the fair, one cannot evade the impression that Sweden endures under a tyranny of simple forms and solid bright colors. As Svetlana Alpers (1990:29) states, "When exhibited together certain objects in any class might repay attentive looking more than others." At the Stockholm Furniture Fair, the largest show of Nordic furniture in the world, the spectacle of so many similar objects *forces* attentive looking so as to make real distinctions in the crowd. The place is predominantly suffused not with a variety of different kinds of objects, but rather with a variety of different objects of the same general kind. Tables on one side of the hall look like benches on the other, while chairs made in competing factories appear virtually indistinguishable to the untrained eye. The sense of similarity is overwhelming—the bluntest reminder in the exhibitionary complex that Swedish style exists in the contemporary world and originates in actual material forms.

The National Museum and Design 1900–2000: Commerce as Art

The Furniture Fair is a large, if temporary, collection of cutting-edge Swedish design, but it makes no attempt to educate its visitors overtly. Whereas both collecting and educating were tasks the civic expositions were created to handle, those functions have for the most part been bequeathed to an array of different private and public venues today. In contrast to the ephemeral Furniture Fair, venerable art institutions, including the National Museum in Stockholm and the Röhsska Museum in Gothenburg, hold within their walls permanent collections of everyday objects that for one reason or another have been deemed proper examples of "good Swedish design." These exhibits highlight design as a historically situated process, with the objects of each stage—always small things, furniture and household objects—serving to satisfy the particular socioeconomic conditions of the time. While there is an obvious educational aspect in this, the primary purpose of these collections is to gather together everything that *counts*, and in so doing to transform what was once *the everyday* not only into "art," but also into "our heritage," as if to say, "These common objects—dinner plates, dish brushes and bread knives—this is how we got here, and this is who we are."[7]

The Nationalmuseum, the National Museum of Fine Arts in Stockholm, is Sweden's premier institution for showcasing Swedish art and culture from the 1500s (when the collection was first initiated) to the present day. It is also the country's largest art museum. In contrast to Stockholm's Nordic Museum (Nordiska Museet), whose ethnological collections focus on the folk life and cultural history of premodern Scandinavia, the National Museum gathers some of the most renowned art pieces—paintings, sketches, prints, photographs, sculptures, and design objects—created by Swedish and European artists. The Modern Art Museum (Modernamuseet), whose mission is less focused on Swedish or Scandinavian art than on international contemporary art in various media, is a much more recently established institution, along with the Architecture Museum, which shares the same building. These four museums, each with its own collection, organizational structure and bureaucracy, and mission statement, form the core of Stockholm's network of art museums, selecting the official state tokens of aesthetic Swedishness and presenting them to the public.

While all of these museums include design objects of one form or another in their archives, the National Museum is the only one that displays them as part of its permanent collection. The modern design exhibit, which first opened in 1999, is entitled Design 19002000 and covers the past one hundred years or so of small-object design. The bulk of the material on display originated in Sweden, but there are objects by designers from Norway, Denmark, and Finland, as well as a few from several other nations.

The National Museum is housed in a nineteenth-century building, and the curators of Design 19002000 have gone to great lengths to disguise that fact and "modernize" the exhibit facilities, at least superficially. The round, weight-bearing columns that pierce the halls are covered with painted foam boards, transforming them into barely noticeable square pillars. Most of the walls in the exhibit rooms are painted black, with glass-fronted display cases inset throughout. Along the top of the walls runs a simple time line, painted in white, loosely marking which decades the objects in each display case roughly belong to. Certain periods are marked with terms to neatly signify them, like Samhällsfokus (Focus on Society) from 1970 to 1974, and Nyenkelhet (New Simplicity) from 1989 to 1993, which are accompanied by short descriptions of what the phrases refer to. Much of the exhibit's textual material calls special attention to the social conditions from which the objects arose, or in some instances the obvious *lack* of social content, such as the postmodernist turn of the 1980s. Inside each case various small, everyday objects are assembled—plates, dishes, cups, telephones, brushes, small appliances, as well as a few graphic design pieces like books and food packaging, much of it crafted with the cultural geometry—some accompanied by brief descriptions of their origins, many left standing alone as one piece among several. A few walls are made entirely of glass, behind which sit objects selected for more explicit viewing—for instance, a collection of glass housewares that spans multiple decades. On the floor in the center of the rooms stand short podiums holding different pieces of furniture—chairs, tables, sofas, desks—each positioned near the time line that corresponds to the period in which the object was produced. Finally, on several white walls are painted words and phrases representing critical themes in the development of Swedish design—*Ergonomi* (Ergonomics), *Billigt och Flexibelt* (Cheap and Flexible), and *Minimalism*—next to the display cases containing representative objects, followed by a paragraph or two teasing out, if only briefly, the conceptual matter unifying the items inside.

Cilla Robach is one of three curators of the National Museum's design collection and was a main player in conceiving and constructing the exhibition. As a curator she is responsible for several different tasks, including procuring items for the collection, choosing which objects to put on display, and maintaining contacts with the outside, including schools, journalists, and researchers. She also writes articles on design for local Stockholm and national publications as well as research pieces in journals and edited volumes. Additionally, she manages to organize temporary design exhibitions at the National Museum, like the *konceptdesign* exhibition in 2005 (see chapter 3). Though she is loath to acknowledge it, Cilla is a powerful figure in the world of contemporary Swedish design.

When I interviewed Cilla about how Design 19002000 was envisioned and built, she pointed to the centrality of the indexical relation between form and *time* in how the exhibit was initially imagined. First and foremost the curators wished to tell a story about the development of Swedish design, and a time line was the best way to narrate visually what they considered to be the most crucial events in the story. However, this structure made it difficult to elaborate or problematize some aspects of the story, so the display elements tackling deeper issues were placed on different walls and podiums away from the time line—a decision that, in effect, removed more complex topics from the exhibit's much more dominant temporal framework:

> If you've never visited the exhibition and you need some light version or quick version, then you could stick to the black wall. But all the rest, the glass section or the furniture on the podiums, and the white walls, there you could work with much more variation. . . . The black wall could be sort of a handle to hold, to guide you through what we wanted, the history, the light version. And then you should find deeper information, or many more problems around that destroys this picture in the other sections. [But] it hasn't really happened.

Time more than topic is the prevailing ordering mechanism in the exhibition. To be sure, as Robach notes, the curators considered it critical to present the temporal development of Swedish design—their version of the story—to the visiting crowds. But they also wished to problematize that story and challenge its dominance in Swedish culture. However, their attempt to do so has not really worked out, according to Robach, and she would change this if she could redesign the exhibition. For the time being, though, because of a lack of funding, Design 19002000 is rather stuck in its current form:

> It was supposed to be more changeable. It has been built so that you should be able to comment on different periods, I mean, that you could sort of for some months make a deep cut into the 1930s or something. You could take away some of the other periods a little bit, or make them smaller, and then you could sort of emphasize this period and make some questions about it or something. But it has never worked like that.

Thus the exhibit has taken on a vibrancy of its own, independent of the social agents responsible for its creation and despite their desires for change. Swedish design as a unified temporal story, a teleological material evolution spurred on by the vulgar social conditions of a given time period—this is the version of reality that goes unchallenged without notice, at least in this heterotopic space. While Design 19002000 does indeed offer resources for visitors to more deeply involve themselves in critiquing these ideas, those resources are largely lost in the exhibit's design.

What does often happen, though, is that visitors feel special connections to the objects on display. The organizers exploited this and intentionally tried to shape the experiences of visitors as they view the dishes, typewriters, and lamps in their showcases to increase visitors' feelings of familiarity and association. This was not too difficult to accomplish. Though residing in a museum, these objects are not, after all, resoundingly bizarre. Most of them are everyday items and somewhat familiar to almost any viewer, though more as usable market goods than as museum pieces. Playing on this tension, the curators contracted a company that designs retail interiors to construct the exhibit display cases:

> It's like we wanted also to comment on how these are market products, they're not museum products. Of course the nice textiles from the 1500s and so on [in other exhibits] have also been used, but they were more precious

kinds of objects when they were made. And this is kind of like things you—you know what it feels like to hold these cups and so on. It should emphasize that.

This kind of thinking is a core motivation for the construction of index-icalizing heterotopias. Recognizing that by placing everyday objects in a display case they are transforming the familiar into the foreign, the curators attempted to partially overcome the museumification problem by constructing cases that evoke a sense that one is window-shopping when peering inside, that the feeling of the object can be remembered or easily imagined. Molding the visitor's experience, then, altering perceptions of the place, was a conscious tactic for jolting the visitor into looking at the heteroglossic artifacts of Swedish design in a particular way, in this case as both commodities and temporally bound cultural symbols simultaneously. Sometimes, however, this strategy is a double-edged sword:

> I think very many come there and say, "Oh that cup, my grandmother had that one." "Oh, remember these chairs when they came out?" It's very much a personal way that you don't have with art. . . . I would like to try to get people to think more about design, and not just remember, "Oh I have that one. I wonder what that's worth? It's in the National Museum. Maybe I can sell it." To come above that level and see the objects as symbols of ideas and times and so on.

Robach laments that the window-shopping displays might not be entirely didactically effective. While from her experience visitors do indeed forge connections to the objects on display, remembering what they or their family members may have once owned, and dreaming about its monetary value, they do not often think beyond that level. The pieces themselves are self-evidently symbols of some sort of heritage because they are on display at the National Museum in Stockholm. But the deeper significance may never reach them, at least in a direct way.

Ikea Home Furnishings and the Spirit of Sweden

Perhaps the most prominent heir to the civic expositions of old is the one that seems most obvious. It is hard to overstate the social presence and deep cultural significance of Ikea in Sweden.[8] Square tables, ergonomic chairs, rectangular trash cans, all mostly monochromatic but also often bright, along with lightly patterned textiles, bookcases, desks, lamps, and a seemingly infinite range of other household objects both large and small, these are the mark of Ikea, and almost every home in Sweden is marked. The company has arguably been as strong a force for change in Sweden as the Stockholm Exhibition of 1930, though today the presence of Ikea furniture in the Swedish wild is so pervasive that it is almost "translucent" (Lewis 2005) to most Swedes. Perhaps that is the goal that Paulsson and other activists had in mind. Ikea certainly attempts to display a socially conscious orientation to the world, especially in relation to environmental concerns. According to the company's 2011 *Sustainability Report*—on page 7 of which appears the phrase "What is good for society is good for us," in large bold letters—since the early 1990s Ikea has banned the use of wood from nonresponsible forests, and has printed its ubiquitous catalog on environmentally friendly chlorine-free paper (Ikea 2011; see also Håkansson and Waluszewksi 2002). The flat-pack concept of self-assembly furniture, which the company helped pioneer, not only reduces the cost of its products, but also allows more pallets to be shipped in fewer containers. But this "caring" corporate attitude is not necessarily a cynical attempt to curry favor with certain customers or ward off government regulations (see Carroll 1999). It also deeply underpins the company's corporate identity (see Salzer 1994; Salzer-Mörling 1998), and has motivated Ikea's business model from the start: "To create a better everyday life for the many," wrote Ingvar Kamprad, the company's founder, "we shall offer a wider range of well designed products at prices so low that as many people as possible will be able to afford them" (quoted in Salzer 1994:255–256).

As a marketing strategy this social orientation has worked, and Ikea is now the largest furniture company in the world. But as a more subtle piece of political rhetoric, it has also left an indelible imprint on the fabric of the Swedish moral order. Using the language of class solidarity that characterized the construction of the *folkhem*, Ikea has transformed the way Swedes conceive of their domestic surroundings and, thus, their sense of private space. What once was an attitude that only the rich could afford to have beautiful things has been replaced by a principled conviction that everybody *should* be able to create a beautiful home if they so choose. In other words, Ikea has strongly pushed the idea that a home makes one feel comfortable through its material accoutrements, and over time this idea has assumed the status of a basic human right in Sweden.

The "corporate saga" (Salzer-Mörling 1998) of Ikea is well known in Sweden, and according to many of my informants, is taught in Swedish schools as an ideal model for how to develop and run a successful business. And lest shoppers forget this saga, Ikea will remind them. In the warehouse section of an Ikea store in Stockholm in 2012, a large banner hung conspicuously over one of the center aisles. On the banner, above a photograph of a simple three-legged, leaf-shaped end table, one aspect of the company's origin myth was explicitly called out:

> It all started when we removed the legs from this table in 1956. The box got considerably smaller, and suddenly we could transport lots of tables, where before we could only move a few. This meant fewer trucks on the roads.
>
> Today all of our products are packed smartly, which saves a tremendous amount of gas, lowers carbon dioxide emissions, and makes it easier for you to take things home.[9]

Ingvar Kamprad first began selling furniture via mail order, an endeavor that had sprung from his boyhood business of peddling useful trinkets like pens and matches door-to-door. The company's name is an acronym, composed of Kamprad's initials, and the first letters of the names of his family farm, Elmtaryd, and his hometown region of Agunnaryd. When Kamprad first decided to expand his products to include furniture—mostly items made by local craftsmen in the Småland region where he grew up—he used newspaper supplements, addressed "To the People of the Countryside," with pictures and descriptions of the pieces Ikea sold. By 1951 the supplements morphed into more complete catalogs presenting a larger assortment of household goods.[10] Though this business was successful, customers would often complain about the quality of the furniture they received in the mail. Kamprad and his associates realized that the most obvious shortcoming of their catalog—in Kamprad's words, "that the customers themselves could not touch the goods but had to rely on descriptions" (Torekull 1998:24)—could have an impact on the viability of their growing business. In response Kamprad decided to redirect the purpose of the catalog. No longer would it be primarily an instrument for ordering furniture for delivery; instead it would be an instrument of enticement, a tool for luring customers to visit an Ikea showroom, where they could not only see the furniture firsthand, but test it before bringing it home. In 1953 Kamprad bought a small factory building in the town of Älmhult, and inside he set up a small showroom full of Ikea furniture, arranged in a few modest model rooms. He invited customers to visit the showroom and experience Ikea furniture in as direct a way as possible—by seeing it, touching it, and using it. At first the furniture was still delivered by mail, but in 1958 the first official Ikea store was opened nearby, and since the late 1950s business has strongly and steadily increased. As of late 2014 Ikea had opened 19 stores in Sweden, and a total of 362 stores in forty-five countries, and still today, almost every store follows the same basic plan that originated in Älmhult: look and touch before you buy.

A shuttle bus takes shoppers from downtown Stockholm to the largest Ikea store in the world, which lies outside the city in Kungens Kurva.[11] The building is huge, as most Ikea stores are, and stands prominently on the landscape, a massive circular turret—the store's original structure, built in 1965, which at Kamprad's request was designed to resemble the Guggenheim Museum in New York (Wickman 2009)—fronting a newer, even larger rectangular box. The external walls of the building (again, like all Ikea stores globally) are painted blue and yellow, the colors of Sweden's national flag (a bit of unsubtle symbolism that Paulsson and Asplund would be proud of), and the company name is spelled out in enormous yellow letters affixed close to the line of the roof. Inside the atmosphere is bright, colorful, and loud—and usually stuffed with bodies of various sizes. Families make outings to Ikea, eat meals there, and spend the whole day there. To the world outside Sweden the food served at Ikea—sausages, meatballs, potatoes, and lingonberries—is typically Swedish, but Swedes recognize these dishes as country food native to Kamprad's home region of Småland. There are indoor playgrounds for children to romp in, while in the core of the building parents discover their own fun, strolling along a path through seemingly countless carefully arranged showrooms—starting on the top floor, in the living rooms—before finally landing in the ground-floor warehouse, where the flat-packed furniture on display upstairs can be picked up and taken to the cash registers.

There are collections at Ikea, of course, the latest selection of armchairs and bookcases standing alongside bins stuffed with innumerable replications of the same dish brush and the same bath mat, each item individually named according to a carefully ordered set of rules. Many of the gathered objects also have small, stylized photographs of their designers attached to their information tags or hanging on banners above them—the design group Front has created a number of items for Ikea's PS line and is often prominently featured (fig. 14)—and sometimes these pictures are accompanied by quotations from the designers meant to illuminate the objects in some way. For instance, a paragraph-long quotation from Tord Björklund, designer of the now-retired EXPEDIT line of furniture, placed below a black-and-white head shot, begins: "EXPEDIT has exactly what I like: simple, clean lines and a severe cubical formal language."[12] On a nearby wall a large poster presents an array of different objects for sale in that section—a smoke detector, reflective vests, fire extinguishers, a baby monitor, all gathered under the heading "A safer life at home."[13]

Figure 14. A placard featuring a picture of the Front designers, hung in the Ikea showroom alongside the lamp they created for the company's PS line of furniture. The accompanying text explains the group's design process. Photograph by the author.

While the collections of gathered objects at Ikea are a powerful indirect index of the widespread presence of Swedish design, just as the Stockholm Exhibition was in 1930, the rhetoric of the place is in the model rooms (fig. 15). Shoppers wander from bedrooms to dining rooms, lying on beds, testing out chairs, and peeking behind the closed doors of mock closets, all the while imagining, "How can I make this stuff useful to me?" A wife and husband discuss their needs while sitting on an unfolded sofa bed, through their words and gestures laminating the details they see before them onto their memories of the room they plan to change back home. A young man leaving his parents' house for the first time calibrates his small budget with the floor plan of his equally small apartment. A toddler hops up and down on a child's bed and confidently declares it to be the one she would like to sleep on.

Social imagineering like this is Ikea's specialty. In its showrooms the company meticulously constructs fragments of a mundane dreamworld, frameworks for an ordered way of living predicated entirely on household objects. These rooms are colorful and bright, neatly arranged curio-cabinets

Figure 15. A typical Ikea showroom, set up to look like a small living room.
Photograph by the author.

scaled to human bodies that perfectly coordinate the cultural geometry and animate its real-world potential. When shoppers enter a mock bedroom or mock living room, they temporarily enter a prototype of the possible, a version of reality ambiently indexed at once as both an infrastructure of everyday well-being and a collection of particularly Swedish things. In these rooms they experience the diagram of Swedish design firsthand, witnessing its lines of visibility and absorbing its lines of enunciation holistically through sight, sound, smell, and touch. What Ikea offers in these spaces is a stewardship of imagination, the building blocks for assembling an image not only of one's own lived world, but of the lived worlds one shares with others. It is, in a way, a simple microcosm of the social democratic order, a top-down provision of basic raw materials that support and encourage the ongoing self-assembly of a better social world.

Displaying Design, Displaying Force

There is a discernible genealogical continuity from civic expositions to trade fairs, from museums to Ikea, all of which are related not necessarily through direct descent, but rather through repeated details linked by family resemblance. Together these indexicalizing heterotopias, where Swedish design's lines of visibility and lines of enunciation are most readily brought together and laid bare, assume the task of "inscribing and broadcasting the messages of power" (Bennett 1988:74), not through official media forms sanctioned by the state, but instead through the more banal and ubiquitous material forms of everyday household objects. They work to enregister objects as Swedish design by gathering tokens of the cultural geometry together and presenting them to consuming audiences in particular semiotic configurations, distilling and constraining both the formal totality of Swedish design and its possible meanings. It is a process largely achieved through social imagineering, the use of pleasurable experience to create and reinforce particular social and semiotic relations in a more or less unnoticed manner.

The real social power of this exhibitionary complex, though, is in how the relations it projects within its heterotopic spaces seep out as experiential residue into the everyday lived world. Entering into these spaces—fairs, trade shows, museums, and department stores—provokes an outward clash in the experience of the visitor, a brute confrontation with a semiotic landscape that is at once familiar and unfamiliar. Such landscapes bear a family resemblance, sometimes more than passing, to the domestic spheres of the world outside, and while they rarely present as instances of exactly the same thing, the fit is usually close enough for the former to serve as a credible visual proxy for the latter. The semiotic relations that the exhibitionary complex casts—between objects and ideologies, between forms and meanings—evoke in visitors an afterimage, reinforced by the outward clash that occurs when moving into and out of these spaces, that flickers between the experience of the heterotopia and what is experienced at home. Tables and lamps, straight lines and simple curves, all retain their heterotopic descriptions, not so much in any obvious way, but humming along in the background of daily life—they are democratic and functional and modern and Swedish. They are ours, and they are caring.

Because the relationship between the exhibitionary complex and the outside world is asymptotic, where the two approach identity with one another but never quite get there, the afterimages produced by the traversal of indexicalizing spaces are fundamentally unstable. The redundancy built into the system, then—spatial and temporal redundancies echoing through time and resounding from node to node, continuously reimprinting afterimages in the experience of the Swedish public—is a crucial precondition for the perpetuation of Swedish design.

The four institutions that I have identified as components of the exhibitionary complex—civic exposition, the Stockholm Furniture Fair, the National Museum, and Ikea—are all, of course, quite different from one another, but at their cores they share a set of common features that help trace out the diagram of Swedish design and give it cultural substance. First, they all manipulate visitors' experience of time, though they do it with different inflections. The museum is primarily retrospective, representing a *past* that is bounded by very recent events but extends far back in time. While some objects are of recent provenance, most are preserved from long-gone historical epochs. The civic expositions, in contrast, were primarily prospective and oriented toward the *future*. Many of the products presented were not yet available for purchase, but they hinted at a possible world constituted primarily through technology and efficiency. The mock rooms improved the show, affording visitors the chance to experience that world firsthand, as it would be ordered in the inhabited space of everyday life. Finally both the Furniture Fair and Ikea are firmly set in the *present*—though they ride on a current of forward momentum. More accurately, like the expositions, they both subsist in the present but reflect a future, though that future is much closer at hand than it was at the expositions. After standing in an Ikea showroom and imagining a life as depicted in that space, a shopper need only proceed to the building's ground floor and fetch the necessary pieces. It is a future that is immediately achievable.

Second, these institutions all rely on a certain kind of embodied experience to present Swedish design persuasively as a resonant cultural category. While they all focus on *showing* design as a physical entity, rather than heavily relying on verbal descriptions and textual elaborations, some, like Ikea and the Furniture Fair, invite additional sensory experiences, such as touching or actually using the objects for their intended purposes. The museum is the only institution that restricts touching, but in exchange visitors are encouraged to read informed texts and consider more intricate ideas.

Third, while each institution, as a heterotopia, is spatially distinct from real space and obliges a transitional passage to enter or exit, each also uses space *within* its boundaries to transform how things and people relate to one another. Objects are ordered in compartmentalized displays and arranged by a small set of possible criteria: by time period (museum), material (expositions, museum), function (Ikea, expositions), or producer (Furniture Fair, Ikea). Likewise the space for motion is restricted, as visitors move from display to display in the pattern deemed appropriate by each institution. Ikea takes this format to an extreme by painting arrows on the floor and designing the basic interior plan of each of its stores almost precisely alike. And in most cases—Ikea again, but also the expositions and even some displays at the Furniture Fair—mock rooms are constructed so as to represent real space, a virtual portal out of the heterotopia and back into real space, a reminder that the order of things as presented inside is not as different from reality as it might seem.

Fourth, the four institutions also promote a modesty of scale in what counts as Swedish design. Some smaller objects, like cutlery and toy cars, fit in one's hand, while others, like sofas and chairs, are meant to hold whole human bodies. Since so much design work in Sweden is focused on the home, few examples of typical Swedish design extend beyond human scale—Volvos and Saabs might represent the outer limit. Almost everything fits in an ordinary room, and almost everything is familiar and experience-near, no matter how radical the design may be.

Finally, these four institutions are all self-consciously Swedish in their being, and that identity is practically permanently affixed onto the objects on display. The National Museum is situated in the capital and stands as the nation's most important repository for Swedish art and aesthetic culture. The national significance is clear. The early expositions, especially the Stockholm Exhibition of 1930, were subsidized by the national government and explicitly oriented toward promoting Swedish industry and lending a hand to the nation's poor. The Stockholm Furniture Fair is peppered with companies with names like Skandiform and Swedese, subtly reminding visitors of the regional or national origins of the furniture surrounding them. And of course there is Ikea, a massive architectural Swedish flag that serves traditional Swedish food, names many products with Swedish names, and hangs posters in its aisles celebrating its commitment to *demokratisk design* and inexpensive light fixtures.

On my first trip to Stockholm in 2003 I wandered into the Svensk Form gallery space on the island of Skeppsholmen. It is a small space, just a few rooms with walls painted white, and it is used to house short-term shows throughout the year. The exhibition going on at the time was called *Made in Sweden?*, and scattered throughout the rooms on low-slung platforms were a number of simple modernist pieces of design, all of which looked very much "Swedish" in appearance. And that "look" was in fact the organizing principle of the show. Some of the objects (placed on blue carpet) were made by Swedish companies but designed by non-Swedish designers. The others (placed on green carpet) were designed by Swedes but manufactured outside of Sweden. The question mark in the exhibit's title was a challenge to the viewer "to find the Swedish expression, or the lack of it" in the items on display, as a poster on the wall suggested. One of the goals of the exhibition was to highlight international collaboration in the Swedish design industry. But another, perhaps more subtle goal was to incite visitors to consider the Swedishness not just of the objects on display before them, but also of the objects they used and experienced in their own daily lives. A quote from an Italian manufacturer prominently displayed on the wall staked one strong claim: "The Swedish style is special. It has something that can be easily recognized as Swedish. We cannot say exactly what it is, but you can feel it." The implicit challenge to the viewer was, *If he can see it, can you?*

Conclusion

Designing a Social Cosmology

I have argued in this book that the expertise required to cultivate and re-produce Swedish design—and to enregister its forms as stable, recogniz-able, and meaningful—is distributed and dispersed, and in many ways necessarily so. I began by outlining the basic contours of the final vo-cabulary of Swedish design—functional, ethical, accessible, democratic, egalitarian—highlighting a parallel moral of "care" shared between de-scriptions of both social democratic ideologies and design in Sweden. Such discourse, often taking the form of ambient material and linguistic "enunciations," saturates the everyday lived world in Sweden. It appears in newspapers, magazines, and street advertisements, in store catalogs and displays, on television programs and in museum exhibitions, its force but-tressed by the ubiquitous presence of design tokens in the experienced built environment. Indeed, this discourse is not configured as a distant or disembodied appeal to a utopic vision of *the way life should be*, but rather is squarely oriented toward reminding the public that *this is the way life is*, a life enhanced by the ostensibly obvious power of everyday goods.

But as I also admitted at the start, in order to understand the logics, trajectories, and forms of how design works in Sweden as a kind of soft power, I have consciously overstated my point. The spread of objects that bear the cultural geometry is quite wide in Sweden, but it is not utterly endemic. The final vocabulary is well known and easily recognizable, but it is not on the lips of every Swedish man, woman, and child. Indeed, the politics of form is sometimes very explicit, but most of the time it is subtle and understated, if it is even stated outright at all. And while twenty-first-century Sweden remains a welfare society through and through, the *folkhem*, both the resonant concept and the strong welfare state that it represented, has been dismantled. And while modernist design still holds strong sway in Sweden, it is not the only lauded style in the Swedish design world. Nonetheless *svensk design*, and the family resemblances linking political ideas and material forms in the everyday world, carry on.

This study emerged from a long-term ethnographic project in Stockholm attuned to the multiple rich textures of social life in Sweden, and as such has attempted to account for and draw out a collection of different contexts in which both the lines of visibility and the lines of enunciation that detail the diagram of Swedish design thrive. I have followed a range of seemingly disparate symbolic domains alongside one another not because they all necessarily relate in any *direct* fashion, but because they all in their own ways—making design, marking design, and making design mean—constitute the complex and continuous reinstantiation of Swedish design as a politico-material assemblage, submerged in the everyday world, which, despite its uneven ontological state, resonates palpably in Swedish society.

I began my analysis in the home, where *svensk design* first crystallized at the intersection of domestic life, form, beauty, and social improvement. In the late nineteenth and early twentieth centuries the home emerged as a material/ideological formation seized on by both social activists and the Social Democratic Party in Sweden as a critical site for incrementally instantiating political reform in everyday life. Technocratic experts like Gunnar and Alva Myrdal worked to link the "real conditions" of the mundane world to the objectives of social policy—that is, they pushed a political goal to transform society for the better by developing and reconfiguring the circumstances in the home, the most basic and common sort of occupied social space. But this was not simply a matter of socially engineering the material conditions of domestic life. Alongside their housing reform enterprise the Social Democrats pushed a resonant discursive frame, the *folkhem*, as a metaphorical reglossing of the welfare state project, effectively recasting the nature of the state in terms of the familiar textures of everyday living. As these political aspirations emerged and matured, prominent activists like Ellen Key and Gregor Paulsson strongly advocated a considered sort of beauty—not just in art, but also in everyday objects and interiors—as a key ethical mechanism for enacting social change in everyday life. And as modernist style evolved and spread across Europe and in Sweden, a set of particular simple and rational design forms surfaced as the principal tokens of a kind of beauty that was treated as the most effective for initiating the sort of social change the Social Democrats had envisioned. In the early days, when both the final vocabulary and cultural geometry were new and vibrant, the politics of *svensk design* was rather clear and overt, an aim the authors of the hugely influential *acceptera* had set out to accomplish. But as time moved on, the explicit complementarity of ideology and form became increasingly more subtle and muted, and in some respects, increasingly taken for granted.

Jumping forward in time to the contemporary design world, where the cultural geometry persists but the final vocabulary is considered old-fashioned and outdated, the ideological conditions originally established by those early twentieth-century activists and technocrats continue to powerfully give shape and sentiment to the work that young designers do. Very few designers consider themselves to be social interventionists whose work directly solves some specific and pressing social problem. But they do see their work as inflected with an ethics of care, even if that ethics is less direct than what the progenitors of *svensk design* had advocated. Yet even as young designers resist the overdetermined politics of design, they still participate in its reproduction. In their efforts to run a viable design firm, to make a name for themselves and earn enough money to live successful, comfortable lives, designers oscillate between anxiously overlapping economic, aesthetic, and social fields—an oscillation that renders the objects they design semiotically unstable and subject to certain politicized glosses and redescriptions. In seeking meaningful recognition that might redound to their identities not as technicians but as artisans, designers place their work—their heteroglossic artifacts—in domains like exhibitions, magazines, and books that are in large part controlled by differently interested social actors, and it is here, despite the designers' desires to depoliticize their work, where the lines of visibility and enunciation are most often drawn together. Thus in the everyday textures of the Swedish design world the politics of design is variably articulated—sometimes easy, and sometimes uncomfortable—but always imminently haunting the objects that designers produce.

The cultural geometry, though, remains quite durable in the objects those designers create. The political glossings and redescriptions that curators, authors, and design historians bring to Swedish design cannot simply be asserted. They need forms that credibly tolerate those glossings, which modernist forms—simple, rational, functional forms that, it is argued, resemble the contours of welfare politics—have historically done. While the semiotic flows linking many of the most prominent sites within the design world produce artifacts that are, from one perspective, heteroglossic, imbued with the voices of the different social actors who contribute to their production, the design studio itself often operates as a machine for preserving and regenerating the cultural geometry. The studio is not a domain of politics, but a domain of form, where the lines of visibility are crafted and recrafted within the language games that constitute designing in practice. Amid the order-words that structure ways of working, talking, and thinking in the studio the cultural geometry is kept alive and granted a privileged position over other sorts of forms. Rarely does the final vocabulary seep into these interactions, and rarely is the cultural geometry invoked as an explicit formal ideal. Instead habitual, structured, and utterly mundane linguistic, gestural, and graphic practices, in combination and over time, continually contribute to the replication of a relatively small set of formal features in design objects. Interactional practices between designers are, then, in a very real sense, a critical and indeed fundamental site for the reproduction of Swedish design.

One of the most common points where the design world and the everyday world converge outside of the domestic sphere itself is in particular sites of display. Across Sweden a network of institutions like museums, galleries, stores, and trade shows harness direct experience both to mark everyday objects as "Swedish," interpellating Swedish design as a culturally significant category, and to manifest a politics of comfort and care in the particular arrangement of domestically oriented artifacts. If the beautiful home has historically been treated as a site of political reform in Sweden, these indexicalizing heterotopias do the work of revealing the semiotic links between home life and a politics of care in Swedish design by offering the opportunity to experience this relationship firsthand. The family resemblances linking these sites and their work have echoed through Swedish society for over a century. Civic expositions like Stockholm 1930 and Helsingborg 1955 were quite explicitly politically inclined and significantly promoted the Swedish design industry. Today the National Museum's design exhibit collects and curates heritage tokens of Swedish design, and smaller temporary shows in museums and galleries celebrate the output of contemporary Swedish designers. Ikea, too, explicitly celebrates Swedish design, while exploiting the final vocabulary in its branding and product descriptions. Moreover, Ikea, like the Stockholm Furniture Fair, mirrors the form of old civic expositions in the construction of consumer sites, recreating comfortable domestic spaces that iconically represent possible real homes, promoting a subtle ambient semiosis that indirectly indexes a long history of politicized living spaces. In these sites Swedes are reminded that Swedish design exists and of what it looks like and what it does.

Swedish design, then, is enregistered as a culturally durable set of things and ideas through the variegated interrelations among such symbolic domains as history, markets, design interactions, and the dynamics of social space, including public and private environments, city neighborhoods, and various design-oriented heterotopias. The levels of symbolic manipulation and the different ways in which they impinge on the production of design as a cultural system rely on "semiosis across encounters," in Asif Agha's (2005) phrasing, throughout an array of contexts in which the products of human action flow. Indeed, each such context leaves behind its own patina of semiotic residue on objects passing through, sometimes readily noticeable and sometimes unconsciously intuited as objects travel from domain to domain. Interactions weave into the fabric of history as the residue of design activities is left in forms. The communicative force of aesthetic forms accrues to common household goods as the residue of art settles on commercial objects. Displayed in heterotopic spaces and configured alongside statements of the final vocabulary, these objects acquire specific ideological associations that bleed into everyday life once they are sold and bought.

Lines of enunciation—politicized utterances focused on beauty, care, practicality, rationality, and egalitarianism—and lines of visibility—unadorned forms like straight lines, right angles, and clear surfaces that ostensibly bear some iconic family resemblance to those utterances—these are what constitute the diagram of Swedish design, all of which are drawn together as they move through the cultural domains I have just elaborated. To be sure design is in general *political* in all sorts of ways in all sorts of contexts, and the Swedish case is not in its broadest strokes unique. However, there is, I have argued, something particular about the way design works in Sweden that I think lends this diagram a distinct inflection. If such a thing can be said to exist, its Swedishness derives from the particularities of the trajectories of both politics and the design industry in Sweden, and the relations that have historically held between them. Over the course of the twentieth century an otherwise widely shared social democratic political system developed in specific ways in Sweden, distinct even from its Nordic neighbors, the hallmarks of which included a commitment to particular morally inclined ideals like cross-class solidarity, the intentional construction of a large middle class, and a commitment to broad-based participatory democracy as the core political form. Moreover, Sweden's neutral stance during both world wars contributed significantly to the uninterrupted development and implementation of social democratic policies and ideologies, a situation unparalleled in other European states. What that means is that the ideas and ideals underpinning social democracy have dominated Swedish politics for decades, so much so that they have become over time immanent features of Swedish cultural life.

From the start, collaboration between those with political power and those working in design has mattered, giving form to Swedish society. Ellen Key's participation in the initial formation of the SAP, and the friendships between Gunnar and Alvar Myrdal and the organizers of the Stockholm Exhibition of 1930 (and the authors of *acceptera*) prefigure contemporary associations between the Swedish government and organizations like Svensk Form tasked with promoting and cultivating Swedish design in a wider public context. And contemporary Swedish firms with international reputations, like Volvo, H&M, and especially Ikea (even if, as in the case of Volvo, they are no longer Swedish-owned), rely on design as a key feature of their global brands, thereby reinforcing the significance of Swedish design both inside and outside Sweden.

There is, of course, plenty of critique of this neat and tidy picture of Swedishness and Swedish design circulating in Sweden, much of which often invokes the language of "myth" (e.g., Ahl and Olsson 2002; Halén and Wickman 2003; Tell 2004), in the "not true" sense of the word. But I think that such a reading misses the point. Whether or not everyday goods are "true" reflections of social democratic ideologies is ultimately an unverifiable point. It is a claim, an argument, a language game of sorts, and as such it is always subject to the details constituting the contexts in which the claim is made. However, there is certainly something quite *hegemonic* about the relationship between welfare politics and design in Sweden, in Antonio Gramsci's original sense of that term.

For Gramsci, hegemony centered on moral leadership and class solidarity as core requirements for effecting wide-scale social change. In contrast to the way the term is often used, hegemony was not a totalizing authoritarian structure designed to dupe individuals through the imposition of false consciousness, but rather a mechanism geared, in part, toward shaping collective consensual belief, or what Gramsci called "common sense." But while common sense may be broadly shared, it is by no means innate or basic—instead it is always "a product of history and a part of the historical process" (Gramsci 2000:327). Critical in this process, though, is the necessary plausibility of ideology. For Gramsci hegemonic political systems may work to help give shape to common sense, but that shaping unfolds not through dominance or coercion, but through the persuasive pull of plausibility:

> It is evident that this kind of mass construction cannot just happen "arbitrarily," around any ideology, simply because of the formally constructive will of a personality or a group which puts it forward solely on the basis of its own fanatical philosophical or religious convictions. Mass adhesion or non-adhesion to an ideology is the very critical test of the rationality and historicity of modes of thinking. Any arbitrary constructions are pretty rapidly eliminated by historical competition, even if sometimes, through a combination of immediately favorable circumstances, they manage to enjoy popularity of a kind; whereas constructions which respond to the demands of a complex organic period of history always impose themselves and prevail in the end, even though they may pass through several intermediary phases during which they affirm themselves only in more or less bizarre and heterogeneous combinations. (341)

In other words, the persistence of ideologies and the cultural forms in which they manifest is not determined solely by the imposition of force or political will but is always sustained by real, felt connections between ideologies and material conditions. From this perspective, then, the final vocabulary and cultural geometry, conspicuous manifestations of social democratic hegemony, function as "forms of cultural organization which keep the ideological world in movement" (342) in Sweden not because the state and other social actors have, through the years, forcefully *insisted* on it, but because the insisted claims have in various ways resonated with people's experiences.

To be sure, the particular moral accents that color the relationship between politics and design can be read in several different ways from the same set of facts. In this book I have taken seriously the relatively positive valence of Swedish design that posits a harmonious relationship between the goals of social democratic governance and the development of *svensk design*. Among other reasons, I have followed this line partly because, despite periodic opposition, it is the dominant form the Swedish design narrative has taken, and as such that form deserves consideration and contemplation rather than immediate critique. But another reason—one that is harder to admit to—is because, as an outsider to the system, a peripheral character in the narrative, I feel like there really is something to it. But to recognize that "something" does not, of course, foreclose other possible critical interpretations. It is quite conceivable to discern the socially beneficial sides of Swedish design while at the same time recognizing its function as an apparatus of mundane governance that instantiates a situated "grid of intelligibility of the social order" (Foucault 1978:93) for both a state in need of controlling its citizens and a public pressed into conformity. Indeed, maintaining "the simple economic geometry of a 'house of certainty'" (Foucault 1977:202) is a necessary procedure for any state project invested in politicized design, whether those politics lean more toward advantaging populations and individuals than disadvantaging them. In other words, whether the political utility of design like the kind evident in Sweden is for liberal or illiberal purposes, the mechanism of its operation is largely the same. How one glosses it, though, is a matter of rhetoric, disposition, and interpretation.

In this book I have also made an argument for analytically detaching symbols from closed contexts of interpretation and expanding the scope of inquiry to encompass a wider view of how symbols are crafted at multiple degrees of magnification. In particular, this entails examining how certain forms become imbued with cultural meanings in a range of different contexts and looking closely at how particular semiotic relationships are brought together, patterned, and naturalized across time and social space. Moreover, I have argued for understanding how processes of symbolization are accomplished and put into motion. Cultural meanings are *made* meanings, achieved through the actions of those who hold some stake in their continued existence. To be sure, culture itself, an intricate lattice-work of mere phenomena artificially transformed into symbols, is "an 'as if' made into an 'is' by the seriousness of those who use it" (Wagner 1986:8). Only through active and sustained *engagement* with signs across diverse cultural domains—creating them and recreating them, challenging them and defending them—can cultural meanings persist, develop, and indeed compel individuals to invest in them. All of the practices in which the Swedish cultural geometry and final vocabulary are reproduced, from design activities to turning on a lamp, reveal a literal "cosmology in the making," to borrow Fredrik Barth's (1987) phrase, a careful shaping of the physical contours of the Swedish social universe.

Thus the myth of Swedish design is, in fact, real. Perhaps one reason people in Sweden are invested in maintaining design as a system of reified cultural values is because of its role as a material component of the Swedish social cosmology (cf. Fehérváry 2012). After decades of almost uninter-rupted Social Democratic control of national politics, most Swedes have grown accustomed to viewing the world through a lens of welfare eco-nomics, and this has in turn colored beliefs about how social relations are morally required to work. Cosmologies are, in Tambiah's (1985:3) words, "frameworks of concepts and relations which treat the universe or cosmos as an ordered system, describing it in terms of space, time, matter, and motion." While cosmologies are traditionally conceived as *religiously* sig-nificant ways for explaining the mechanics of how the wider world works, *secular* cosmologies are a similarly potent means for instantiating the moral order in commonly shared beliefs. A social cosmology allocates positions and clarifies relations among social beings. It provides "common sense," a means for explaining and mapping out how the social universe does and should work, and helps individuals reckon their place in a grander order of things.

In Sweden, a society whose public face is thoroughly secular, the social cosmology (which is decidedly not to say the actual workings of society) treats all people as fundamentally free and fundamentally equal to one another. At the same time individuals are also obliged to minimize their own negative impact on the world and their peers, and thus their freedom is tempered by an acute awareness of how they and others should and do behave. However, the cosmological view also admits that individuals face potentially intractable problems they are unable to solve through their own means, and thus a corollary to freedom is the ideal that hardship and adversity should and can be managed through channels external to the individual but available to everyone. To that end the Swedish social cosmology places great faith in the "higher power" of the social collective, which, because the cosmology stems from a democratic political system, is represented by a regulatory government—at local, regional, and national levels—charged with enacting the will of the group.

The welfare system, run by the state, is a significant but impersonal means for people to receive external care. Design, too, follows a similar pattern by providing impersonal, external care in everyday life. The ordering of the Swedish social cosmology is symbolically reinforced by the widespread presence of common household goods that perform much of the everyday work of managing mundane hardship. They are not just tools for accomplishing some given task at hand—sitting, sleeping, cutting; they simultaneously become signs used by individuals to enact the spirit of the cosmological attitude and thereby engage in the reproduction of culture. At the same time these objects, never entirely extracted from the final vocabulary even in everyday life, morally skew perceptions of the material world in their use. Symbolic manipulations, and indeed all ideological processes, are concerned at the core with cognition. Inasmuch as animals, as Lévi-Strauss (1971:89) asserts, figure so prominently in the cosmologies of traditional societies because they are "good to think," so too does the artifice of the everyday function in the Swedish social cosmology. The extensive existence of objects designed to anticipate and meet the needs of users transforms the exceptionality of such objects into taken-for-granted facts about the way the world *should be* structured and what that structure *should* accomplish.

This is, in a word, a cosmology of modernity that reshapes the natural world to conform to human will. It is the construction of an "artificial nature" populated by citizens, workers, and consumers instead of gods, spirits, and demons. It is divinity replaced by civility, the purposeful ordering and structuring of the social universe according not to the unknowable whims of a heavenly deity, but to the familiar needs of more worldly beings. Modern nation-states maintain an interest in resculpting the natural world for a number of logistical and economic reasons, one of the most central of which is making populations more "legible" (Scott 1998) and easy to control, and the Swedish state is no exception. In the Swedish social cosmology, after decades of social engineering and social imagineering projects, state ideology, cultural attitudes, and social norms have coalesced to the point that such categories are in practice indistinguishable from one another. Critical in this process has been the cultivation of design as a rational and thoroughly artificial alternative to strict reliance on the natural universe to satisfy all human needs.

Lukács (1968), following Marx, argued that objects acquire a reified "otherness" in the objectification of labor. The temporal flow of the labor process becomes spatialized in the form of objects, which themselves then come to stand in for the very labor processes from which they emerged. In this way objects take on what Lukács calls a "second nature" as not just things-as-they-are, but also as taken-for-granted tokens of human toil. In a similar sense, we might describe the creation and spread of everyday objects crafted in the mold of Swedish design as the reification of the sociopolitical values of the social cosmology, a "second nature," *another* nature that exists alongside the physical reality of the natural world, but is fundamentally rational, controlled, and human—two natures aligned in everyday life. As I have mentioned or discussed at various points in this book, Swedes maintain a deep respect for the natural environment, an affection whose patent fervor rarely goes unremarked in books written by foreigners for general outsider audiences (e.g., Austin 1968). Recycling is a way of life in Sweden, partially mandated by government policy, but also widely advocated as the right thing to do (Isenhour 2010). Skiing, skating, and ice fishing are popular activities during the winter, despite the cold and darkness, and typical summertime events, especially at Midsummer, involve retreating to the countryside—preferably by the ocean or one of the country's countless lakes—to spend time with family and friends. Indeed, both individuals and the social collective preserve intimate connections with the natural world in Sweden, and even design itself, conventionally crafted in wood, steel, glass, and other sustainable materials, tends to interact with the environment in nondestructive ways. Thus the construction of an artificial "second" nature in Sweden is not aimed at *supplanting* the already given natural world—a common goal, or perhaps by-product, of many state-sponsored modernization projects (see, e.g., Scott 1998; Holston 1989)—but instead at *supplementing* it with a responsible, cooperative system better equipped to handle the social consequences entailed in building a modern society.

Finally, although I have focused in this book on the cultural particulars of Swedish design, I hope that such research has broader implications. Fundamentally, I would like to advocate the position that by examining the *semiotics of material production* we can link up ground-level dynamics of language use to the ideological forces within which materiality helps shape culture. Moreover, as I see it, there are at least three further thematic areas to consider. First, an anthropology of design highlights the contributions to political theater and social life made by designers, a significant but otherwise overlooked group of social agents responsible for manufacturing the set pieces of everyday life. An anthropology of design, focused on how physical worlds and moral orders are meaningfully and purposefully structured, can shed light on how cultural knowledge, values, and norms are consciously put to use in fabricating materials that create, support, and challenge ideologies. Second, an anthropology of design contributes to a general understanding of the relationship between the broad categories of material culture, style, and politics, and how these relate to on-the-ground practices of creation and planning. Finally, an anthropology of design provides an ideal ground both to document the processes by which certain "designed" objects are transformed into "culture," and to refine the conceptual apparatus required for understanding how such processes function more generally.

In designing objects designers are, of course, making *things*, commodities intended to be bought and sold. But they are, with the help of various other social actors and institutions, simultaneously crafting and naturalizing *signs*, constructing an always emergent but nonetheless stable semiotic system with deep significance and resonance in modern Swedish society. I have tried to examine thing-making (the cultural geometry) and meaning-making (the final vocabulary) as interrelated social processes, each with its own dynamics, but whose products possess a unified symbolic identity in the social world. While language is a crucial semiotic resource for constructing such cultural symbols, it is by no means the only, or even primary one. Like the objects of design themselves, the language of design circulates within, between, and around innumerable symbolic domains and settles in the most obvious and most obscure corners of culture. The challenge, then, is to pull both objects and language out from those corners and place them together, front and center, as one way to understand how they relate both to each other and to the wider sociocultural world.

NOTES

Introduction

1. As of yet there are not many in-depth ethnographic studies of design from an anthropological point of view; however, a few recent works have begun to address Suchman's call in different ways. Jakob Krause-Jensen's (2010) study of Danish electronics producer Bang and Olufsen examines how the circulation of corporate values helps employees both maintain solidarity and form deep divisions within the company's organizational structure. Natasha Dow Schüll's (2012) detailed examination of "machine gambling" in Las Vegas reveals the many subtle ways in which slot machine design and casino interior design help capture gamblers in spheres of addiction.

2. There are a number of good overviews of Swedish and Scandinavian design available in English: Fiell and Fiell 2002; Helgeson and Nyberg 2002; Nelson 2004; Sommar 2011. For several important early Swedish design texts, with comprehensive commentary, see Creagh, Kåberg, and Lane (2008). Mattsson and Wallenstein (2010) offer a more historical view of design and society in Sweden in the twentieth century, and Fallan (2012) is a useful critical rereading of Scandinavian design history.

3. See Yaneva (2009) for an insightful ethnographic look into the design practices of one of the most highly regarded international architects, Rem Koolhaas.

4. For anthropologists familiar with the name, yes, it's the same Wenner-Gren. Axel Wenner-Gren was a Swedish businessman and designer who, in the 1930s, played a pivotal role in the development of the home vacuum cleaner when he worked for the company Electrolux. He went on to develop a number of other products, but is perhaps best known for building and

advocating monorail transportation systems in the 1960s. In 1941 he founded the Viking Fund to support anthropological research, which is now known as the Wenner-Gren Foundation.

5. For an overview of early generations of Swedish anthropologists, most of whom were not conducting research in Sweden, see Hannerz (1982, 1985).

6. It is important to note, though, that while there are many high-level similarities across the political systems within the Nordic region, these systems are not, in any monolithic sense, the same (Mjøset 1992). Knudsen and Rothstein (1994), for instance, argue that while both Denmark and Sweden may nominally operate according to a shared Scandinavian political model, the two nations have constructed their respective systems, including institutions like the military and civil administration, along historically distinct lines. And while the Nordic countries have gone through periods of both similarity and difference over the past several decades with regard to gender-equality policy (especially around issues of mothering and work), today there are relatively stark differences in the degree to which states officially enforce these policies (Sweden and Norway regulate, while Denmark does not; see Melby, Ravn, and Wetterberg 2009; see also Bergqvist et al. 1999). The Nordic model of welfare, then, and Sweden's adherence to it, in as much as it represents a set of real policies, tax schemes, and orientations that extend across the Nordic countries, should also be treated as a usefully blunt category—and a blunt category with deep resonance in Sweden and the other Nordic countries—and viewed within a broader cultural project in which Norden itself is continually constructed and recast in light of changing social and economic conditions.

7. For details on the lead-up to the crisis, see Englund (1999) and Llewellyn (1992); for details on how the crisis was handled, see Larsson (2003).

8. Importantly, it seems that the SAP's success in the 2014 election has less to do with a newfound appeal of left-leaning policies than with shifting party dynamics across the political spectrum. The Social Democrats and the Left Party saw only very modest increases in their vote tallies over the 2010 election, while the Greens lost votes, and many voters on the left threw in with the Feminist Initiative (Feministiskt Initiativ), a small party that wasn't able to secure enough votes to seat any members in parliament. The biggest shift, however, occurred on the right, where the nationalist, anti-immigration party, the Sweden Democrats (Sverigedemokraterna, SD), were able to capture almost 13 percent of the vote, becoming the third largest party in Sweden behind the SAP and Moderaterna. Because the conservative Alliance refused to collaborate with SD, a weak red-green alliance was able to win the election.

9. Links between furniture and nationalist sentiment have also been described in other contexts (e.g., Auslander 1996; Arnadottir 1999), and a link between mundane aesthetics and "national character" has been described in other countries, such as Japan (Riessland 1997; Madge 1997; McVeigh 2000).

1. The Diagram of Swedish Design

1. For more on the retrospective creation of "modernism" as a distinct aesthetic style, see Banham (1967), Goldhagen (2005), and Pevsner (1960).

2. With the exception of Peter and Matti (chapter 4), all of the names used to identify informants (individuals or groups) are pseudonyms. I use Peter's and Matti's real names because their work, which I describe in detail, is so connected to who they are that pseudonyms wouldn't function as intended. This is also true of the design group Front, which is the collective's real name. Other names identified as well-known contemporary or historical figures in design are also real.

3. See Doordan (1995), Sparke (1988, 1998), and Sabatino (2010) for more on the development of Italian modernist design.

2. Building the Beautiful Home

1. For more on national romanticism in other parts of Scandinavia, see Falnes (1933) and Lane (2000).

2. Unless otherwise noted, all translations of Swedish sources are my own. In most instances, for readability's sake, I don't provide the original Swedish alongside my English translations. However, with some texts in particular—Ellen Key's being a good example—I've chosen to include the original Swedish because it displays an important rhetorical force that I think gets lost in translation. If English-language versions of these texts exist, I cite those, too. Additionally, in some cases I'll quote and cite an English translation instead of the original Swedish version because the English-language sources are easier for readers to track down, should they choose to do so.

3. For a full translation of Key's essay, along with two other important early texts in Swedish design history, see Creagh, Kåberg, and Lane (2008).

4. Nordstrom (2000), Tomasson (1970), and especially Scott (1988) offer comprehensive and accessible presentations of the social and political landscape in prewar Sweden. For more details on the general political system, see Andersson (2006), Hadenius (1990), Lewin (1988), and Tilton (1990), and on the development of the *folkhem* in particular, see Berman (1998, 2004, 2006).

5. The sources I am drawing on here with regard to the life and work of Gunnar Myrdal, including the political-economic situation in 1930s Sweden, are Appelqvist and Anderson (2005), Barber (2008), Eliaeson (2000), Gill (1992), Jackson (1990), Lalonde (1992), and Tilton (1992); on Alva Myrdal see Hirdman's (2008) comprehensive biography; and for more on both Myrdals and their collaborations, see Carlson (1990), Eyerman (1985), and Hirdman (1994).

6. Hirdman (1992) provides a critical analysis of the SAP's early efforts in social engineering, including the central roles played by Gunnar and Alva Myrdal. See also Hirdman (1994, 2008) and Therborn (1989).

7. An English-language version of the Swedish constitution can be found on the Riksdag's website: http://www.riksdagen.se/en/Documents-and-laws/Laws/The-Constitution/.

3. In the Design World

1. This stance conforms to a general cultural tendency in Sweden to avoid boastfulness and project humility when discussing one's own achievements, which when translated into the practice of business, has potential effects on how the business grows. While the hypercognized cultural trait of humility is by no means unique to Sweden (Daun 1998), it has become a form of what Herzfeld (2005) calls "cultural intimacy" there—that which when seen from the outside seems slightly embarrassing but which nevertheless furnishes insiders with a deeply felt sense of familiarity. This articulated humility is strongly expressed throughout Scandinavia, and has been codified across the region as "Jante's law"—*jantelagen* in Swedish. The phrase was coined by Norwegian author Aksel Sandemose, who, in one of his novels, drew up a tongue-in-cheek list of ten inviolable laws, all of which more or less amount to "Don't think you're better than anyone else." This maxim has resonated well enough in Sweden to have become a nationally recognized cultural trait. *Jante*, as it is colloquially known, is widely followed in Swedish social interaction, and many Swedes consider it to be a core element of so-called Swedishness (Daun 1998). Some even consider *jante* to underpin the continued perseverance of the Swedish welfare state (Henningsen 2001). It also influences an almost universal resistance among designers in Sweden to self-promotion and prevents them from pitching their designs to potential paying clients. As a result, their income stream is fundamentally limited to and reliant on producers who happen to notice their work and actively seek them out for assignments.

2. While "network" has been the dominant metaphor used to describe the structure of most art worlds, Giuffre (1999) remarks that these communities more often take the form of what she calls a "sandpile": as any one individual navigates the art world its shape changes, altering the terrain and its possible through-points for those who follow.

3. In Sweden the *kommun*, sometimes translated as "municipality," is a level of local government that is smaller than the county (*län*) but often larger than a single community. Much of the provision of welfare services (e.g., child care, early education, elder care) is handled at the level of the *kommun*.

4. In the Studio

1. I am working here within the parameters of existing studies of conversation in design interactions (Ivarsson 2010; Lymer 2009; Lymer, Ivarsson, and Lindwall 2009; Luck 2009, 2010; Murphy 2004, 2005, 2012; Oak 2011; Reid and Reed 2007), which tend to highlight the role of linguistically mediated action as central for mobilizing design knowledge in practice.

2. While Austin's theory has had widespread influence on social scientific theory—for instance, the study of gender performativity (see Hall 2000; Morris 1995) and Callon's theory of markets (MacKenzie, Muniesa, and Siu 2008), the intricate, underlying mechanics of speech act theory have also been critiqued from a number of different angles (Rosaldo 1982; Silverstein 1979; Streeck 1980). Perlocutionary effects themselves have typically been underexamined in the range of scholarship influenced by speech act theory, at least those areas concerned with the kinds of linguistically mediated contexts that Austin first identified (Cohen 1973). This stems partly from analytical methods traditionally used by philosophers and some linguists that favor imagined examples over real-world data, which afford closer attention to locutions and illocutions, as well as an orientation to perlocutions as strictly affective and immaterial (see Ricoeur 1976). Yet even when the force of language is explored in naturally occurring speech (see Duranti 2011), it is often very difficult to measure or even identify a clear relation between a given utterance and a given effect. One notable exception is Butler's (1993:7) famous discussion of "girling" in which upon the pronouncement "It's a girl" a female infant is "brought into the domain of language and kinship through the interpellation of gender." Ironically, the later Butler (2010), distancing herself from perlocutionary acts, seems to disagree with the characterization that relatively little attention has been paid to perlocutions. She states in her analysis of Callon (1998) that "within the social sciences more generally ... performativity has become a way to think about 'effects', in particular, to supply an alternative to causal frameworks for thinking about effects" (Butler 2010:147). While this may arguably be the case for various conceptual extensions of Austin's theory to broad processes of social formation, it does not apply to the way perlocutions have been taken up in the study of on-the-ground communicative behavior.

3. Conventions used in the transcripts: — = cut-off speech; (.) = short pause; (1.0) = timed pause, in seconds; words enclosed in single parentheses ( ) = best guess of unclear speech; material enclosed in double parentheses (( )) = contextual information; [= overlapping speech.

4. This is a pseudonym.

5. Displays of Force

1. Compare the opening of this text to that of a large poster greeting visitors at American Ikea stores in early 2008: "We *believe* that *home* is the most important place in the world.

2. The Deutscher Werkbund (German Work Association) was founded in Germany in 1907 by a group of architects and designers interested in protecting traditional aesthetic culture from the potentially devastating effects of industrialization (see Campbell 1978). They did not work against mass production but sought to find ways to integrate handicrafts and other forms of traditional artistry into emerging methods of production (see also Overy 2004).

3. This description is after Rudberg (1999) and Pred (1995). See also Rudberg (1995), Råberg (1970), Fant (1985), and Koinberg (1985).

4. See Lövgren (1993) for an in-depth discussion of HFI—and its relation to Svenska Slöjdföreningen—and the improvement of women's social position in Swedish society through the politicization of housework.

5. For more on H55, see also Silow (1995); Wickman (1985, 1995); Andersson (1993); Johnson (1985); Bengtsson (1993); and Hald (1970).

6. The problem is largely restricted to the Anglophone world, where two separate versions of the original lecture, one called "Of Other Spaces" (Foucault 1986) and the other called "Different Spaces" (Foucault 1998), have circulated with small but significant deviations in the translations of some key terms.

7. Donald Horne (1984) describes European museums as "dreamlands" where states cynically attempt to reinscribe official, often totalizing versions of history in more or less explicit ways. He does note, however, that Sweden—which he characterizes as "a paragon of soullessness" (144)—is, compared to other European nations, generally restrained in its museum representations of social democratic success.

8. The most comprehensive sources for all sorts of information about Ikea are Bengtsson's 2010 and Bjarnestam's 2009 works, both of which the company itself had a hand in producing. Indeed, as Lewis (2005) notes in the foreword to her book about Ikea, the company tends to be rather touchy about reporters and academics other than those interested in the organizational side of things (e.g., Salzer 1994; Björk 1998) snooping around too much. There is also a minor genre of literature critical of Ikea, or of its founder Ingvar Kamprad (e.g., Stenebo 2009, 2011; Åsbrink 2011).

9. "Allt började med att vi tog av benen från den här bordet 1956. Lådan blev betydligt mindre och plötsligt kunde vi transportera mängder av bord där bara några få hade få plats förut. Det betydde färre lastbilar på vägarna.

Idag är alla våra produkter förpackade på ett smart sätt vilket spårar ofantliga mängder olja, sänker koldioxidutsläppen och gör det lättare för dig att ta med sakerna hem."

10. Today the Ikea catalog is one of the most widely distributed publications in the world—apocryphally surpassing even the Bible's popularity—with over two hundred million copies printed each year in twenty-nine different languages. The catalog also serves as a two-dimensional print version of the showroom experience that Ikea stores provide (Edvardsson, Enquist, and Johnston 2005), prominently featuring glossy photographs of elaborate life scenes unfolding in Ikea-furnished rooms. In Sweden the release of the annual catalog is a major media event, covered by newspapers all over the country and some of the major television networks.

11. In a 2004 interview with Swedish newspaper *Svenska Dagbladet* (Blomgren 2004), Ingvar Kamprad admitted that he preferred to take the subway and the Ikea shuttle to the Kungens Kurva location when he was visiting Stockholm from his home in Switzerland.

12. "EXPEDIT har precis det jag tycker om: enkla, rena linjer och ett stramt, kubiskt formspråk."

13. "Ett tryggare liv hemma."

REFERENCES

Agha, A. 2003. "The Social Life of Cultural Value." *Language and Communication* 23 (3–4): 231–273.

———. 2005. "Introduction: Semiosis across Encounters." *Journal of Linguistic Anthropology* 15 (1): 1–5.

Ahl, Z., and E. Olsson. 2002. *Svensk Smak: Myter om den Moderna Formen*. Stockholm: Ordfront Förlag.

Ahlgren, P. 1978. *Tilltalsordet "Ni": Dess Semantik och Användning i Historiskt Perspektiv*. Uppsala: Almqvist and Wiksell.

Åhren, U., G. Asplund, W. Gahn, S. Markelius, G. Paulsson, and E. Sundahl. 1931. *Acceptera*. Stockholm: Tryckeriaktiebolaget Tiden.

———. 2008. "Acceptera." In *Modern Swedish Design: Three Founding Texts*, edited by L. Creagh, H. Kåberg, and B. M. Lane, 140–347. New York: The Museum of Modern Art.

Akner-Kohler, C. 2007. *Form and Formlessness: Questioning Aesthetic Abstractions through Art Projects, Cross-Disciplinary Studies and Product Design Education*. Stockholm: Konstfack University College of Arts.

Alpers, S. 1990. "The Museum as a Way of Seeing." In *Exhibiting Cultures: The Poetics and Politics of Museum Display*, edited by I. Karp and S. D. Lavine, 25–32. Washington, DC: Smithsonian Institution Press.

Andersson, F. 1993. "I Människans Tjänst." *Utblick Landskap* 2: 32–33.

Andersson, J. 2006. *Between Growth and Democracy: Swedish Social Democracy from a Strong Society to a Third Way*. Manchester: Manchester University Press.

Appelqvist, Ö. and S. Anderson, eds. 2005. *The Essential Gunnar Myrdal*. New York: The New Press.

Arnadottir, A. A. 1999. "Vernacular Furniture Crafts to Design: Icelandic Furniture, 1900–1945." *Scandinavian Journal of Design History* 9: 74–93.

Åsbrink, E. 2011. *Och i Weinerwald Står Träden Kvar*. Stockholm: Natur och Kultur.

Auslander, L. 1996. *Taste and Power: Furnishing Modern France*. Berkeley: University of California Press.

Austin, J. L. 1962. *How to Do Things with Words*. Cambridge, MA: Harvard University Press.

Austin, P. B. 1968. *On Being Swedish: Reflections towards a Better Understanding of the Swedish Character*. London: Secker and Warburg.

Aylott, N., and N. Bolin. 2007. "Towards a Two-Party System? The Swedish Parliamentary Election of September 2006." *West European Politics* 30 (3): 621–633.

Aynsley, J. 2000. *Graphic Design in Germany, 1890–1945*. Berkeley: University of California Press.

Baer, L. D., and B. Ravneberg. 2008. "The Outside and Inside in Norwegian and English Prisons." *Geografiska Annaler: Series B, Human Geography* 90 (2): 205–216.

Bakhtin, M. 1981. "Discourse in the Novel." In *The Dialogic Imagination*, 259–422. Austin: University of Texas Press.

Banarjee, M., and D. Miller. 2003. *The Sari*. Oxford: Berg.

Banham, R. 1967. *Theory and Design in the First Machine Age*. New York: Frederick A. Praeger Publishers.

Barber, W. J. 2008. *Gunnar Myrdal: An Intellectual Biography*. New York: Palgrave.

Barth, F. 1987. *Cosmologies in the Making: A Generative Approach to Cultural Variation in Inner New Guinea*. Cambridge: Cambridge University Press.

Barthes, R. 1986. "The Reality Effect." In *The Rustle of Language*, 141–148. Oxford: Blackwell.

Bateson, G. 1979. *Mind and Nature: A Necessary Unity*. New York: Bantam.

Baudrillard, J. 1996. *The System of Objects*. London: Verso.

Becker, H. S. 1982. *Art Worlds*. Berkeley: University of California Press.

Belfrage, C. 2008. "Towards 'Universal Financialisation' in Sweden?" *Contemporary Politics* 14 (3): 277–296.

Bengtsson, A. 1993. "En Oförglömlig Fest." *Utblick Landskap* 2: 34–37.

Bengtsson, S. 2010. *IKEA the Book: Designers, Products, and Other Stuff*. Stockholm: Arvinius Förlag.

Bennett, T. 1988. "The Exhibitionary Complex." *New Formations* 4: 73–102.

Berdahl, D. 1999. "'(N)Ostalgie' for the Present: Memory, Longing, and East German Things." *Ethnos* 64 (2): 192–211.

Bergqvist, C., A. Borchorst, A.-D. Christensen, V. Ramstedt-Silén, and A. Styrkársdóttir, eds. 1999. *Equal Democracies? Gender and Politics in the Nordic Countries*. Oslo: Scandinavian University Press.

Berkling, A. L. 1982. *Från Fram till Folkhemmet: Per Albin Hansson som Tidningsman och Talare*. Stockholm: Metodica Press.

Berman, S. 1998. *The Social Democratic Moment: Ideas and Politics in the Making of Interwar Europe*. Cambridge, MA: Harvard University Press.

———. 2004. "The Folkhem Was a Success Story." In *The Swedish Success Story?*, edited by K. Almqvist and K. Glans, 61–66. Stockholm: Axel & Margaret Axson Johnson Foundation.

———. 2006. *The Primacy of Politics: Social Democracy and the Making of Europe's Twentieth Century*. Cambridge: Cambridge University Press.

Berner, B. 1998. "The Meaning of Cleaning: The Creation of Harmony and Hygiene in the Home." *History and Technology* 14: 313–352.

Betts, P. 2000. "The Twilight of the Idols: East German Memory and Material Culture." *Journal of Modern History* 72 (3): 731–765.

———. 2002. "The New Fascination with Fascism: The Case of Nazi Modernism." *Journal of Contemporary History* 37 (4): 541–558.

———. 2004. *The Authority of Everyday Objects: A Cultural History of West German Industrial Design*. Berkeley: University of California Press.

Billig, M. 1995. *Banal Nationalism*. London: SAGE.

Bjarnestam, E. A. 2009. *IKEA: Design och Identitet*. Stockholm: Bokförlaget Arena.

Björk, S. 1998. *IKEA: Entreprenören, Affärsiden, Kulturen*. Stockholm: Svenska Förlag.

Blomgren, J. 2004. "Kamprad Tar T-banan till Sitt Varuhus." *Svenska Dagbladet*, March 29.

Bourdieu, P. 1993a. "The Field of Cultural Production, or: The Economic World Reversed." In *The Field of Cultural Production*, 29–73. New York: Columbia University Press.

———. 1993b. "The Market of Symbolic Goods." In *The Field of Cultural Production*, 112–141 New York: Columbia University Press.

———. 1993c. "The Production of Belief: Contribution to an Economy of Symbolic Goods." In *The Field of Cultural Production*, 74–111. New York: Columbia University Press.

Boyer, D. 2001. "The Impact and Embodiment of Western Expertise in the Restructuring of the Eastern German Media after 1990." *Anthropology of East Europe Review* 19 (1): 77–84.

———. 2005a. The Corporeality of Expertise. *Ethnos* 70 (2): 243–266.

———. 2005b. *Spirit and System: Media, Intellectuals, and the Dialectic in Modern German Culture*. Chicago: University of Chicago Press.

———. 2006. "Ostalgie and the Politics of the Future in Eastern Germany." *Public Culture* 18 (2): 361–381.

Brinton, C. 1916. "The Swedish Art Exhibition." *Fine Arts Journal* 34 (8): 402–415.

Butler, J. 1993. *Bodies That Matter: On the Discursive Limits of "Sex."* New York: Routledge.

———. 2010. "Performative Agency." *Journal of Cultural Economy* 3 (2): 147–161.

Bydler, C. 2004. *The Global ArtWorld Inc.: On the Globalization of Contemporary Art*. Uppsala: Uppsala University.

Callon, M. 1986. "Some Elements of a Sociology of Translation: Domestication of the Scallops and the Fishermen of St. Brieuc Bay." In *Power, Action and Belief: A New Sociology of Knowledge?*, edited by John Law, 196–223. London: Routledge.

———. 1987. "Society in the Making: The Study of Technology as a Tool for Sociological Analysis." In *The Social Construction of Technological Systems: New Directions in the Sociology and History of Technology*, edited by W. E. Bijker, T. P. Hughes, and T. Pinch, 85–103. Cambridge, MA: MIT Press.

———, ed. 1998. *Laws of the Markets*. London: Routledge.

Campbell, J. 1978. *The German Werkbund: The Politics of Reform in the Applied Arts*. Princeton, NJ: Princeton University Press.

Carlson, A. 1990. *The Swedish Experiment in Family Politics: The Myrdals and the Interwar Population Crisis*. London: Transaction Publishers.

Carroll, A. B. 1999. "Corporate Social Responsibility: Evolution of a Definitional Construct." *Business and Society* 38 (3): 268–295.

Castañeda, Q. E. 2004. "Art-Writing in the Modern Maya Art World of Chichen Itza: Transcultural Ethnography and Experimental Fieldwork." *American Ethnologist* 31 (1): 21–42.

Castillo, G. 2010. *Cold War on the Home Front: The Soft Power of Midcentury Design*. Minneapolis: University of Minnesota Press.

Childs, M. W. 1936. *Sweden: The Middle Way*. New Haven, CT: Yale University Press.

Christophers, B. 2013. "A Monstrous Hybrid: The Political Economy of Housing in Early Twenty-First Century Sweden." *New Political Economy* 18 (6): 885–911.

Clarke, A. J. 2010. *Design Anthropology: Object Culture in the 21st Century*. New York: Springer.

Cohen, T. 1973. "Illocutions and Perlocutions." *Foundations of Language* 9 (4): 492–503.

Cohn, C. 1987. "Sex and Death in the Rational World of Defense Intellectuals." *Signs* 12 (4): 687–718.

Cornell, P. 2005. "Ting som Tänker." *Expressen*, May 3, 6.

Creagh, L., H. Kåberg, and B. M. Lane, eds. 2008. *Modern Swedish Design: Three Founding Texts*. New York: The Museum of Modern Art.

Crouch, C. 1999. *Modernism in Art, Design, and Architecture*. New York: St. Martin's Press.

Daniels, R., and G. Brandwood, eds. 2003. *Ruskin and Architecture*. Reading: Spire Books.

Danto, A. C. 1964. "The Artworld." *Journal of Philosophy* 61 (19): 571–584.

———. 1974. "The Transfiguration of the Commonplace." *Journal of Aesthetics and Art Criticism* 33 (2): 139–148.

———. 1981. *The Transfiguration of the Commonplace: A Philosophy of Art*. Cambridge, MA: Harvard University Press.

Daun, Å. 1991. "Individualism and Collectivity among Swedes." *Ethnos* 56 (3–4): 165–172.

———. 1996. *Swedish Mentality*. University Park: Pennsylvania State University Press.

———. 1998. "Describing a National Culture—Is It at All Possible?" *Ethnologia Scandinavica* 28: 5–19.

De Certeau, M. 1984. *The Practice of Everyday Life*. Berkeley: University of California Press.

Deland, M. 2001. *The Social City: Middle-Way Approaches to Housing and Suburban Governmentality in Southern Stockholm, 1900–1945*. Stockholm: Stads-och Kommun-Historiska Institutet.

Deleuze, G. 1988. *Foucault*. Minneapolis: University of Minnesota Press.

———. 1992. "What Is a Dispositif?" In *Michel Foucault: Philosopher*, edited by T. J. Armstrong, 159–168. Hemel Hempstead: Harvester Wheatsheaf.

Deleuze, G., and F. Guattari. 1987. *A Thousand Plateaus: Capitalism and Schizophrenia*. Minneapolis: University of Minnesota Press.

Dewey, J. 1934. *Art as Experience*. New York: Capricorn.

Donzelot, J. 1979. *The Policing of Families*. Baltimore: Johns Hopkins University Press.

Doordan, D. P. 1995. "Political Things: Design in Fascist Italy." In *Designing Modernity: The Arts of Reform and Persuasion, 1885–1945*, edited by W. Kaplan, 225–255. London: Thames and Hudson.

Dumit, J. 2003. *Picturing Personhood: Brains Scans and Biomedical America*. Princeton, NJ: Princeton University Press.

Duranti, A. 2011. "Linguistic Anthropology: The Study of Language as a Non-neutral Medium." In *The Cambridge Handbook of Sociolinguistics*, edited by R. Mesthrie, 28–46. Cambridge: Cambridge University Press.

Eade, J. C. 1983. *Romantic Nationalism in Europe*. Canberra: Humanities Research Centre, Australian National University.

Edvardsson, B., B. Enquist, and R. Johnston. 2005. "Cocreating Customer Value through Hyperreality in the Prepurchase Service Experience." *Journal of Service Research* 8 (2): 149–161.

Eitner, L. 1957. "Industrial Design in Postwar Germany." *Design Quarterly* 40: 1–27.

Ekström, A., S. Julich, and P. Snickars, eds. 2006. *1897: Mediehistorier kring Stockholmsutställningen*. Stockholm: Mediehistoriskt Arkiv.

Eliaeson, S. 2000. "Gunnar Myrdal: A Theorist of Modernity." *Acta Sociologica* 43 (4): 331–341.

Engelbrektsson, U.-B. 1986. "Ethnicity in the Local Context: Italians and Greeks in a Swedish Town." *Ethnos* 51 (3–4): 148–172.

Englund, P. 1999. "The Swedish Banking Crisis: Roots and Consequences." *Oxford Review of Economic Policy* 15 (3): 80–97.

Ericson, D. 1988. *In the Stockholm Art World*. Stockholm: Stockholm Studies in Social Anthropology.

Esperanza, J. S. 2008. "Outsourcing Otherness: Crafting and Marketing Culture in the Global Handicrafts Market." *Research in Economic Anthropology* 28: 71–95.

———. 2010. "Bali's Ethnic Arts Industry: Global Identities amidst a National Tourist Agenda." *Material Culture Review* 71: 14–23.

Esping-Andersen, G. 1985. *Politics against Markets: The Social Democratic Road to Power*. Princeton, NJ: Princeton University Press.

———. 1990. *The Three Worlds of Welfare Capitalism*. Princeton, NJ: Princeton University Press.

Evans, R. 1995. *The Projective Cast: Architecture and Its Three Geometries.* Cambridge, MA: MIT Press.

Eyerman, R. 1985. "Rationalizing Intellectuals: Sweden in the 1930s and 1940s." *Theory and Society* 14 (6): 777–807.

Facos, M. 1998. *Nationalism and the Nordic Imagination: Swedish Art of the 1890s.* Berkeley: University of California Press.

Fallan, K., ed. 2012. *Scandinavian Design: Alternative Histories.* London: Berg.

Falnes, O. J. 1933. *National Romanticism in Norway.* New York: Columbia University Press.

Fant, Å. 1985. "Några Aspekter på Stockholmsutställningen 1930." In *Årsbok 1985*, 66–77. Stockholm: Arkitekturmuseet.

Fehérváry, K. 2009. "Goods and States: The Political Logic of State-Socialist Material Culture." *Comparative Studies in Society and History* 51 (2): 426–459.

———. 2012. "From Socialist Modern to Super-Natural Organicism: Cosmological Transformations through Home Decor." *Cultural Anthropology* 27 (4): 615–640.

———. 2013. *Politics in Color and Concrete: Socialist Materialities and the Middle Class in Hungary.* Bloomington: Indiana University Press.

Fennell, C. 2011. " 'Project Heat' and Sensory Politics in Redeveloping Chicago Public Housing." *Ethnography* 12 (1): 40–64.

———. 2012. "The Museum of Resilience: Raising a Sympathetic Public in Postwelfare Chicago." *Cultural Anthropology* 27 (4): 641–666.

Fiell, C., and P. Fiell. 2002. *Scandinavian Design.* Cologne: Taschen.

Foster, H. 2003. "Brow Beaten." *Design and Crime and Other Diatribes.* New York: Verso.

Foucault, M. 1970. *The Order of Things: An Archaeology of the Human Sciences.* New York: Vintage.

———. 1977. *Discipline and Punish: The Birth of the Prison.* New York: Pantheon.

———. 1978. *The History of Sexuality.* Vol. 1, *An Introduction.* New York: Vintage.

———. 1986. "Of Other Spaces." *Diacritics* 16 (1): 22–27.

———. 1998. "Different Spaces." In *Aesthetics, Method, and Epistemology*, edited by J. D. Faubion, 175–186. New York: The New Press.

Frick, G. 1978. *Svenska Slöjdföreningen och Konstindustrin före 1905.* Stockholm: Nordiska Museet.

Frykman, J. 1993. "Becoming the Perfect Swede: Modernity, Body Politics, and National Processes in Twentieth-Century Sweden." *Ethnos* 58 (3/4): 259–274.

———. 1995. "The Informalization of National Identity." *Ethnologia Europaea* 25: 5–15.

Frykman, J., and O. Löfgren. 1987. *Culture Builders: A Historical Anthropology of Middle-Class Life.* New Brunswick, NJ: Rutgers University Press.

Garvey, P. 2003. "How to Have a 'Good Home': The Practical Aesthetic and Normativity in Norway." *Journal of Design History* 16 (3): 241–251.

———. 2005. "Domestic Boundaries: Privacy, Visibility and the Norwegian Window." *Journal of Material Culture* 10 (2): 157–176.

———. 2008. "The Norwegian Country Cabin and Functionalism: A Tale of Two Modernities." *Social Anthropology* 16 (2): 203–220.

Gaunt, D., and O. Löfgren. 1984. *Myter om Svensken*. Stockholm: LiberFörlag.

Gell, A. 1998. *Art and Agency: An Anthropological Theory*. Oxford: Clarendon.

Gill, L. 1992. "Myrdal and 'The Third Way.'" In *Gunnar Myrdal and His Works*, edited by G. Dosaler, D. Ethier, and L. Lepage, 52–67. Montreal: Harvest House.

Gille, H. 1948. "Recent Developments in Swedish Population Policy, Part I." *Population Studies* 2 (1): 3–70.

Giuffre, K. 1999. "Sandpiles of Opportunity: Success in the Art World." *Social Forces* 77 (3): 815–832.

Goldhagen, S. W. 2005. "Something to Talk About: Modernism, Discourse, Style." *Journal of the Society of Architectural Historians* 64 (2): 144–167.

Goodman, N. 1978. *Ways of Worldmaking*. Cambridge, MA: Hackett Publishing.

Goodwin, C. 1994. "Professional Vision." *American Anthropologist* 96 (3): 606–633.

———. 2003. "Embedded Context." *Research on Language and Social Interaction* 36 (4): 323–350.

Gowlland, G. 2009. "Learning to See Value: Exchange and the Politics of Vision in a Chinese Craft." *Ethnos* 74 (2): 229–250.

Gramsci, A. 2000. "Philosophy, Common Sense, Language, and Folklore." In *The Antonio Gramsci Reader: Selected Writings, 1916–1935*, edited by D. Forgacs, 323–362. New York: New York University Press.

Grasseni, C., ed. 2009. *Skilled Visions: Between Apprenticeship and Standards*. London: Berghan.

Grisham, T. 1991. "Linguistics as an Indiscipline: Deleuze and Guattari's Pragmatics." *SubStance* 20 (3): 36–54.

Guldberg, J. 2011. "'Scandinavian Design' as Discourse: The Exhibition Design in Scandinavia, 1954–57." *Design Issues* 27 (2): 41–58.

Gullestad, M. 1989a. *Kultur og Hverdagsliv: På Sporet av det Moderne Norge*. Oslo: Universitetsforlaget.

———. 1989b. "Small Facts and Large Issues: The Anthropology of Contemporary Scandinavian Society." *Annual Review of Anthropology* 18: 71–93.

———. 2001. *Kitchen-Table Society: A Case Study of the Family Life and Friendships of Young Working-Class Mothers in Urban Norway*. Oslo: Universitetsforlaget.

Gunn, W., and J. Donovan, eds. 2012. *Design and Anthropology*. London: Ashgate.

Gunn, W., T. Otto, and R. C. Smith, eds. 2013. *Design Anthropology: Between Theory and Practice*. London: Berg.

Hacker, J. S. 2002. *The Divided Welfare State: The Battle over Public and Private Social Benefits in the United States*. Cambridge: Cambridge University Press.

Hadenius, S. 1990. *Swedish Politics During the Twentieth Century*. Stockholm: The Swedish Institute.

Hagströmer, D. 2001. *Swedish Design*. Stockholm: The Swedish Institute.

Hagtvet, B., and E. Rudeng. 1984. "Scandinavia: Achievements, Dilemmas, Challenges." *Daedalus* 113: 227–256.

Håkansson, H., and A. Waluszewski. 2002. *Managing Technological Development: IKEA, the Environment and Technology*. London: Routledge.

Hald, A. 1970. "50-Talet—Tingens Årtionde." *Form* 66 (6–7): 303–307.

Hall, K. 2000. "Performativity." *Journal of Linguistic Anthropology* 9 (1–2): 184–187.

Hall, T., and S. Vidén. 2005. "The Million Homes Programme: A Review of the Great Swedish Planning Project." *Planning Perspectives* 20 (3): 301–328.

Hannerz, U. 1982. "Twenty Years of Swedish Social Anthropology: 1960–1980." *Ethnos* 47 (1–2): 150–171.

——. 1985. "History and Anthropology in Scandinavia: An Introduction." *Ethnos* 50 (3–4): 165–167.

Hansen, J. F. 1976. "The Proxemics of Danish Daily Life." *Studies in the Anthropology of Visual Communication* 3 (1): 52–62.

Harper, D. 1987. *Working Knowledge: Skill and Community in a Small Shop*. Berkeley: University of California Press.

Hedqvist, H. 2002. *Svensk Form Internationell Design*. Stockholm: Bokförlaget DN.

Helgeson, S., and Nyberg, K., eds. 2002. *Swedish Design: The Best in Swedish Design Today*. London: Octopus Publishing.

Heller, S., and L. Fili. 1998. *German Modern: Graphic Design from Wilhelm to Weimar*. San Francisco: Chronicle Books.

Henderson, W. 2000. *John Ruskin's Political Economy*. London: Routledge.

Henningsen, B. 2001. "Jante, or the Scandinavian Law of Mediocrity: One Factor in the Identity of the Welfare State." In *The Swedish Success Story?*, edited by K. Almqvist and K. Glans, 161–174. Stockholm: Margaret Axson Johnson Foundation.

Heritage, J. 1984. *Garfinkel and Ethnomethodology*. Cambridge: Polity Press.

Herzfeld, M. 2004. *The Body Impolitic: Artisans and Artifice in the Global Hierarchy of Value*. Chicago: University of Chicago Press.

——. 2005. *Cultural Intimacy: Social Poetics in the Nation-State*. 2nd ed. New York: Routledge.

Hetherington, K. 1997. *The Badlands of Modernity: Heterotopia and Social Ordering*. New York: Routledge.

——. 2011. "Foucault, the Museum and the Diagram." *Sociological Review* 59 (3): 457–475.

Hilson, M. 2008. *The Nordic Model: Scandinavia since 1945*. London: Reaktion Books.

Hirdman, Y. 1989. *Att Lägga Livet Tillrätta: Studier i Svensk Folkhemspolitik*. Stockholm: Carlsson Bokförlag.

——. 1992. "Utopia in the Home." *International Journal of Political Economy* 22 (2): 5–99.

——. 1994. "Social Engineering and the Woman Question: Sweden in the Thirties." *Studies in Political Economy* 44: 73–94.

——. 2008. *Alva Myrdal: The Passionate Mind*. Bloomington: Indiana University Press.

Holston, J. 1989. *The Modernist City: An Anthropological Critique of Brasilia*. Chicago: University of Chicago Press.

Horne, D. 1984. *The Great Museum: The Re-Presentation of History*. London: Pluto Press.

Horst, H., and D. Miller. 2006. *The Cell Phone: An Anthropology of Communication*. Oxford: Berg.

Ikea. 2011. *Sustainability Report 2011*. Stockholm: Ikea Group.

Ingold, T. 2010a. "Bringing Things to Life: Creative Entanglements in a World of Materials." NCRM Working Paper. Realities/Morgan Centre, University of Manchester, Manchester, UK.

———. 2010b. "The Textility of Making." *Cambridge Journal of Economics* 34 (1): 91–102.

———. 2012. "Toward an Ecology of Materials." *Annual Review of Anthropology* 41 (1): 427–442.

Isenhour, C. 2010. "Building Sustainable Societies: A Swedish Case Study on the Limits of Reflexive Modernization." *American Ethnologist* 37 (3): 511–525.

———. 2011. "How the Grass Became Greener in the City: Urban Imaginings and Practices of Sustainability." *City and Society* 23 (2): 118–138.

———. 2013. "On the Politics of Climate Knowledge: Sir Giddens, Sweden and the Paradox of Climate (In)Justice." *Local Environment: International Journal of Justice and Sustainability* 18 (2): 201–216.

Ivanov, V. 2000. "Heteroglossia." *Journal of Linguistic Anthropology* 9: 100–102.

Ivarsson, J. 2010. "Developing the Construction Sight: Architectural Education and Technological Change." *Visual Communication* 9 (2): 171–191.

Jackson, W. A. 1990. *Gunnar Myrdal and America's Conscience: Social Engineering and Racial Liberalism, 1938–1987*. Chapel Hill: University of North Carolina Press.

Jakobson, R. 1971. "The Dominant." In *Readings in Russian Poetics: Formalist and Structuralist Views*, edited by L. Matejka and K. Pomorska, 82–87. Cambridge, MA: MIT Press.

Johnson, E. 1961. "Mellan Idyll och Hemskhet." In *Perspektiv på 30-Talet*, edited by B. Christofferson and T. von Vegesack, 25–30. Stockholm: Wahlström and Widstrand.

Johnson, G. 1985. "H55 i Helsingborg." *Utblick Landskap* 2/3: 20–21.

Johnson, J. 1988. "Mixing Humans and Nonhumans Together: The Sociology of a Door-Closer." *Social Problems* 35 (3): 298–310.

Johnson, P. 2006. "Unravelling Foucault's 'Different Spaces.'" *History of the Human Sciences* 19 (4): 75–90.

———. 2008. "The Modern Cemetery: A Design for Life." *Social and Cultural Geography* 9 (7): 777–790.

Jones, C. A. 2000. "The Modernist Paradigm: The Artworld and Thomas Kuhn." *Critical Inquiry* 26 (3): 488–528.

Jones, G. M. 2011. *Tricks of the Trade: Inside the Magician's Craft*. Berkeley: University of California Press.

Jones, P. B. 2006. *Gunnar Asplund*. New York: Phaidon.

Jonsson, S. 2003. "Vilse i Designatlasen." *Dagens Nyheter*, December 22.

Kahn, M. 1995. "Heterotopic Dissonance in the Museum Representation of Pacific Island Cultures." *American Anthropologist* 97 (2): 324–338.

Kavanagh, G. 2000. *Dream Spaces: Memory and the Museum*. London: Leicester University Press.

Keane, W. 2003. "Semiotics and the Social Analysis of Material Things." *Language and Communication* 23 (3–4): 409–425.

Key, E. 2006. *Skönhet för Alla*. Ödeshög: Ellen Keyinstitut.

234   *References*

———. 2008. "Beauty in the Home." In *Modern Swedish Design: Three Founding Texts*, edited by L. Creagh, H. Kåberg, and B. M. Lane, 32–57. New York: The Museum of Modern Art.

Koinberg, S. 1985. "Stockholmsutställningen 1930." *Utblick Landskap* 2/3: 15–17.

Kolko, J. 2010. "Abductive Thinking and Sensemaking: The Drivers of Design Synthesis." *Design Issues* 26 (1): 15–28.

Kondo, D. 1990. *Crafting Selves: Power, Gender, and Discourses of Identity in a Japanese Workplace*. Chicago: University of Chicago Press.

Korff, G. 2002. "Fremde (the Foreign, Strange, Other) and the Museum." *Journal of the Society for the Anthropology of Europe* 2 (2): 29–34.

Knudsen, T., ed. 2000. *Den Nordiske Protestantisme og Velfaerdsstaten*. Aarhus: Aarhus University Press.

Knudsen, T., and B. Rothstein. 1994. "State Building in Scandinavia." *Comparative Politics* 26 (2): 203–20.

Kratz, C. A. 2011. "Rhetorics of Value: Constituting Worth and Meaning through Cultural Display." *Visual Anthropology Review* 27 (1): 21–48

Krause-Jensen, J. 2010. *Flexible Firm: The Design of Culture at Bang and Olufsen*. New York: Berghahn Books.

Kulick, D. 2003. "Sex in the New Europe: The Criminalization of Clients and Swedish Fear of Penetration." *Anthropological Theory* 3 (2): 199–218.

———. 2005. "Four Hundred Thousand Swedish Perverts." *GLQ: A Journal of Lesbian and Gay Studies* 11 (2): 205–235.

Lalonde, F. 1992. "Gunnar Myrdal and Social Democracy." In *Gunnar Myrdal and His Works*, edited by G. Dosaler, D. Ethier, and L. Lepage, 37–51. Montreal: Harvest House.

Lane, B. M. 2000. *National Romanticism and Modern Architecture in Germany and the Scandinavian Countries*. Cambridge: Cambridge University Press.

———. 1968. *Architecture and Politics in Germany, 1918–1945*. Cambridge, MA: Harvard University Press.

Langby, E. 1984. *Vinter i Välfärdslandet*. Stockholm: Brombergs.

Langer, S. K. 1953. *Feeling and Form*. New York: Scribner.

———. 1957. *Problems of Art: Ten Philosophical Lectures*. New York: Scribner.

Larsson, B. 2003. "Neo-Liberalism and Polycontextuality: Banking Crisis and Re-Regulation in Sweden." *Economy and Society* 32 (3): 428–448.

Latour, B. 1993. *We Have Never Been Modern*. Cambridge, MA: Harvard University Press.

———. 2007. *Reassembling the Social: An Introduction to Actor-Network-Theory*. Oxford: Oxford University Press.

———. 2008. "A Cautious Prometheus? A Few Steps toward a Philosophy of Design (with Special Attention to Peter Sloterdijk)." Keynote lecture presented at the Networks of Design meeting of the Design Historical Society, Falmouth, Cornwall, UK, September 2008.

Latour, B., and S. Woolgar. 1986. *Laboratory Life: The Construction of Scientific Facts*. Princeton, NJ: Princeton University Press.

Law, J. 1987. "Technology and Heterogeneous Engineering: The Case of Portuguese Expansion." In *The Social Construction of Technological Systems: New Directions in the Sociology and History of Technology*, edited by W. E. Bijker, T. P. Hughes, and T. Pinch, 111–134. Cambridge, MA: MIT Press.

———. 1992. "Notes on the Theory of the Actor-Network: Ordering, Strategy and Heterogeneity." *Systems Practice* 5 (4): 379–393.

Lecercle, J.-J. 2002. *Deleuze and Language*. New York: Palgrave.

Lengborn, T. 2002. *Ellen Key och Skönheten: Estetiska och Konstpedagogiska Utvecklingslinjer i Ellen Keys Föfattarskap 1891–1906*. Stockholm: Gidlunds.

Levi-Strauss, C. 1971. *Totemism*. Boston: Beacon Press.

Lewin, L. 1988. *Ideology and Strategy: A Century of Swedish Politics*. Cambridge: Cambridge University Press.

Lewis, E. 2005. *Great Ikea! A Brand for All the People*. London: Cyan.

Lin, K. 2004. "Sectors, Agents and Rationale: A Study of the Scandinavian States with Special Reference to the Society Model." *Acta Sociologica* 47 (2): 141–157.

Lind, I. 1970. "Hemutställningen 1917." *Form* 66 (6/7): 273–281.

Lindén, C. 2006. "Ellen Keys Feministiska Estetik." Foreword to *Skönhet för Alla*, by E. Key, 7–23. Ödeshög: Ellen Keyinstitut.

Lindkvist, L. 1982. "Better Everyday Goods and a New Sensuality: Some Thoughts on Swedish Design." In *Scandinavian Modern Design: 1880–1980*, edited by D. R. McFadden, 259–260. New York: Harry N. Abrams.

Lindwall, J., and B. Rothstein. 2006. Sweden: The Fall of the Strong State." *Scandinavian Political Studies* 29 (1): 47–63.

Llewellyn, D. T. 1992. "The Performance of Banks in the UK and Scandinavia: A Case Study in Competition and Reregulation." *Sveriges Riksbanks Quarterly Review* 3: 20–30.

Löfgren, O. 1987. "Deconstructing Swedishness: Culture and Class in Modern Sweden." In *Anthropology at Home*, edited by A. Jackson, 74–93. London: Association of Social Anthropologists.

———. 1988. *Hej, Det Är från Försäkringskassan! Informaliseringen av Sverige*. Stockholm: Natur och Kultur.

———. 1991. "Att Nationalisera Moderniteten." In *Nationella Identiteter i Norden—Ett Fullbordat Projekt?*, edited by A. Linde-Laursen and J. O. Nilsson, 101–116. Stockholm: Nordiska Rådet.

———. 1993. "Materializing the Nation in Sweden and America." *Ethnos* 58 (3/4): 161–196.

———. 1997. "Scenes from a Troubled Marriage: Swedish Ethnology and Material Culture Studies." *Journal of Material Culture* 2 (1): 95–113.

———. 1999. "Feeling at Home: The Politics and Practices of National Belonging." *Anthropological Journal on European Cultures* 8 (1): 79–97.

———. 2000. "The Disappearance and Return of the National: The Swedish Experience, 1950–2000." In *Folklore, Heritage Politics and Ethnic Diversity*, edited by P. Anttonen, 230–252. Botkyrka: The Multicultural Centre.

Lord, B. 2006. "Foucault's Museum: Difference, Representation, and Genealogy." *Museum and Society* 4 (4): 1–14.

Lövgren, B. 1993. *Hemarbete som Politik: Diskussioner om Hemarbete, Sverige 1930–40-talen, och Tillkomsten av Hemmens Forskningsinstitut*. Stockholm: Almqvist and Wiksell.

Luck, R. 2009. "'Does This Compromise Your Design?' Interactionally Producing a Design Concept in Talk." *CoDesign* 5 (1): 21–34.

——. 2010. "Using Objects to Coordinate Design Activity in Interaction." *Construction Management and Economics* 28 (7): 641–655.

Lukács, G. 1968. *History and Class Consciousness: Studies in Marxist Dialectics*. Cambridge, MA: MIT Press.

Lymer, G. 2009. "Demonstrating Professional Vision: The Work of Critique in Architectural Education." *Mind, Culture, and Activity* 16: 145–171.

Lymer, G., J. Ivarsson, and O. Lindwall. 2009. "Contrasting the Use of Tools for Presentation and Critique: Some Cases from Architectural Education." *International Journal of Computer-Supported Collaborative Learning* 4 (4): 423–444.

MacKenzie, D. A., F. Muniesa, and L. Siu. 2008. *Do Economists Make Markets? On the Performativity of Economics*. Princeton, NJ: Princeton University Press.

Madestrand, B. 2005. "Konceptdesign mer än Försäljningssiffror." *Dagens Nyheter*, June 5, C07.

Madge, L. 1997. "Capitalizing on 'Cuteness': The Aesthetics of Social Relations in a New Postwar Japanese Order." *Japanstudien* 9: 155–174.

Makovicky, N. 2010. "'Something to Talk About': Notation and Knowledge-Making among Central Slovak Lace-Makers." *Journal of the Royal Anthropological Institute (New Series)* 16 (s1): S80–S99.

Marchand, T. 2010. "Embodied Cognition and Communication: Studies with British Fine Woodworkers." *Journal of the Royal Anthropological Institute (New Series)* 16 (s1): S100–S120.

Marcus, G. E., and F. R. Myers. 1995. *The Traffic in Culture: Refiguring Art and Anthropology*. Berkeley: University of California Press.

Mattsson, H., and S.-O. Wallenstein. 2009. *Den Svenska Modernismen vid Vägskälet/ Swedish Modernism at the Crossroads*. Stockholm: Axl Books.

——, eds. 2010. *Swedish Modernism: Architecture, Consumption, and the Welfare State*. London: Black Dog.

Mazzarella, W. 2003. *Shoveling Smoke: Advertising and Globalization in Contemporary India*. Durham, NC: Duke University Press.

McVeigh, B. 2000. "How Hello Kitty Commodifies the Cute, Cool and Camp: 'Consumutopia' versus 'Control' in Japan." *Journal of Material Culture* 5 (2): 225–245.

Melby, K., A.-B. Ravn, and C. C. Wetterberg. 2009. "A Nordic Model of Gender Equality? Introduction." In *Gender Equality and Welfare Politics in Scandinavia: The Limits of Political Ambition*, edited by K. Melby, A.-B. Ravn, and C. C. Wetterberg, 1–24. Bristol: Policy Press.

Mettler, S. 2011. *The Submerged State: How Invisible Government Policies Undermine American Democracy*. Chicago: University of Chicago Press.

Milani, T. M. 2008. "Language Testing and Citizenship: A Language Ideological Debate in Sweden." *Language and Society* 37: 27–59.

Milani, T. M., and R. Jonsson. 2012. "Who's Afraid of Rinkeby Swedish? Stylization, Complicity, Resistance." *Journal of Linguistic Anthropology* 22 (1): 44–63.

Miller, D. 1987. *Material Culture and Mass Consumption*. Oxford: Blackwell.

——, ed. 1998a. *Material Cultures: Why Some Things Matter*. Chicago: University of Chicago Press.

——. 1998b. *A Theory of Shopping*. Chicago: University of Chicago Press.

——, ed. 2001a. *Car Cultures*. Oxford: Berg.

——. 2001b. *The Dialectics of Shopping*. Chicago: University of Chicago Press.

——. 2001c. *Home Possessions: Material Culture behind Closed Doors*. New York: Berg.

——, ed. 2005. *Materiality*. Durham, NC: Duke University Press.

——. 2008. *The Comfort of Things*. Cambridge: Polity.

——. 2010. *Stuff*. Cambridge: Polity.

——. 2012. *Consumption and Its Consequences*. Cambridge: Polity.

Miller, D., and S. Woodward. 2012. *Blue Jeans: The Art of the Ordinary*. Berkeley: University of California Press.

Mjøset, L. 1992. "The Nordic Model Never Existed, but Does It Have a Future?" *Scandinavian Studies* 64 (4): 652–671.

Montoya, M. 2011. *Making the Mexican Diabetic: Race, Science, and the Genetics of Inequality*. Berkeley: University of California Press.

Morris, R. C. 1995. "All Made Up: Performance Theory and the New Anthropology of Sex and Gender." *Annual Review of Anthropology* 24: 567–592.

Morris, W. 1882. *Hopes and Fears for Art*. Boston: Roberts Brothers.

——. 1902. *Architecture, Industry and Wealth: Collected Papers*. London: Longmans, Green and Co.

Moschonas, G. 2011. "Historical Decline or Change of Scale? The Electoral Dynamics of European Social Democratic Parties, 1950–2009." In *What's Left of the Left: Democrats and Social Democrats in Challenging Times*, edited by J. Cronin, G. Ross, and J. Schoch, 50–85. Durham, NC: Duke University Press.

Mukarovsky, J. 1977. "The Aesthetic Norm." In *Structure, Sign, and Function*, edited by J. Burbank and P. Steiner, 49–56. New Haven, CT: Yale University Press.

Murphy, K. M. 2004. "Imagination as Joint Activity: The Case of Architectural Interaction." *Mind, Culture, and Activity* 11 (4): 267–278.

——. 2005. "Collaborative Imagining: The Interactive Use of Gestures, Talk and Graphic Representation in Architectural Practice." *Semiotica* 156: 113–145.

——. 2012. "Transmodality and Temporality in Design Interactions." *Journal of Pragmatics* 44: 1966–1981.

——. 2013. "A Cultural Geometry: Designing Political Things in Sweden." *American Ethnologist* 40 (1): 118–131.

Myrdal, A. 1945. *Nation and Family: The Swedish Experiment in Democratic Family and Population Policy*. London: Kegan Paul, Trench, Trubner and Co.

Myrdal, A., and G. Myrdal. 1934. *Kris i Befolkningsfrågan*. Stockholm: Bonniers.

Myrdal, G. 2005. "Dilemma of Social Welfare Policy." In *The Essential Gunnar Myrdal*, edited by Ö. Appelqvist and S. Andersson, 88–91. New York: The New Press.

Myrdal, G., and U. Åhrén. 1933. *Bostadsfrågan såsom Socialt Planläggningsproblem*. Stockholm: Kooperativa Förbundet.

Nelson, K. E. 2004. *New Scandinavian Design*. San Francisco: Chronicle Books.

Nilsson, J. O. 1991. "Modernt, Allt för Modernt Speglingar." In *Nationella Identiteter i Norden—Ett Fullbordat Projekt?*, edited by A. Linde-Laursen and J. O. Nilsson, 59–100. Stockholm: Nordiska Rådet.

Nordstrom, B. J. 2000. *Scandinavia since 1500*. Minneapolis: University of Minnesota Press.

Nye, J. S. 2004. *Soft Power: The Means to Success in World Politics*. New York: Public Affairs.

Nyström-Hamilton, L. 1913. *Ellen Key: Her Life and Her Work*. New York: G. P. Putnam's Sons.

Oak, A. 2011. "What Can Talk Tell Us about Design? Analyzing Conversation to Understand Practice." *Design Studies* 32 (3): 211–234.

O'Dell, T. 1993. "'Chevrolet … That's a Real Raggarbil': The American Car and the Production of Swedish Identities." *Journal of Folklore Research* 30: 61–74.

———. 1997. *Culture Unbound: Americanization and Everyday Life in Sweden*. Lund: Nordic Academic Press.

———. 1998. "Junctures of Swedishness: Reconsidering Representations of the National." *Ethnologia Scandinavica* 28: 20–37.

Ohlsson, C. 2004. "Designåret—Satsning med Liten Budget." *Göteborgs-Posten*, December 23, 57.

Orr, J. E. 1996. *Talking about Machines: An Ethnography of a Modern Job*. Ithaca, NY: Cornell University Press.

Overy, P. 2004. "Visions of the Future and the Immediate Past: The Werkbund Exhibition, Paris 1930." *Journal of Design History* 17 (4): 337–357.

Owens, B. M. 2002. "Monumentality, Identity, and the State: Local Practice, World Heritage, and Heterotopia at Swayambhu, Nepal." *Anthropological Quarterly* 75 (2): 269–316.

Padgett, S., and W. E. Paterson. 1991. *The History of Social Democracy in Postwar Europe*. London: Longman.

Parr, J. 2002. "Introduction: Modern Kitchen, Strong Nation." *Technology and Culture* 43 (4): 657–667.

Paulsson, G. 1916. *Den Nya Arkitekturen*. Stockholm: P.A. Norstedt och Söners Förlag.

———. 1919. *Vackrare Vardagsvara*. Stockholm: Svenska Slöjdföreningen.

———. 1927. *Swedish Contemporary Decorative Arts*. New York: The Metropolitan Museum of Art.

———. 1939. *Ny Svensk Arkitektur/New Swedish Architecture*. Stockholm: Svenska Arkitekturs Riksförbund.

———. 2008. "Better Things for Everyday Life." In *Modern Swedish Design: Three Founding Texts*, edited by L. Creagh, H. Kåberg, and B. M. Lane, 72–125. New York: The Museum of Modern Art.

Paulsson, G., and N. Paulsson. 1957. *Tingens Bruk och Prägel*. Stockholm: Kooperativa Förbundets Bokförlag.

Peebles, G. 2011. *The Euro and Its Rivals: Currency and the Construction of a Transnational City*. Bloomington: University of Indiana Press.

Peirce, C. P. 1955. "Abduction and Induction." In *Philosophical Writings of Peirce*, edited by J. Buchler, 150–156. Mineola, NY: Dover.

———. 1992a. "Deduction, Induction, and Hypothesis." In *The Essential Peirce: Selected Philosophical Writings*, vol. 1, *1867–1893*, edited by N. Houser and C. J. W. Kloesel, 186–199. Bloomington, IN: Indiana University Press.

———. 1992b. "An American Plato: Review of Royce's Religious Aspect of Philosophy." In *The Essential Peirce: Selected Philosophical Writings*, vol. 1, *1867–1893*, edited by N. Houser and C. J. W. Kloesel, 229–241. Bloomington, IN: Indiana University Press.

Pevsner, N. 1960. *Pioneers of Modern Design*. New York: Penguin.

Pontusson, J. 2011. "Once Again a Model: Nordic Social Democracy in a Globalized World." In *What's Left of the Left: Democrats and Social Democrats in Challenging Times*, edited by J. Cronin, G. Ross, and J. Schoch, 89–115. Durham, NC: Duke University Press.

Popper, K. 1971. *The Open Society and Its Enemies*. Vol. 1, *Plato*. Princeton, NJ: Princeton University Press.

Power, D., J. Lindström, and D. Hallencreutz. 2004. *Country Report: The Swedish Design Industry*. Oslo: The Nordic Innovation Center.

Pred, A. 1991. "Spectacular Articulations of Modernity: The Stockholm Exhibition of 1897." *Geografiska Annaler: Series B, Human Geography* 73 (1): 45–84.

———. 1995. *Recognizing European Modernities: A Montage of the Present*. London: Routledge.

Råberg, P.-G. 1970. "Stockholmsutställningen 1930." *Form* 66 (6/7): 286–293.

Rampell, L. 2003. *Designatlas: En Resa Genom Designteori 1845–2002*. Stockholm: Gabor Palotai.

Reeves, S., B. Brown, and E. Laurier. 2009. "Experts at Play: Understanding Skilled Expertise." *Games and Culture* 4 (3): 205–227.

Reid, F. J. M., and S. E. Reed. 2007. "Conversational Grounding and Visual Access in Collaborative Design." *CoDesign* 3 (2): 111–122.

Remlov, A. 1954. *Design in Scandinavia: An Exhibition of Objects for the Home from Denmark, Finland, Norway, Sweden*. Oslo: Saugbrugsforeningen.

Ricoeur, P. 1976. *Interpretation Theory: Discourse and the Surplus of Meaning*. Fort Worth: Texas Christian University.

———. 2004. *Memory, History, Forgetting*. Chicago: University of Chicago Press.

Riessland, A. 1997. "Sweet Spots: The Use of Cuteness in Japanese Advertising." *Japanstudien* 9: 129–154.

Robach, C. 2005. "Rapport från Nuläget." In *Konceptdesign*, edited by C. Robach, 7–23. Stockholm: Nationalmuseum.

Robertson, A. 1988. "Welfare State and Welfare Society." *Social Policy and Administration* 22 (3): 222–234.

Rojas, M. 1996. *Efter Folkhemmet: En Agenda för Sveriges Fornyelse*. Stockholm: Timbro.

Rörby, M., ed. 1996. *En Miljon Bostäder: Arkitekturmuseet Årsbok 1996*. Stockholm: Arkitekturmuseet.

Rorty, R. 1989. *Contingency, Irony, and Solidarity*. Cambridge: Cambridge University Press.

Rosaldo, M. Z. 1982. "The Things We Do with Words: Ilongot Speech Acts and Speech Act Theory in Philosophy." *Language in Society* 11 (2): 203–237.

Rubin, E. 2006. "The Form of Socialism without Ornament: Consumption, Ideology, and the Fall and Rise of Modernist Design in the German Democratic Republic." *Journal of Design History* 19 (2): 155–168.

Rudberg, E. 1995. "Rakkniven och Lösmanschetten." In *Formens Rörelse*, edited by K. Wickman, 122–140. Stockholm: Föreningen Svensk Form.

———. 1999. *The Stockholm Exhibition 1930: Modernism's Breakthrough in Swedish Architecture*. Stockholm: Stockholmia Förlag.

Ruskin, J. 1890. *The Seven Lamps of Architecture*. New York: John Wiley.

———. 1907. *The Stones of Venice*. London: J. M. Dent and Co.

Sabatino, M. 2010. *Pride in Modesty: Modernist Architecture and the Vernacular Tradition in Italy*. Toronto: University of Toronto Press.

Sachs, L. 1986. "Fertility and Birth in an Unfamiliar Environment: The Case of Turkish Migrant Women in Sweden." *Ethnos* 51 (3–4): 223–245.

Saldanha, A. 2008. "Heterotopia and Structuralism." *Environment and Planning A* 40 (9): 2080–2096.

Salzer, M. 1994. "Identity across Borders: A Study in the 'IKEA-World.'" Department of Management and Economics, Linköping University.

Salzer-Mörling, M. 1998. "As God Created the Earth … A Saga That Makes Sense." In *Discourse and Organization*, edited by D. Grant, T. Keenoy, and C. Oswick, 104–118. London: Sage.

Sawyer, L. 2002. "Routings: 'Race,' African Diasporas, and Swedish Belonging." *Transforming Anthropology* 11 (1): 13–35.

Schön, D. 1984. "The Architectural Studio as an Exemplar of Education for Reflection-in-Action." *Journal of Architectural Education* 38 (1): 2–9.

———. 1985. *The Design Studio: Explorations of Its Traditions and Potential*. London: Riba.

Schüll, N. D. 2012. *Addiction by Design: Machine Gambling in Las Vegas*. Princeton, NJ: Princeton University Press.

Sclafani, R. J. 1973. "Artworks, Art Theory, and the Artworld." *Theoria* 39 (1–3): 18–34.

Scott, F. D. 1988. *Sweden: The Nation's History*. Carbondale: Southern Illinois University Press.

Scott, J. C. 1998. *Seeing Like a State: How Certain Schemes to Improve the Human Condition Have Failed*. New Haven, CT: Yale University Press.

Silow, S. 1995. "H55—Med Ansiktet Vänt mot Framtiden." In *Formens Rörelse*, edited by K. Wickman, 176–219. Stockholm: Föreningen Svensk Form.

Silverstein, M. 1979. "Language Structure and Linguistic Ideology." In *The Elements: A Parasession on Linguistic Units and Levels*, edited by R. Clyne, W. F. Hanks, and C. Hofbauer, 193–247. Chicago: Chicago Linguistic Society.

Smith, R. A., and C. M. Smith. 1977. "The Artworld and Aesthetic Skills: A Context for Research and Development." *Journal of Aesthetic Education* 11 (2): 117–132.

Sommar, I. 2011. *Scandinavian Design*. London: Carlton Books.

Sparke, P. 1988. *Italian Design 1870 to the Present*. London: Thames and Hudson.

———. 1998. "The Straw Donkey: Tourist Kitsch or Proto-Design? Craft and Design in Italy, 1945–1960." *Journal of Design History* 11 (1): 59–69.

Štanský, P. 1985. *Redesigning the World: William Morris, the 1880s, and the Arts and Crafts*. Princeton, NJ: Princeton University Press.

Stavenov, Å., M. Hörlen, Å. H. Huldt, and E. Svedberg. 1939. *Swedish Arts and Crafts: Swedish Modern—A Movement in Sanity*. Uppsala: The Royal Swedish Commission.

Stenebo, J. 2009. *Sanningen om IKEA*. Stockholm: ICA Förlag.

———. 2011. *The Truth about IKEA*. London: Gibson Square.

Stenholm, B. 1984. *The Swedish School System*. Stockholm: The Swedish Institute.

Stenius, H. 1997. "The Good Life Is a Life of Conformity: The Impact of Lutheran Tradition on Nordic Political Culture." In *The Cultural Construction of Norden*, edited by Ø. Sørensen and Bo Stråth, 161–171. Oslo: Scandinavian University Press.

Stenius, H., M. Österberg, and J. Östling. 2008. "Nordic Narratives of the Second World War: An Introduction." In *Nordic Narratives of the Second World War*, edited by H. Stenius, M. Österberg, and J. Östling, 9–30. Lund: Nordic Academic Press.

Streeck, J. 1980. "Speech Acts in Interaction: A Critique of Searle." *Discourse Processes* 3: 133–154.

Streeck, J., C. Goodwin, and C. LeBaron. 2011. *Embodied Interaction: Language and Body in the Material World*. Cambridge: Cambridge University Press.

Stromberg, P. G. 1983. "An Anthropological Approach to a Swedish Popular Movement." *Ethnos* 1–2: 69–84.

———. 1986. *Symbols of Community: The Cultural System of a Swedish Church*. Tucson: University of Arizona Press.

Suchman, L. 2011. "Anthropological Relocations and the Limits of Design." *Annual Review of Anthropology* 40 (1): 1–18.

Sudnow, D. 2001. *Ways of the Hand: A Rewritten Account*. Cambridge, MA: MIT Press.

Sunder Rajan, K. 2006. *Biocapital: The Constitution of Postgenomic Life*. Durham, NC: Duke University Press.

Tambiah, S. J. 1985. *Culture, Thought, and Social Action*. Cambridge, MA: Harvard University Press.

Tannen, D. 2010. "Abduction and Identity in Family Interaction: Ventriloquizing as Indirectness." *Journal of Pragmatics* 42 (2): 307–316.

Tell, J. 2004. *Lagom: Sanningar och Myter om det Vi Kallar Svenskt*. Stockholm: Bokförlaget DN.

Terrio, S. J. 1996. "Crafting Grand Cru Chocolates in Contemporary France." *American Anthropologist* 98 (1): 67–79.

Therborn, G. 1989. "Social Steering and Household Strategies: The Macropolitics and the Microsociology of Welfare States." *Journal of Public Policy* 9 (3): 371–397.

Tilton, T. 1990. *The Political Theory of Swedish Social Democracy: Through the Welfare State to Socialism*. Oxford: Clarendon Press.

———. 1992. "Gunnar Myrdal and the Swedish Model." In *Gunnar Myrdal and His Works*, edited by G. Dosaler, D. Ethier, and L. Lepage, 13–36. Montreal: Harvest House.

Tomasson, R. F. 1970. *Sweden: Prototype of Modern Society*. New York: Random House.

Ulrich, R. 2004. Introduction to *DDR Design: 1949–1989*, edited by A. Volk, 13–15. Cologne: Taschen.

Venkatesan, S. 2009. "Rethinking Agency: Persons and Things in the Heterotopia of 'Traditional Indian Craft.'" *Journal of the Royal Anthropological Institute (New Series)* 15: 78–95.

Vinck, D., ed. 2003. *Everyday Engineering: An Ethnography of Design and Innovation*. Cambridge, MA: MIT Press.

Von Zweigbergk, E. 1968. *Hemma Hos Carl Larssons*. Stockholm: Bonniers.

Waever, O. 1992. "Nordic Nostalgia: Northern Europe after the Cold War." *International Affairs* 68 (1): 77–102.

Wagner, R. 1986. *Symbols That Stand for Themselves*. Chicago: University of Chicago Press.

Ward, J. 2001. *Weimar Surfaces: Urban Visual Culture in 1920s Germany*. Berkeley: University of California Press.

Weckström, N. 2006. "Form är Mer än Föremålet." *Hufvudstadsbladet*, January 22.

Welch, D. 1983. Introduction to *Nazi Propaganda: The Power and the Limitations*, edited by D. Welch, 1–9. London: Croom Helm.

White, H. 1973. *Metahistory: The Historical Imagination in Nineteenth-Century Europe*. Baltimore: Johns Hopkins University Press.

———. 1978. *Tropics of Discourse: Essays in Cultural Criticism*. Baltimore: Johns Hopkins University Press.

———. 1987. *The Content of the Form: Narrative Discourse and Historical Representation*. Baltimore: Johns Hopkins University Press.

Wickman, K. 1985. "H55." *Form* 81 (7): 22–29.

———, ed. 1995a. *Formens Rörelse: Svensk Form Genom 150 År*. Stockholm: Carlssons.

———. 1995b. "På en Smal Tunga ut i Havet. Tingen, Leken, Teknologin och de Gemensamma Rummen." In *Formens Rörelse*, edited by K. Wickman, 188–199. Stockholm: Föreningen Svensk Form.

———. 2009. "A Furniture Store for Everyone." In *Ikea at Liljevalchs Konsthall*, edited by S. Bengtsson, 20–51. Stockholm: Liljevalchs Konsthall.

Winner, L. 1980. "Do Artifacts Have Politics?" *Daedalus* 109 (1): 121–136.

———. 1993. Upon Opening the Black Box and Finding It Empty: Social Constructivism and the Technology of Philosophy." *Science, Technology and Human Values* 18 (3): 362–378.

Wittgenstein, L. 2009. *Philosophical Investigations*. Oxford: Blackwell.

Wollheim, R. 1980. *Art and Its Objects*. 2nd ed. Cambridge: Cambridge University Press.

Wrede, S. 1980. *The Architecture of Erik Gunnar Asplund*. Cambridge, MA: MIT Press.

Wurdak, R. D. 1996. "Trade Fairs and Industrial Exhibitions in the Baltic Region." In *The Baltic Sea: New Developments in National Policies and International Cooperation*, edited by R. Platzöder and P. A. Verlaan, 51–84. Leiden: Martinus Nijhoff.

Yaneva, A. 2009. *Made by the Office for Metropolitan Architecture: An Ethnography of Design*. Amsterdam: 010 Publishers.

Zdebik, J. 2012. *Deleuze and the Diagram: Aesthetic Threads in Visual Organization*. London: Continuum.

INDEX

Locators in *italic* refer to figures